Contributions to Economics

More information about this series at
http://www.springer.com/series/1262

Gorana Krstić • Friedrich Schneider
Editors

Formalizing the Shadow Economy in Serbia

Policy Measures and Growth Effects

Translated by Uroš Vasiljević

Springer Open

Editors
Gorana Krstić
Faculty of Economics
University of Belgrade
Belgrade
Serbia

Friedrich Schneider
Department of Economics
University of Linz
Linz
Austria

This publication is made possible by the support of the American People through the United States Agency for International Development (USAID). The contents of this report are the sole responsibility of the authors and do not necessarily reflect the views of USAID or the United States Government.

USAID Business Enabling Project

The work published in this book is supported by the Faculty of Economics, University of Belgrade and FREN (Foundation for the Advancement of Economics) which covered the cost for open access publication. The book only reflects the author's views.

Foundation for the Advancement of Economics

Faculty of Economics
UNIVERSITY OF BELGRADE

ISSN 1431-1933 ISSN 2197-7178 (electronic)
ISBN 978-3-319-36715-6 ISBN 978-3-319-13437-6 (eBook)
DOI 10.1007/978-3-319-13437-6
Springer Cham Heidelberg New York Dordrecht London

Printed on acid-free paper

Springer is part of Springer Science+Business Media (www.springer.com)

Preface

This report presents the results and recommendations of a comprehensive study of the shadow economy in Serbia prepared by the Foundation for the Advancement of Economics for the USAID Business Enabling Project (BEP). The report is based on the results of an analysis of the relevant statistical data, information obtained from the *Survey on Conditions for Doing Business* carried out on a sample of registered businesses and entrepreneurs in Serbia, as well as the findings of qualitative research covering the key stakeholders.

The overall goal of this study is to develop a strategy and specific recommendations that will enhance the formalisation of the shadow economy in order to improve the competitiveness of the Serbian economy and contribute to economic growth. The specific objectives of this study are as follows:

- To increase awareness of the actual size of the shadow economy and its impact on the business community by estimating its aggregate size and its distribution across key business sectors and different regions in Serbia.
- To identify the main causes of the shadow economy, especially in terms of the types of informal activities that are being undertaken and the reasons businesses are engaging in those activities, so that policy recommendations and actions for the formalisation of the shadow economy will address its root causes.
- To develop a strategy for the formalisation of the shadow economy and to provide specific recommendations, policies, and programmes concerning fiscal and labour market policy and financial sector development that will enhance the formalisation of the shadow economy, improve the competitiveness of the Serbian economy, and contribute to economic growth.

Many institutions and individuals provided assistance and support during our work on this report. We are very grateful to USAID, which provided financial support for this research project, and to the team of the USAID Business Enabling Project for their outstanding cooperation during the preparation of the report and their valuable suggestions, which proved extremely useful in producing the final draft. Thanks are also due to Ipsos Strategic Marketing, which conducted the Survey on Conditions for Doing Business in Serbia, for their professional assistance and suggestions regarding the survey questionnaire. We owe a great debt of gratitude to Prof. Boško Živković for his invaluable suggestions and selfless assistance in our efforts to shed more light on this subject, and to Dr. Aleksandra Nojković for her help in collecting and analysing data for the econometric assessment of the shadow economy in Central and Eastern Europe and Serbia.

Furthermore, the editors of this volume would like to extend their thanks to the Springer team for the smooth cooperation in finalising this book. We are very grateful to the Faculty of Economics, University of Belgrade, which supported this publication, under the projects of the Ministry of Education, Science and Technology of the Republic of Serbia (No. 179005, 179065) and FREN (Foundation for the Advancement of the Economics). Our special gratitude goes to Prof. Branko Urošević, Prof. Branislav Boričić, Prof. Božidar Cerović (Faculty of Economics, University of Belgrade) and Dr. Jelena Žarković Rakić (FREN), who recognised the importance of this publication. Without their support, this e-book would not have been possible.

Finally, we are very grateful for the comments received from the reviewers of the book, Prof. Barry Reilly, Dr. Peter Sanfey and Prof. Branko Urošević.

Belgrade, Serbia
Linz, Austria
October 2014

Gorana Krstić
Friedrich Schneider

Contents

Contributors

Mihail Arandarenko Faculty of Economics, University of Belgrade, Belgrade, Serbia

Milojko Arsić Faculty of Economics, University of Belgrade, Belgrade, Serbia

Irena Janković Faculty of Economics, University of Belgrade, Belgrade, Serbia

Gorana Krstić Faculty of Economics, University of Belgrade, Belgrade, Serbia

Branko Radulović Faculty of Law, University of Belgrade, Belgrade, Serbia

Saša Ranđelović Faculty of Economics, University of Belgrade, Belgrade, Serbia

Friedrich Schneider Department of Economics, University of Linz, Linz, Austria

Chapter 1
Introduction

Gorana Krstić

1.1 Introduction

The shadow economy is one of the biggest challenges to the Serbian economy, with its consequences in terms of tax evasion, labour market distortion, unfair competition, and inefficient allocation of resources. In many transition countries and in Serbia it is a major obstacle to the development of a strong business sector and to the building of a well-functioning market economy. Even though the shadow economy is still an important safety net for many individuals and households in Serbia, the disadvantages for workers, business, and society at large far outweigh the advantages.

During the economic crisis in Serbia since 2008 the need to deeply understand the shadow economy and to find ways to reduce it through formalisation has become acute. In times of crisis it becomes more apparent that the shadow economy is not only a consequence but also a cause of the greater decline in gross domestic product, and can spread the crisis further. Thus, the overall goal of this study is to develop a strategy and specific recommendations that will enhance the formalisation of the shadow economy in order to improve the competitiveness of the Serbian economy and contribute to economic growth.

We define the shadow economy as the ensemble of all market-based legal production activities that are deliberately concealed from public authorities for one or more reasons: to evade payment of income, value added, or other taxes; to evade payment of social security contributions; to evade certain legal labour market standards, such as the minimum wage, maximum working hours, safety standards, etc.; and to evade certain administrative procedures, such as completing statistical questionnaires or administrative forms (Schneider et al. 2010).

G. Krstić (✉)
Faculty of Economics, University of Belgrade, Belgrade, Serbia
e-mail: gkrstic@ekof.bg.ac.rs

G. Krstić, F. Schneider (eds.), *Formalizing the Shadow Economy in Serbia*, Contributions to Economics, DOI 10.1007/978-3-319-13437-6_1

For the purpose of this research, a special Survey on Conditions for Doing Business in Serbia was designed and implemented on a representative sample of 1,251 registered businesses and entrepreneurs in Serbia. This survey allows us to explore the shadow economy in Serbia from the business perspective for the first time, as all previous research has been based on household surveys.

In this study we apply an approach that combines elements of macro- and micro-economic analysis using all relevant statistical data, data from the survey on registered businesses and entrepreneurs, and qualitative research involving interviews with key informants and stakeholders. More specifically, the macro estimates of the shadow economy are based on two methods: the MIMIC approach (multiple indicators, multiple causes) and the Household Tax Compliance approach. Micro-estimates are based on the survey data, identifying the types of shadow economy that exist within the formal sector across the various sectors of economic activity, region, firm size, and other business characteristics. In addition to estimating the extent of the shadow economy we also estimated the tax evasion gap—the difference between evaded taxes and statutory tax liabilities.

It is worth mentioning that in 2013–2014, after the final version of the study was completed in March 2013, the Serbian government implemented a few of the proposed policy measures for formalising the shadow economy presented in the study.

The report is organized as follows. The next chapter by Mihail Arandarenko reviews the various negative consequences and positive effects of the shadow economy in Serbia over the last decade. Chapter 3 by Gorana Krstić describes the design and methodology of the survey of registered businesses and entrepreneurs. Chapter 4 by Milojko Arsić, Mihail Arandarenko, Branko Radulović, Saša Ranđelović, and Irena Janković identifies the main causes of the shadow economy concerning the tax system, labour market institutions, and the financial sector, as well as other institutional and economic causes of the shadow economy. Chapter 5 by Friedrich Schneider, Gorana Krstić, Milojko Arsić, and Saša Ranđelović presents estimates of the shadow economy in Serbia using different methods, while Chap. 6 by Gorana Krstić and Branko Radulović introduces estimates of the main types of shadow economy among business entities, determinants of their participation in the shadow economy, and the impact of competition from the informal sector on businesses. Chapter 7 by Milojko Arsić and Gorana Krstić provides estimates of the potential fiscal effects of reducing the shadow economy to the level observed in more developed countries and the effects that formalisation of the shadow economy can have on economic growth. Chapter 8 by Mihail Arandarenko reviews the institutional capacity, inter-governmental coordination, and policy framework for fighting shadow economic activity. Chapter 9 by Gorana Krstić, Friedrich Schneider, Mihail Arandarenko, Milojko Arsić, Branko Radulović, Saša Ranđelović, and Irena Janković presents the main findings and specific recommendations, policies, and programmes concerning fiscal and labour market policy and financial sector development to enhance the formalisation of the shadow economy. Chapter 10 by Gorana Krstić, Friedrich Schneider, Mihail Arandarenko, Milojko

Arsić, Branko Radulović, Saša Ranđelović and Irena Janković provides an executive summary.

Reference

Schneider F, Buehn A, Montenegro CE (2010) New estimates for the shadow economies all over the world. Int Econ J 24(4):443–461

Chapter 2
The Shadow Economy: Challenges to Economic and Social Policy

Mihail Arandarenko

2.1 Features of the Shadow Economy

The shadow economy is a multi-dimensional, multi-faceted phenomenon, which inevitably accompanies formal economies throughout the world. However, its characteristics and dimensions can be vastly different: from relatively benign, stable, and acceptable to extremely destructive to the economic tissue and long-term economic growth. In countries where shadow economies are present to a large extent or where they show upward trends, these informal sectors are invariably a symptom of deeper disturbances in the economic structure, regulation, and institutions.

In an environment dominated by the economic crisis—present in Serbia since 2008 both statistically and, particularly, in the public's perception—the need to deeply understand the shadow economy and find ways to reduce it through formalisation grows acute. In times of crisis it becomes more apparent that the shadow economy can be not only a consequence but also a cause of greater decline in the gross domestic product, and can spread the crisis further. The shadow economy becomes part of a vicious circle where one of the consequences of recession is flight from formal to shadow trading, which reduces tax revenue, thus increasing the fiscal deficit. The growing deficit must, in turn, be compensated for by higher tax rates: higher taxes drive more companies and workers into the shadow economy, or, even more devastatingly, out of the economy altogether. This downward spiral keeps repeating itself, always at a lower level of GDP and employment. The empirical mechanisms behind this vicious circle are complex, and include the impact of inflation, declining real wages, and growing unemployment on the increase of the informal economy, and vice versa.

M. Arandarenko (✉)
Faculty of Economics, University of Belgrade, Belgrade, Serbia
e-mail: arandarenko@ekof.bg.ac.rs

G. Krstić, F. Schneider (eds.), *Formalizing the Shadow Economy in Serbia*,
Contributions to Economics, DOI 10.1007/978-3-319-13437-6_2

On the other hand, in an abstract economic context the shadow economy can be viewed as a specific market 'anti-institution'. In this light it can be claimed that the shadow economy can eliminate tax and other wedges that institutions create between labour supply and labour demand or product supply and product demand, thereby creating employment or products that would otherwise not have been created, and extending the cost-effectiveness margin for both individuals and businesses.

In a hypothetical market free of taxes and other costs associated with the running of institutions, all economic activity is 'in the shadow'. In reality, formal and informal economies exist in parallel, which introduces distortions and allocates resources sub-optimally. Schneider and Enste (2000) underline the ambivalence of the effects of the shadow economy on the formal economy. On the one hand, the informal economy leads to allocation distortions because resources and production factors are not used as efficiently as possible. On the other hand, income generated in the shadow economy is mainly spent in the formal economy (as much as three-quarters, according to surveys carried out in Germany), which has a stimulating effect on it.

In order to be efficient, measures designed to foster the formalisation of the shadow economy have to be based on knowledge of the causes and structure of informal activity. A particular problem in designing these measures is that information about the shadow economy is necessarily unreliable and incomplete. Further, the shadow economy is inherently very heterogeneous, while economic policy measures, to be implementable in practice, should be simple and, in the main, universally applicable—at any rate, less selective than is desirable from the point of view of optimal targeting.

From the standpoint of economic and social effects, and given the need to develop a formalisation strategy for the shadow economy, it is very important to have a clear perspective of the dominant character of the shadow economy in any particular country and to know whether it is primarily a consequence of voluntary or forced exit, or of exclusion. Voluntary exit means that particular individuals, with specific preferences and mind-sets (say, strong individualists or people more likely to take risks), decide to engage in economic activity outside of the formal economy, even though they are able to find employment in the formal sector. Voluntary exit from the formal economy with the aim of maximising profits or personal income can be reinforced by inadequate penal policy or the lack of implementation of legal sanctions. Forced exit means that individuals or firms are pressured to leave the formal economy due to their own failure in the market, negative trends in the business environment, or rigid regulation. For these entities the shadow economy is the last resort. Exclusion means that certain individuals or groups have never been part of the formal economy, nor have ever had any realistic opportunity to join it.

The two main groups of entities engaged in the shadow economy are businesses and the population. 'Diagnosing' the shadow economy, as a precondition for successfully tackling it, entails answering many specific structural questions that relate to both of these large groups of stakeholders. It is important to learn more about the levels of education and human capital of the segments of the population that participate in the shadow economy, as well as their geographical distribution and structure by type of locality (urban/rural population), structure by age, gender, and social status, the average amount and distribution of wages in the shadow economy, and working hours and modes of employment (primary vs. secondary or supplementary).

Detailed structural information is also needed on businesses and entrepreneurs. These include both basic data (total revenue, profit, number of employees, industry, registration status, etc.) and information on participation in the shadow economy, ranging from evasion of taxes and other dues payable to the state, to non-compliance with regulations and standards that entail expenses.

More information is available on the participation of the population in the Serbian shadow economy than on businesses, owing to regular semi-annual Labour Force Surveys carried out by the Statistical Office of the Republic of Serbia. The survey implemented in this study, aimed primarily at businesses and entrepreneurs, will therefore fill a major void in the available knowledge base for pursuing evidence-based economic and social policies designed to formalise the shadow economy.

2.2 Brief History of the Shadow Economy in Serbia

Over the last quarter of a century Serbia's economy has undergone tectonic changes. In the late 1980s the economic system was still based on socialist self-management, rooted in self-managing socially owned businesses. There was a shadow economy, but it was confined to the then-small private sector and households, mainly in agriculture and through supplementary work. This situation underwent fundamental change from the early 1990s as the federal state disintegrated: business legislation was amended in the 'first transition' while initial privatisation took place; hyperinflation ravaged the country between 1992 and 1994; international sanctions were introduced in 1992—with Serbia virtually living in a state of war. All of these factors contributed to the creation of a lawless business environment in which the shadow economy flourished. In the 1990s even the central authorities operated informally in many important aspects of the economy such as customs and foreign trade. The parallel existence of private, social, and state property stimulated a great deal of abuse. Faced with loss of income or even property, households turned in large numbers to the shadow economy as their primary or supplementary source of income. Workers, although generally retaining formal jobs, nonetheless lost reasonable or indeed any wages, and supplemented them by finding employment in the shadow economy. Many businesses also turned to the shadow economy, with socially owned companies largely evading the payment of payroll taxes, while the newly established private firms often evaded taxes and failed to declare their employees. Parallel trade in consumer goods, particularly those subject to excise duty, reached extreme levels.

Estimates of the extent of the shadow economy in the 1990s on the one hand show extremely high levels and on the other substantial volatility. The halting of hyperinflation in 1994 and the removal of most of the sanctions imposed by the international community resulted in a drop in the volume of the informal economy after the 1993 peak when the share of the shadow economy reached 54.4 % of GDP. In 1995 this figure declined to 40.8 %, and fell again to 34.5 % in 1997 (Krstić et al. 1998). In all likelihood the relative size of the shadow economy grew again after the bombing campaign against Serbia in 1999.

Macroeconomic stabilisation and economic reforms, including European integration, begun after the ousting of the Milošević regime in 2000, had been expected to bring about a quick decline in the extent of the shadow economy. This, however, failed to materialise, both in terms of the reduction seen and the time it took for improvements to take place. There are several potential explanations for this. Firstly, the period after 2000 was marked by accelerating transition, including mass privatisation and restructuring, which introduced additional instability. Secondly, there are strong arguments in favour of the claim that inappropriate taxation policy, particularly in the field of labour taxation,[1] incentivised flight into the informal sector rather than the formalisation of businesses and employment. Further, inefficient and selective law enforcement was the hallmark of this entire period, which again failed to create sufficient incentives for entities to leave the shadow economy.

Yet it cannot be disputed that the 2000s saw changes in the relative size and character of the shadow economy. The development of the shadow economy over the last decade has been studied more extensively from the point of view of households than from that of businesses. It can be monitored through the three waves of the Living Standards Measurement Study (2002, 2003, 2007) and, since 2008, through semi-annual Labour Force Surveys as well.

Informal employment can be defined in various ways. Basically, people working without formal contracts and unable to exercise their social insurance rights are employed informally. They may work for a wage, be self-employed, or work as helping members of households—with this last category being informal by definition.

Krstić and Sanfey (2011) compared data on informal employment obtained from the Living Standards Measurement Survey at two points in time, 2002 and 2007, which correspond to the early and mature phase, respectively, of Serbia's post-2000 transition. By their own admission, they obtained counterintuitive results that indicate that the level of informal employment increased significantly over those 5 years, from 28 % of total employment in 2002 to 35 % in 2007. Secondly, they also found that the informal nature of employment was a significant determinant of inequality in 2007, but not so in 2002—in other words, transition saw a 'dipping' of

[1] This primarily refers to the very high tax burden at low wage levels, which resulted in very high average and marginal tax rates for the minimum wage, the natural point of entry into the formal economy. This issue will be dealt with in greater detail in Chap. 3.

informal employment towards the bottom of the wage distribution, in parallel with the growth in its volume. Thus the authors found that informal workers earned less than formal workers in monthly net amounts, even when all other characteristics were controlled for. In an endeavour to discover the potential causes of the increase in informal employment and the rise in the advantage enjoyed by the wages of formal workers, the authors point to the regressive labour taxation system as one of the likely causes of these unexpected and unfavourable trends.

Although the Labour Force Survey as carried out prior to 2008 did not contain questions that would enable employment to unambiguously be categorised into one of two mutually exclusive categories—formal or informal—efforts were made to estimate informal employment using Labour Force Survey data. Thus, under a World Bank (2006) classification, the group of those in informal employment includes: (1) self-employed people without a university degree; (2) all helping members of households; and (3) salaried employees and owners of private companies with fewer than ten staff. All salaried employees of state and socially owned businesses are deemed to be formally employed. According to the definition used in this World Bank report, Serbia's informal sector was very large in 2005, comprising 43 % of all those in employment and 27 % of all salaried employees. Although informal economy is overestimated by the arbitrary inclusion of the micro-business and entrepreneurs in the informal economy, the structural findings are distinctive and for the most part convincing, and are also borne out by other analyses. The study also found that informal employment is linked to low income, poverty, and vulnerability. Further, there is an above-average share of the young and the undereducated among those in informal employment. Professional experience and wages are much lower in the informal than in the formal economy. The wage premium for those in formal work stood at around 20 %.

Interestingly, data from the 2008 Labour Force Survey show much lower levels of informal employment than those presented above. Another interesting finding, available since the Labour Force Survey made it possible to monitor informal employment, is that informal employment was slower to decline during the crisis. Thus, as shown in Table 2.1, the share of informal employment in total adult employment according to the 2008 Labour Force Survey stood at 23 %. This figure dropped to 21 % in 2009, fell again to 19.6 % in 2010, only to decline yet again to just 17 % by April 2012.

It should be borne in mind that, under the definition used by the Statistical Office of the Republic of Serbia, informal employment includes: (1) workers at unregistered privately held companies; (2) workers at registered companies employed without a written contract and without paid social insurance contributions; and (3) helping family members. Krstić (2012) uses a more standard definition, which also includes workers employed under a written contract but without paid contributions. Consequently, this study found greater rates of informal employment, as shown in Table 2.2.

A finding of this study, which is both interesting and difficult to explain, is the substantial decline in informal work seen since the start of this crisis. It does not fit

Table 2.1 Serbia: Labour market and informal employment indicators, 2006–2012

	2006	2007	2008	2009	2010	2011	2012
Participation rate (%)	63.6	63.4	62.7	60.6	59.0	59.9	59.7
Employment rate (%)	49.8	51.5	53.7	50.4	47.2	45.3	44.2
Unemployment rate (%)	21.6	18.8	14.4	16.9	20.0	24.4	26.1
Informal employment (in % of population aged 15 years and over)	–	–	23.0	20.6	19.6	17.8	17.0

Source: Labour Force Survey, Statistical Office of the Republic of Serbia

Table 2.2 Informal employment based on broader definition, October 2010–October 2011

	October 2010	April 2011	October 2011
Informal employment (in % of total employment, 15+)	25.8	25.1	24.1
Informal employment (in % of total employment, 15–64)	23.1	22.5	21.8
Informal employment outside agriculture	9.2	9.5	8.5

Source: Krstić (2012); Estimates based on panel observations. Labour Force Survey, Statistical Office of the Republic of Serbia

into the standard assumption of the counter-cyclical or at least ambivalent character of informal employment.

A newer comparative study carried out by the International Labour Organisation (ILO 2011) found that Serbia had the lowest level of non-agricultural informal employment among a group of 44 mostly middle- and lower-income countries. Data for Serbia were collected using the Labour Force Survey, which, it was recently claimed, has categorisation issues that probably make it underestimate the actual number of those in informal employment (Krstić 2012). Nevertheless, the conclusion that the level of non-agricultural informal employment in Serbia is lower than would be expected based on its GDP is certainly valid—placing Serbia among countries with relatively low levels of non-agricultural informal employment (ILO 2011).

Be that as it may, research into the informal economy from the population standpoint undoubtedly shows that the informal sector has substantially changed in character over the last decade. Let us note that the standard theoretical explanation for informal employment (at least for salaried employment) is that both the employee and the employer have an interest in splitting the 'excess' that appears when the payment of social contributions is evaded. In this context, an informal wage is greater than a salary in addition to which contributions must be paid, but, in terms of total labour costs, it is lower than the total labour costs of a formal salary. While at the beginning of the decade the informal sector, obviously taking its cue from the disorderly 1990s, comprised employees with widely varying and not necessarily inferior characteristics, who did not earn less than their formal counterparts (see, for instance, the findings of Lokshin and Jovanović 2003), by the end of the 2000s it was no smaller in size but its structure had taken a dramatic turn for the worse, as had its exposure to discrimination and poverty. If this had been a sector of voluntary 'exit' at the beginning of the decade, by its end it had become predominantly a sector of 'exclusion' (cf. Oviedo et al. 2009).

Findings about the volume, structure, and features of informal employment are of great importance in designing economic and social policies aimed at tackling the shadow economy. Data available from the Labour Force Survey, as well as deeper research based on various sources that we have presented in brief, indicate that informal employment is today primarily the last refuge of those forced out of the formal economy during the transition and traditionally excluded groups. Consequently, when developing and implementing measures to formalise informal employment, incentives should take precedence over sanctions.

Why did we need this brief summary of the development of the shadow economy in Serbia? It was needed because it serves as a reminder of the multi-faceted, heterogeneous, and simultaneously stubborn, deeply rooted nature of this phenomenon. In the early 1990s the shadow economy became an acceptable survival mechanism for businesses, entrepreneurs, and households, in answer to the multiple shocks that they faced. At the time, liberal economists mainly underlined the positive role of neo-liberal economics in co-ordinating the market and fostering entrepreneurship. Yet the shadow economy mangled the rules and institutions of the market economy, incentivised corruption, and undermined fiscal morality and the trust of the population in the state. In various forms, the entire society took part in the shadow economy. For instance, the official foreign currency exchange rate usually deviated from the market exchange rate, sometimes even by a multiple of the official figure, but transactions in foreign currency nonetheless took place at the market exchange rate.

The negative economic and social effects of the informal economy first became an issue in the 2000s. Starting in 2001, the Ministry of Finance undertook periodical publicity campaigns to raise the profile of tax compliance, particularly that accompanying the introduction of VAT and fiscal receipts. A survey recently carried out by the Employers' Association and the Association of Independent Trade Unions confirmed that business entities generally viewed the informal economy in a negative light.

However, as with many other areas of the economy, government authorities and economic policymakers are yet to systematically tackle this issue. There is no clear commitment or strategy to the fight against the shadow economy. The past decade again saw permitted exceptions that damaged equality of the participants in the formal market: for instance, 'linking' workers' years of service to compensate for unpaid contributions, cancelling back taxes and other arrears, and tolerating the non-payment of social security contributions by public businesses. Socially owned companies in restructuring even enjoyed, for a long period of time, formal statutory protection from actions that might have led to their insolvency (under the latest amendments to the Law on Privatisation, this protection is set to expire in mid-2014), and were thus able to run up huge debts in unpaid employee contributions to social security funds. There were several waves of what is termed "linking employees' years of service", where the government pays staff contributions at troubled companies—thereby attempting to sway public opinion, but also acting as accessory to the undermining of fiscal morals. This practice of socialising costs, of course, has a negative demonstration effect on employers who comply with all of their statutory obligations to their staff. In other cases, objectively marginal from the point of view of public interest, the state was extraordinarily efficient, even brutal, when collecting certain dues (e.g., performance rights charges).

Serbia's experience over a lengthy period of time demonstrates the shadow economy's distorting and negative effect on balanced economic growth, particularly in times of economic crisis. Displacement and substitution effects dominate employment trends. To paraphrase Gresham's law, no net new jobs are created—bad jobs just drive out the good ones.

Although current economic conditions are much more favourable than those that prevailed during the last decade of the twentieth century, and the shadow economy shows no signs of overflowing its admittedly broad and comfortable basin, it poses at least a threefold challenge to economic policymakers. Firstly, it directly hurts public finances and often threatens public safety and health. Secondly, it is a symptom of institutional weakness and an unfavourable business environment, which jeopardises long-term growth. Thirdly, although it may at first sight seem to serve as a refuge for vulnerable groups, the shadow economy is in reality a trap, perpetuating instead of eliminating their poverty and exclusion.

References

International Labour Office (2011) Statistical update on employment in the informal economy. ILO Department of Statistics

Krstić G (2012) Labour force flows and informal economy in Serbia. In: International conference from global crisis to economic growth. Which way to take? The Faculty of Economics, University of Belgrade, September 2012

Krstić G, Sanfey P (2011) Earnings inequality and the informal economy: evidence from Serbia. Econ Transit 19(1)

Krstić G et al (1998) Analysis of the grey economy in the FRY with estimates of its volume for 1997 and recommendations for its legalisation. Economics Institute Belgrade

Lokshin M, Jovanović B (2003) Wage differentials and state-private sector employment choice in Yugoslavia. Econ Transit 11

Oviedo et al (2009) Economic informality: causes, costs and policies – a literature survey. World Bank Working Paper No. 167, Washington, DC

Schneider F, Enste D (2000) Shadow economies: size, causes and consequences. J Econ Lit 38 (1):77–114

World Bank (2006) Serbia: labor market assessment, report no. 36576-YU, Washington, DC

Chapter 3
The Concept of the Survey of Businesses and Entrepreneurs Operating Informally

Gorana Krstić

3.1 Aim and Content of the Survey

The principal aim of the survey of businesses and entrepreneurs operating informally in Serbia is to assess the various forms of the shadow economy, as well as to analyse the forms of the shadow economy according to the relevant characteristics of business entities. In addition, the survey provides insight into the causes and motives of businesses operating in the shadow economy, which is important when drafting recommendations for shifting businesses from the shadow to the formal economy. The sample consisted of 1,251 business entities (businesses and entrepreneurs), and the survey was carried out from 16 to 22 October 2012 throughout Serbia.

This survey has, for the very first time, made it possible to explore the shadow economy in Serbia from the point of view of businesses, as all previous research has been based on household surveys (Krstić et al. 1998, 2001).[1] Research on employment in the shadow economy has recently been conducted in many countries (EC 2007) in addition to standard and regular Labour Force Surveys, but similar studies on the informal operation of businesses have been relatively rare, as will be discussed in greater detail in Chap. 6. This is due to the substantial risk that business owners/managers will refuse to take part in such a survey, or, when they do take part, will provide misleading answers to questions regarding their involvement in the various forms of the informal economy such as shadow employment (evasion of wage tax and social security contributions); shadow trading (evasion of value added tax); and evasion of other taxes, customs duties, and the like. This concern is also present when surveying the general population, but seems to be less pronounced.

[1] The surveys were carried out in 1997 and 2002, respectively.

G. Krstić (✉)
Faculty of Economics, University of Belgrade, Belgrade, Serbia
e-mail: gkrstic@ekof.bg.ac.rs

G. Krstić, F. Schneider (eds.), *Formalizing the Shadow Economy in Serbia*,
Contributions to Economics, DOI 10.1007/978-3-319-13437-6_3

This is borne out by the results of this study, which show that activities in the shadow economy are more acceptable where individuals rather than legal entities engage in them: legal entities are thus less likely to report such activities in interviews than individuals. Similar results were obtained in a Eurobarometer survey covering 26,755 people aged 15 and over in 27 EU member states, where undeclared work by individuals for private households is deemed more acceptable than undeclared work by businesses (EC 2007).

Notwithstanding the risks inherent in such measurement, the survey of businesses and entrepreneurs operating in the shadow economy in Serbia was successfully carried out on the planned sample, with a large percentage of respondents answering nearly all the questions posed in the questionnaire.

Most of the respondents were either owners of business entities or entrepreneurs. The data were collected using face-to-face interviews.

To reduce the impact of the concealment of undeclared work on the results of the survey, the content of the questions and their wording and order in the questionnaire, as well as the approach employed by the interviewers, were tested in a pilot study[2] and were subsequently adjusted so as to affect respondent bias as little as possible. Various techniques were used that had in previous research shown their effectiveness in eliciting answers that were as honest as possible (e.g., Gerxhani 2007; Kazemier and van Eck 1992; Hanousek and Palda 2004; Krstić et al. 1998). This entails, among other things, gradually introducing respondents to the most sensitive questions, which will usually be posed after the less sensitive ones. The title of the survey (Survey on Conditions for Doing Business in Serbia) was carefully worded so as not to be perceived negatively by the potential respondents i.e., representatives of businesses.

In addition to questions relating to the participation of the surveyed businesses in particular forms of the shadow economy, questions were also asked regarding the subjective attitudes of business owners/managers to the participation of other businesses from the same sector in these activities. This approach has been described as a method that yields more honest responses (Gerxhani 2007) and was used in the studies carried out by Hanousek and Palda (2004), Sauka (2008), and Putninš and Sauka (2011). For the most significant forms of the shadow economy, the same questions were posed to business owners/managers regarding the participation of their own business in the shadow economy and their perception of the participation of other businesses from the same sector in these activities. Sauka (2008) found that, although the questions were posed indirectly, owner/manager responses could be applicable to their own businesses. In this study we assumed that data obtained on the basis of biased owner/manager responses regarding the participation of their own businesses in informal operations could be considered the lower limit of the extent of the shadow economy, while the data obtained on the basis of their subjective perceptions on the participation of other businesses from the same sector could be considered the upper limit.

[2] The pilot study encompassed ten businesses and ten entrepreneurs.

The questionnaire was made up of multiple modules. The first module was devoted to general information about the business (type, size, ownership, year of incorporation, sector of activity, turnover, etc.). The second module was designed to capture data on the activities of each business, starting from less sensitive questions and ending with those dealing with cash payments. The next set of questions related to the position of the business in the market, relative to its competitors. In this part of the questionnaire the business owner/manager was expected to present his or her own subjective view of the participation of other businesses from the same sector of economic activity in the shadow economy (trading, employment, and the like) and the 'justification' of informal operation (individuals vs. legal entities). The last part of this section contained questions that the pilot survey revealed as the most sensitive and the least likely to be answered by respondents. These questions dealt with informal employment (whether any workers were employed in this manner, and, if so, what their number and wages were). The third part of the questionnaire related to the causes of informal operation and the motives of participants in the shadow economy, while the fourth part dealt with the abilities of tax and inspection authorities. These were followed by a section relating to remittances from abroad received through both formal and informal channels by the households of the entrepreneurs interviewed. The final section of the questionnaire covered proposals to develop policies leading to a reduction in informal operations.

3.2 Research Methodology

3.2.1 Definition of 'Shadow Economy' Used in the Survey

Although the subject of this survey was the participation of businesses and entrepreneurs in the shadow economy, the term 'informal operation' was used rather than the expression 'shadow economy'. Where respondents asked for clarification of this term, they were shown a card containing the following definition: "Informal operation is operation that is not fully in compliance with particular laws and regulations governing the operation of businesses, or is not fully governed by law." This definition is rather broad and general in scope so as not to overly discourage respondents from providing answers that are as honest as possible. It corresponds to the definition used in the macro assessment of the shadow economy in Serbia (see Chap. 5), which states that the shadow economy comprises all market-based legal production activities that are deliberately concealed from public authorities for one or more reasons: to evade payment of income, value added, or other taxes; to evade payment of social security contributions; to evade certain legal labour market standards, such as minimum wages, maximum working hours, safety standards, etc.; and to evade certain administrative procedures, such as completing statistical questionnaires or administrative forms (Schneider et al. 2010).

We need to underline that the survey encompassed only formally registered businesses and entrepreneurs, while unregistered companies and/or small privately owned businesses not formally incorporated as legal entities were not covered. In other words, the survey encompassed only a portion of businesses in the shadow economy, the portion involving businesses operating in the formal sector (registered businesses). Shadow economy practices by businesses in the informal sector (unregistered businesses and/or small privately owned businesses not formally incorporated as legal entities) and in households were not examined. It should be borne in mind that estimates of informal employment prepared by the ILO (2011) for nearly all of the world's countries show that employment in unregistered businesses exceeds informal employment in registered businesses and households.

The definition of the shadow economy used in this study is based on the concept of activities that may be declared or undeclared (with tax authorities and other government bodies), rather than on the concept of declared or undeclared businesses or jobs. The first definition has become predominant in Europe and other developed countries as it includes those forms of the shadow economy inherent to a larger degree in developed economies, such as the under-reporting of income by self-employed people and formal businesses, or the payment of a portion of wages in cash (so-called 'envelope wages') that are not covered by the business-based or job-based definition, since the worker is in a formal job and the work takes place in a registered business (Williams et al. 2008).

The shadow economy can be divided into two parts. The first part involves undeclared employment, where entrepreneurs or businesses do not report their employees or declare only a portion of their wages in an attempt to evade or reduce the tax burden (informal employment). These activities are at their most common in the sectors of construction, agriculture, and services performed for households. Another part of the shadow economy entails the underreporting of income, which is most frequent in small shops owned by entrepreneurs that charge in cash and in businesses trading in cash without paying taxes. Schneider (2011) estimated that in Turkey, Spain, Italy, Germany, and Poland the first part accounted for on average two-thirds of the total shadow economy and the second part for the other third.

Taking this concept as the starting point, both of these aspects of business participation in the shadow economy were examined. Business owners/managers were posed questions about the two most important forms of the shadow economy present at their firm: informal employment and evasion of value-added tax i.e., transactions made in cash. The following groups of questions were designed to capture this information:

- Is informal employment present at the company—the most important types of such employment being employing workers without a formal contract, i.e., undeclared employees, and employing workers with a contract but declaring only a portion of their wage? What is the number of such employees? How much do they earn?
- Are payments made through bank accounts, or are payments made partly in cash? What is the frequency of such payments? What is the estimated share of

cash payments in the total? What are the other characteristics of payments made in cash?

In addition to these questions (deemed to be the most important) other forms of the shadow economy were examined by looking at the subjective views of the respondents regarding participation in the shadow economy by other businesses in the same sector of economic activity. The practices analysed included evading property tax or customs duty, and infringement of individual laws and regulations governing business operations.

The percentage of answers to questions posed in the survey was very high, ranging from 92 to 98 %. An exception was the question regarding the number of informally employed workers and their wages, with between 57 and 77 % answering.

3.2.2 Sample

The survey was carried out on a single-stage stratified sample of business entities. The entities were selected from a list of business and entrepreneurs registered with the Business Registries Agency and classified by stratum. The stratification was based on:

- Region: Šumadija and Western Serbia; Southern and Eastern Serbia; Vojvodina.
- Size of entity: up to 4 employees; between 5 and 19 employees; between 20 and 49 employees; between 50 and 249 employees; more than 250 employees.
- Sector of economic activity: agriculture; manufacturing; construction; trade; transportation; catering; other services.

The total sample was allocated by stratum in proportion to the size of each stratum in the initial sample. A simple random sample was used, without replacement by stratum. The sample is representative at the level of Serbia and by stratum (size of entity, sector of economic activity, and region).

3.3 Basic Information on the Business Entities Surveyed

A total of 606 businesses and 645 entrepreneurs were surveyed and the results were presented after weighting by stratum to make the sample representative at the level of Serbia and by stratum.

Most of the respondents were business owners (82 % of all businesses surveyed), with far fewer managing directors (13 %) or chief financial officers (6 %). The sample made it possible to survey business entities of varying sizes. The final sample contained 83 % companies with a few workers (i.e., up to four employees), 13 % with slightly more employees (5–20), while larger companies were less

Table 3.1 Main characteristics of the business entities surveyed (%)

Characteristics of business entities	% of business entities surveyed
Number of employees	
Up to 4	83.3
5–19	13.2
20 or more	3.5
Ownership structure	
Private	97.0
Socially owned	1.9
State	0.4
Other	0.6
VAT payer	
Yes	56.0
No	44.0

Source: Own calculations. Survey on Conditions for Doing Business in Serbia, FREN, 2012

represented (Table 3.1). Just as expected, entrepreneurs were to a greater extent micro-enterprises with fewer than five workers (89 % of all entrepreneurs), since they almost never employ more than 20 workers. According to ownership structure, 91 % of all businesses and nearly 100 % of all entrepreneurs were privately owned (97 % of the total sample), while their equity was nearly always of domestic origin (in 98 % of all cases).

The sample was constructed taking into account the sector of the business entities' economic activity. Most entities represented were engaged in wholesale and retail trade or auto repair (30 %) or other services (26 %) such as: information and communications; financial and insurance services; real estate; public administration; scientific and technical activities; administration; education; healthcare and social security; and other services. These were followed by manufacturing (17 %), construction (9 %), transportation (10 %), catering (7 %) and agriculture (2 %).

Around half of all business entities (56 %) were VAT payers: 83 % of all businesses and 45 % of all entrepreneurs.

Respondents estimated that only 24 % of all businesses and 46 % of entrepreneurs saw their sales increase in 2011 relative to 2010, while all other business entities reported a decline in sales.

References

European Commission (2007) Undeclared work in the European Union, Special Eurobarometer
Gerxhani K (2007) Did you pay your taxes? How (not) to conduct tax evasion in transition countries. Soc Indic Res 80(3):555–581

Hanousek J, Palda F (2004) Quality of government services and the civic duty to pay taxes in the Czech and Slovak Republics and other transition countries. Kyklos 57(2):237–252
International Labour Office (2011) Statistical update on employment in the informal economy. ILO Department of Statistics
Kazemier B, van Eck R (1992) Survey investigations of the hidden economy. J Econ Philos 13
Krstić G et al (1998) Analysis of the grey economy in the FRY with estimates of its volume for 1997 and recommendations for its legalisation. Economics Institute Belgrade
Krstić G et al (2001) Reintegration of the grey economy and development of private sector in Serbia. Economics Institute Belgrade and League of Experts
Putninš TJ, Sauka A (2011) The size and determinants of shadow economies in the Baltic States. Baltic J Econ 11(2)
Sauka A (2008) Productive, unproductive and destructive entrepreneurship: a theoretical and empirical exploration. Peter Lang GmbH, Frankfurt am Main
Schneider F (2011) The shadow economy in Europe – using payment systems to combat the shadow economy. http://www.bblf.bg/uploads/files/file_378.pdf
Schneider F, Buehn A, Montenegro CE (2010) New estimates for the shadow economies all over the world. Int Econ J 24(4):443–461
Williams C, Horlings E, Renooy P (2008) Tackling undeclared work in the EU, European Foundation for the improvement of living and working conditions, 2008

Chapter 4
Causes of the Shadow Economy

Milojko Arsić, Mihail Arandarenko, Branko Radulović, Saša Ranđelović, and Irena Janković

4.1 Causes of the Shadow Economy Rooted in the Tax System

Of all the factors related to the design of the tax system and the institutional environment for its payment, collection, and administration, the following have the most significant impact on the extent of the shadow economy: size and structure of the tax burden; efficiency of the tax administration in collecting taxes; penalty policy; complexity and fairness of the tax system; and compliance costs.

4.1.1 The Size of the Tax Burden

According to the standard (Allingham–Sandmo) model of tax evasion, the size of the tax burden, along with the probability of detection of tax evasion and the possible sanctions, is a fundamental determinant of tax evasion, as well as of the shadow economy as a basis for tax evasion. According to this approach, increasing the tax burden makes it more cost-effective to operate in the informal sector. The total tax burden in Serbia is moderate (as measured by the ratio of tax revenue to GDP) and close to the averages of other Central and Eastern European countries. The situation is different, however, when individual forms of taxes are considered. Thus the general VAT rate is among the lowest in the region (even after the increase

M. Arsić (✉) • M. Arandarenko • S. Ranđelović • I. Janković
Faculty of Economics, University of Belgrade, Belgrade, Serbia
e-mail: arsicm@ekof.bg.ac.rs; arandarenko@ekof.bg.ac.rs; randjelovic@ekof.bg.ac.rs; irenaj@ekof.bg.ac.rs

B. Radulović
Faculty of Law, University of Belgrade, Belgrade, Serbia
e-mail: bradulovic@ius.bg.ac.rs

G. Krstić, F. Schneider (eds.), *Formalizing the Shadow Economy in Serbia*, Contributions to Economics, DOI 10.1007/978-3-319-13437-6_4

to 20 %), while the reduced rate (at 8 %) is about average (Fiscal Council 2012). The rate of excise duty on oil products is slightly higher than the regional average, while the excise on tobacco products is at the level of the regional average (but lower than in developed countries); excise duty on most alcoholic beverages is at the level of the regional average or below. We can therefore conclude that the size of the tax burden on consumption in Serbia is no greater, on average, than in other Central and Eastern European countries, which leads us to conclude that the VAT tax burden is not an important cause of the greater extent of the shadow economy in Serbia in comparison to other countries in the region.

On the other hand, the fiscal burden on labour (as measured by the share of wage tax and social security contributions in total labour costs) is relatively high in Serbia, both in absolute terms and in relation to the country's level of development. This leads us to the conclusion that the size of the tax burden on income (particularly regarding social security contributions) is a major cause of the shadow economy in the field of wages, as well as of the corresponding tax gap in Serbia. Although the overall fiscal burden in Serbia is, realistically, moderate in relation to that in other Central and Eastern European countries, it is perceived as high by most businesses: many respondents in the survey carried out as part of this study identified high taxes as the third most significant cause of the large extent of the shadow economy. As legal entities mainly shift the VAT burden onto end-users, it is realistic to assume that most of them refer to the fiscal burden on labour when discussing fiscal burdens in general.

4.1.2 The Fiscal Burden on Labour

As for the fiscal burden on labour, it is particularly important to underline that, from a comparative standpoint, the labour tax wedge (calculated as the quotient of total wage tax and social contributions and total labour costs) is high at low wage levels and relatively low at high wage levels, a consequence of a proportional income tax system with a relatively small portion of non-taxable wage. At 33 % of the average wage, the tax wedge in Serbia stands at 36.7 %. In Europe, recognised globally as the region with the highest taxes, only Sweden, Hungary, Romania, and the Federation of Bosnia–Herzegovina have greater tax wedges at those wage levels. At the level of the average wage, Serbia's tax wedge is around the European average. The progressiveness of labour taxation is very low: between 33 and 100 % of the average wage, the tax wedge increases by just 2.6 percentage points, while in many European countries the increase is over 10 percentage points (Koettl 2012). It should be noted that taxation was even regressive between 2001 and 2007, with the tax wedge at the level of 33 % of the average wage standing at as much as 47.1 %, while amounting to 42.2 % at the level of the average wage (Arandarenko and Stanić 2006): which could serve as an explanation of the otherwise counterintuitive increase in informal employment seen between 2002 and 2007 (Krstić and Sanfey 2011).

The high tax wedge for low-paid work is a natural incentive to sustain and increase informal employment. When informal businesses (including informal self-proprietorships) are formalised by moving into the formal sector they typically introduce salaries close to the minimum wage. If the tax burden is high at these wage levels, it is a clear obstacle to formalisation on the labour demand side. On the side of labour supply, the productivity of lower-qualified workers in lower-paid, labour-intensive sectors is low; so for many of them their salary is borderline 'cost-effective' when compared to the alternatives, such as social welfare or work in the informal economy. In addition, the existence of a minimum social insurance contribution base (currently standing at 35 % of the average wage) limits formal part-time employment.

4.1.3 The Social Welfare System

The social welfare system in Serbia is conceived in the traditional manner. Most importantly, welfare benefits are withdrawn at a ratio of 1:1 as reported income from labour increases. There is no employee benefits programme. Once a person loses the right to social welfare payments by virtue of finding employment, he or she must go through the entire demanding procedure of collecting documents and undergoing verification to become entitled to social welfare again. As a consequence, many beneficiaries of social welfare opt for a survival strategy where they combine these benefits with unreported, generally occasional, work. The rules of the tax/benefit system as presented here act in synergy to foster informal employment, and consequently the shadow economy.

4.1.4 The Efficiency of the Tax Administration in Collecting Taxes

The efficiency of the tax administration in collecting taxes is also an important determinant of the shadow economy, in the sense that greater probability of detecting tax evasion—all other considerations being equal—leads to a reduction in the shadow economy. Although there are no consistent and comparable data on the probability of detecting tax evasion in Serbia and other Central and Eastern European countries, we estimate, from the results of the survey, that it is relatively low in Serbia. A large number of taxpayers cite that the benefits of tax evasion are greater than potential losses if detected as 8th of the 11 key causes of the shadow economy. This does not mean that the Tax Administration is very effective in uncovering tax evasion, but rather that other factors are seen as more important in maintaining the shadow economy.

The Shadow Economy and Use of State Services Free of Charge
The focus of most research on the shadow economy is on the environmental factors that affect whether individuals decide to take part in the shadow economy. However, it must be borne in mind that people have a propensity to evade paying taxes but to continue using social security, health, education and other services provided by the state. This propensity is borne out by both day-to-day experience and a substantial body of econometric and experimental research. Due to people's preference for free services, there would be tax evasion even if state services were completely aligned with public preferences. To tackle tax evasion, therefore, the elimination of environmental incentives must be accompanied by the establishment of an efficient evasion detection system, and non-selective prosecution of evaders caught. The propensity of the public to use services free of charge can to some degree be reduced by changing the population's values through outreach and the education system.

4.1.5 The Penalties for Tax Evasion

The penalties for tax evasion correlate negatively with the extent of the shadow economy and tax evasion: greater penalties, all other things being equal, bring about a reduction in the volume of the shadow economy and tax evasion. Empirical research shows that the impact of sanction policies on the extent of the shadow economy is lower than that of the probability of discovery (Alm et al. 1992), which leads to the conclusion that inadequate sanctions can be a cause, but not the key cause, of the shadow economy. The system of sanctions for tax evasion in Serbia is relatively well defined in statute, both as regards the penalties themselves and their imposition. Penalties for non-payment of taxes are defined as a function of the tax evaded (rather than of the undeclared tax base), which is an appropriate solution from the point of view of the sanction's desired aim. The sanctions for non-payment of taxes in Serbia comprise the basic penalty (fine or imprisonment) and interest for not having paid the taxes in due time. Although the statutory framework is not structurally deficient, the inappropriate and inconsistent application of the available penal mechanisms fosters the development of the shadow economy in Serbia. It has become standard practice for the Government to write off interest for late payment of taxes, provided that taxpayers continue paying tax regularly. This means that those taxpayers that pay their taxes regularly are put at a disadvantage, increasing moral hazard behaviour that negatively impacts their future readiness to comply with tax rules.

4.1.6 The Probability of Sanctions

The probability of sanctions where evasion is detected also substantially affects the extent of the informal economy. Even with a well-designed statutory framework for sanctioning tax evasion the penalty system can remain an inefficient tool for tackling the shadow economy due to corruption, poor co-ordination between the Tax Administration and other government bodies, and lack of readiness and willingness on the part of the judiciary to process tax evasion cases, particularly with more complex evasion schemes ('VAT carousel' etc.). According to the results of the survey, this is also the case with Serbia, as more than two-thirds of all respondents felt that the probability of being penalised for tax evasion as provided for by law was very low, standing at the level of a random guess (50 %) or even lower.

4.1.7 The Structure of the Tax System

The structure of the tax system is an important factor in the extent of the shadow economy, in the sense that the level of informal activity is lower in countries where the public revenue system is based more on taxing consumption than on taxation of the factors of production. The reason for this lies in the fact that it is easier to evade taxes on the factors of production (particularly personal income tax). The share of taxes on consumption and those on the factors of production in total public revenues is nearly equal in Serbia, but a reform of the tax system involving a reduction in tax on labour and a revenue-neutral increase in consumption taxes could, among other positive economic effects, bring about a partial reduction in the general extent of the shadow economy.

4.1.8 The Complexity of the Tax System

In Serbia there is a large number of types of tax, and the system used to assess individual taxes is very complex. The more different streams of public revenue there are, and the more complex rules to assess and implement taxes, the lower the ability of tax inspectors to audit all types of tax, resulting in a lower probability of detecting tax evasion. In 2011 there were in excess of 370 various charges in Serbia, both fiscal and quasi-fiscal; most were administered by the Tax Administration of the Republic of Serbia and by local Public Revenue Administrations (NALED 2012a). In an environment dominated by such a large number of charges and with few qualified people auditing taxes, the complexity of the tax system is a major cause of the shadow economy. A large number of taxes, including many that are difficult to assess, can also lead to tax evasion by omission, as taxpayers may fail to comply because they are not aware of the requirements or lack the technical knowledge for tax self-assessment. The survey found that quasi-fiscal charges were seen as 5th of the 11 causes of the shadow economy, being ranked after macroeconomic and fiscal factors, lack of trust in the state, and corruption.

This system of quasi-fiscal charges has not been sufficiently transparent: unpredictable changes to it have been made and the main parameters of the charges (base, rate, taxpayer, etc.) have sometimes been arbitrarily defined according to the needs of different public authorities (Arsić et al. 2012). Quasi-fiscal charges have substantially distorted the operations of companies and entrepreneurs.[1] The amount of these charges has often been out of proportion to the financial strength of the taxpayer, value of the service rendered to the taxpayer, amount of natural resources used by the taxpayer, and damage caused to the environment. As the fees and charges have, in some cases, been assessed at a much higher level than appropriate for the purpose of these instruments, they have often been primarily—and sometimes predominantly—taxes in nature.[2] Apart from issues regarding the amounts of the charges, multiple quasi-fiscal fees have often been introduced that have similar purposes (same base, same taxpayer). In addition to introducing distortion, the quasi-fiscal charges have made a major contribution to the opaque tax system and growing tax compliance costs. These charges have to a large extent negated the positive effects of the low rates of basic taxes (corporate income tax, VAT). Some of the fees that have been a major burden in the private sector have had a direct bearing on the decision to start operating in the informal sector or to move a part or all of an operation into the shadow economy. The reform of the system of quasi-fiscal charges carried out in the second half of 2012 has been an important precondition for improving the business environment in Serbia, while the abolishment of some of these charges will certainly reduce start-up costs for small business entities. Appropriate categorisation and naming of the various charges, use of better parameters, and, above all, alignment of the charges with the financial strength of the taxpayer, will all have a major impact on motivating entities not to operate in the shadow economy. The statutory requirement for government bodies to set the amount of fees and charges for the following year by the end of third quarter of the current year could contribute to greater predictability of conditions for doing business in Serbia. Moreover, the proposed requirement to obtain the consent of the Ministry of Finance and Economy for any modification of fees and charges within the remit of local authorities or extra-budgetary institutions could prevent the uncontrolled growth of these burdens, which in the past has been a major incentive for taxpayers to attempt to circumvent them.

---

[1] According to the NALED study, the Government collected in excess of 2 % of GDP through the charges inventoried, but it is clear that the number of these charges and their significance to the balance are greater.

[2] For instance, some classical taxes were treated by statute as fees: the construction land usage fee, which is a typical property tax, as well as the 'signboard fee', which is also a classical tax rather than a fee.

4.1.9 The Fairness of the Tax System

A fair tax system subjects entities at similar levels of financial strength to similar tax burdens. In the Serbian tax system, and particularly in personal and corporate income tax, such fairness is often notably absent. Personal income from various sources is taxed differently, so that individuals with high income from capital are taxed at a lower rate than those with high income from work. There are many tax breaks available to business entities so that entities in different segments pay different levels of tax on the same amount of profit. The real or perceived lack of fairness in taxation is a major driver of resistance to paying taxes. Although the latest changes to the Corporate Income Tax Law, adopted in December 2012, removed a number of tax breaks, the most generous and most frequently used (such as investment tax credit) have been retained. Given the relatively low statutory tax rate, liberal tax breaks are an expensive (in terms of tax expenditure) and inefficient instrument for incentivising investment, as well as one that distorts business behaviour by continuing to treat entities of similar economic power differently.

4.1.10 Tax Compliance Costs

Tax compliance costs are, along with high tax burden, one of the major elements of expenses associated with tax compliance. When costs (time and money) associated with assessing, declaring, and paying taxes are high due to complicated procedures, lack of e-filing opportunities, etc., taxpayers are more incentivised to operate in the informal sector. Serbia is ranked 149th (of 185 countries) for ease of paying taxes in the World Bank's Doing Business 2012 survey: a decline in relation to last year and almost the worst result of all the countries in the region, as well as of all other areas of doing business in Serbia. The high tax compliance costs in Serbia are caused by the large number of payment procedures (as many as 66 times per year, compared to the Eastern European average of 28 times per year) and the substantial time cost of these activities (280 working hours per year, on average). Accordingly, it can be concluded that high tax compliance costs are also a major reason for the increase in the shadow economy in Serbia. According to estimates based on the standard cost model, costs of administering taxes account for 47 % of all administrative costs (Radulović 2011b).

The contribution made by these causes to the extent of the shadow economy in Serbia is difficult to gauge, but can be approximately estimated on the basis of taxpayers' views and their perception of the importance of each of the above causes (Fig. 4.1).

According to the results of the survey, legal taxpaying entities believe that the economic crisis and fewer opportunities for employment, loss of confidence in the government and public institutions, and high taxes are the principal causes of

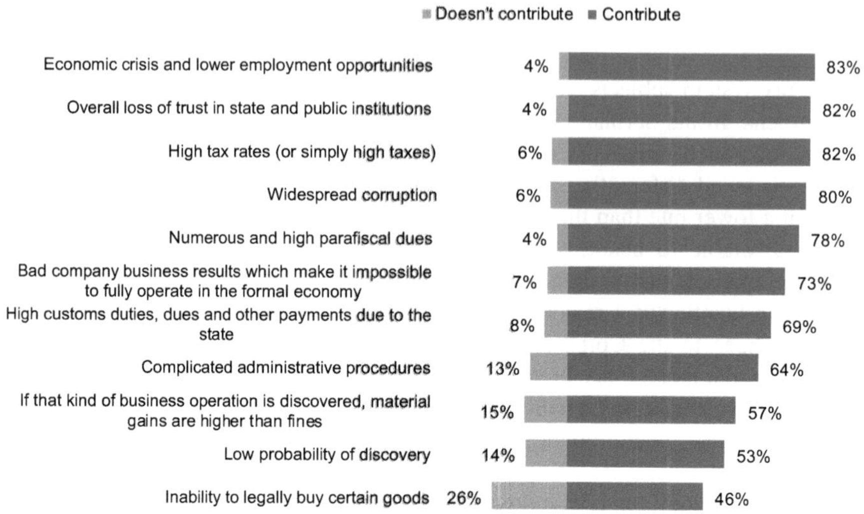

Fig. 4.1 Respondents' views on the contribution made by individual causes to the shadow economy in Serbia. *Source*: Own calculations. Survey on Conditions for Doing Business in Serbia, FREN, 2012

the shadow economy in Serbia. In addition, widespread corruption, numerous quasi-fiscal charges, and poor corporate performance are among the main causes. The problem of being unable to legally purchase certain goods is ranked least significant.

The taxpayer's decision whether or not to fully comply with their tax obligation depends on the objective situation regarding the causes of the shadow economy referred to above, and on their perception of that situation. The survey results on taxpayer views of the importance of the causes of the shadow economy is therefore also relevant in the context of designing measures aimed at tackling the shadow economy in Serbia.

4.2 Labour Market Institutions as an Incentive to the Shadow Economy

Recently it has often been claimed that rigid labour market regulation (particularly hiring and firing rules or more generally, employment protection legislation) is one of the major causes of the shadow economy. However, the regulatory framework for the labour market comprises a large number of other features whose impact on the shadow economy may be equally important. In this section we will briefly consider the influence of some of these diverse factors that we believe could, in their current form, foster the shadow economy.

4.2.1 Minimum Wage

In the simplest theoretical context, the minimum wage in the competitive labour market can artificially constrain demand for labour. If an institutionally imposed lower wage limit means that it is not cost-effective for businesses to pay workers more than the wage that reflects their marginal productivity, such businesses will simply refuse to hire them. Those workers will either remain unemployed or will move to sectors without a minimum wage. If a uniform minimum wage applies across the entire formal sector, as is the case in Serbia, then the informal sector is the only way out for workers whose marginal productivity is lower than the minimum wage.

The amount of the minimum wage is one of the key parameters that define how many workers will be 'squeezed out' of the formal sector. The higher this wage (the amount of which is usually viewed in relation to the average wage, which also makes it comparable internationally), the greater the likelihood that more workers enter the informal sector. Between 2001 and 2010 the minimum wage in Serbia fluctuated in a relatively stable interval of between 35 and 40 % of the average wage (Arandarenko and Avlijaš 2011), which, in international terms, is considered a moderate amount. However, 2011, and particularly 2012, saw a major increase in the minimum wage, which reached a level of approximately 50 % of the average wage in 2012, making the minimum-to-average wage ratio in Serbia higher then the Western Balkans average (Kovtun et al. 2014). This is considered very high and can safely be said to be an incentive to informal employment.

4.2.2 Working Hours

The Labour Law stipulates rules governing working hours. This is a broad body of regulations that includes rules on the length of full-time, part-time, and shortened working hours, overtime and work on holidays, re-allocation of working hours, annual leave, daily rest periods, maternity leave, etc. Generally speaking, the more generous these provisions are to workers (shorter working hours, longer leave, greater reimbursement for overtime, etc.), *ceteris paribus*, the greater the cost to employers and the greater the incentive for them to partially or fully rely on informal workers to whom they can deny statutory rights. Typically, employers operating on the margins of formal sector will tend to extend the working hours of their employees, both formal and informal, without reimbursement for overtime or indeed any reimbursement at all; they are also prone to cutting workers' annual leave and ignoring statutory paid leave periods. It has also been observed that a shorter working week (e.g., of 35 h, as in France) creates incentives for additional informal work among those in formal employment.

OECD (2008) concluded that, when compared to other nations, Serbia had in place balanced and neutral working hours regulations. The 40 h standard working week fits into the international average. The option of reducing the working week to 36 h is rarely used. From a comparative perspective, overtime is rather limited, with 8 h of overtime allowed per week. However, the law is more generous towards employers in terms of re-allocating working hours, since it allows them to require employees to work up to 60 h/week over a rather lengthy period of 6 months.

Thus working hours legislation in Serbia is comparable to the international average for countries at a similar level of development. It is part of a tradition spanning several decades that is rooted among both workers and employers and thus probably does not represent a major primary incentive for exclusion from the formal economy and/or participation in the informal economy.

4.2.3 Employment Protection Legislation

In a narrow sense, employment protection legislation (EPL) is made up of a set of provisions and procedures that apply to the termination of employees. It imposes statutory limitations on the termination of employees and governs compensation payable by employers to employees in the case of both individual and collective termination of open-ended employment contracts. Employment protection legislation has two main cost components: transfers, made up of severance payments and the obligatory notice period, and taxes, which entail the procedural costs of implementing EPL and the payments that need to be made to third parties, such as the state, courts, and legal experts or other consultants. In a broader sense, EPL also includes statutory regulation of hiring rules, including statutory limitations that can be imposed through atypical employment contracts and that limit employee rights in relation to those enjoyed by workers on open-ended employment contracts. In general, the stricter the EPL the greater the incentive for businesses to employ informal workers.

A composite EPL index, developed by the OECD, is used for international comparison of the level of strictness of this framework. Although World Bank and OECD (2008) research found that Serbia had an EPL index of 2.4 (on a scale from 0 to 6, with 0 being the most liberal and 6 the most rigid level of regulation), which is close to the average of OECD countries including comparable Central and Eastern European nations, there are specific and important aspects of EPL that are widely held to have a possible negative impact on formal employment.

Firstly, the amount of the statutory severance pay applicable in Serbia is linked to the entire years of service of an employee, rather than on the years of service with any one employer. This solution is nearly unique globally and must have a detrimental impact on the formal employment of elderly workers, although the intent of the legislator was surely quite the opposite, as it makes it more expensive to fire workers with more years of service.

Secondly, another harmful rule often cited is that under which the most a fixed-term employment contract can be extended is up to 1 year, after which the employer is required either to terminate the employee or to change their contract to an open-ended one. From a global perspective, most countries now allow fixed-term contracts that last or can be extended for more than 1 year as a result of efforts to increase labour market flexibility. However, in practice most companies in Serbia have been known to break this rule with impunity by changing job titles and thus circumventing the statutory provision.

It is interesting to note that the respondents in the Survey on Conditions for Doing Business in Serbia stated that, among the most significant factors that constrain doing business, labour legislation was only marginally restrictive: a mere 3 % of total respondents included labour legislation among the largest constraints. In addition, when respondents were asked what would improve the employee registration process and increase their total wages, 38 % cited a cut in wage taxes and 38 % a cut in contributions, while just 5 % mentioned changes to labour legislation making it easier to terminate workers.

4.2.4 Unemployment Benefits

These benefits are a reserve source of income for workers who lose their jobs, designed to help protect their standard of living and to enable them to devote all of their time to looking for a new job. They therefore represent a natural extension of employment protection legislation during the time that a worker is unemployed. Yet, since entitlement to unemployment benefits is lost when a new formal job is found, beneficiaries are incentivised to combine these benefits and income from informal employment until their unemployment benefits expire.

The new 2009 Law on Employment and Unemployment Insurance reduced these incentives in several aspects. Firstly, the extent of these benefits was reduced by cutting the maximum period to 1 year (or, exceptionally, 2 years for people meeting at least one condition for retirement at the time they lose their job), as well as by establishing lower minimum and maximum benefit amounts ranging from 80 to 160 % of the minimum wage, respectively. Secondly, incentives were introduced for finding formal employment before the expiry of the benefit period in the form of 30 % of the amount that would have been paid if the right to benefits had been exercised to the fullest extent.

As current statutory provisions governing these benefits are comparable with European and regional practice, in addition to which few countries have incentives for early re-employment, the that current rules cannot be changed substantially when it comes to statutorily guaranteed rights. There has, however, been criticism of the National Employment Service, which is believed by some not to be sufficiently efficient in supervising active job seeking by unemployment beneficiaries.

4.2.5 *Retirement Rules*

The parameters governing Serbia's pension system include a relatively low minimum retirement age. In addition, there is no actuarial penalty for early retirement. This creates incentives for people to continue working after retiring, primarily in the informal sector, as formal work by pensioners is highly restricted. The standard retirement age in Serbia is lower than in most other European countries (particularly for women), while the difference between the standard and minimum age is among the greatest, which indicates that this factor could substantially affect the shadow economy among the Serbian population. The minimum retirement age in Serbia is 55 years, or even lower in some sectors of activity (such as the military and the police); thus people who retire relatively young continue working, mainly in the informal sector.

4.3 Other Institutional and Economic Causes of the Shadow Economy in Serbia

The following institutional and economic factors have been estimated to have the greatest impact on the extent of the shadow economy in Serbia: low productivity, the economic crisis and widespread lack of liquidity, inefficient market exit mechanism, high administrative burden, poor regulatory environment and legal insecurity, construction permits for both existing buildings ('legalisation') and new construction, low quality of public services, large number of small business entities, structure of the population's income, high levels of corruption, high tolerance for the shadow economy by the state, high unemployment rate, and low tax morality.[3]

4.3.1 *Low Productivity*

According to the World Bank (2009), the productivity of Serbian businesses (value added per worker) is much lower and their unit costs are much higher than in other countries in the region.[4] Low productivity, coupled with other factors, causes a

[3] For an overview of the relevant causes of the shadow economy, see Schneider and Enste (2000), and GIZ (2010).

[4] Between 2007 and 2009 the added value per worker in Serbia was €12,837 per annum, or on average less than half of the figure recorded in Slovakia (€25,043), or slightly less than half of the amount for Hungary (€20,812). In addition, unlike the situation in EU countries—where medium-sized and large businesses are much more productive than small ones—workers in Serbia's medium-sized businesses are less productive by as much as 20 % than employees in small businesses, while large businesses are only slightly more productive (by a mere 5 %). The

vicious circle in which low productivity makes business entities turn to the informal sector, which, as a rule, decreases productivity further.[5] In these circumstances, the business model of many companies means they can be profitable (or, indeed, even survive) only if they fail to comply with their tax obligations, either wholly or in part.[6]

4.3.2 Economic Crisis and Widespread Lack of Liquidity

In an environment dominated by the economic crisis and a major decline in demand, a number of business entities have been forced to adjust their operations to the emerging circumstances. Some businesses that used to be profitable before the crisis have now been forced to move at least part of their activities into the shadow economy to be able to continue doing business. Other business entities are faced with poor liquidity.[7] Due to widespread liquidity problems, business entities that pay taxes in Serbia often opt for partial compliance with tax legislation, either not paying regularly or not paying the amounts required, giving preference instead to meeting their obligations arising from commercial transactions. To be able to be selective in their payments, business entities often shift part of their operations into the shadow economy and pay their debts according to the significance of each particular creditor to their business. According to the findings of the survey, the economic crisis was identified as the single most important cause of the shadow economy.

difference is even greater when particular sectors are observed (e.g., manufacturing) (World Bank 2011).

[5] Multiple reasons for the lower productivity of the informal sector are usually cited in literature. The first one is the informal sector's limited access to finance. Poorer access to formal finance (see the last section of this chapter) forces these entities to seek finance from more expensive informal sources, or to rely exclusively on their own sources of finance (including borrowing from family and friends). Limited access to finance means that these companies employ less capital: this in turn means that they cannot be more efficient due to division of labour, or achieve economies of scale and size. Consequently, business entities operating in the informal sector tend to use labour-intensive means of production and have lower productivity. The second reason is that the informal sector, as a rule, retains a less productive workforce. The third factor is that these entities cannot seek protection from the state (say, if informal contracts are not met), nor do they have access to the various forms of assistance provided by the state. Finally, these business entities are often unable to report corruption in government bodies, and are thus frequently forced to bribe corrupt officials themselves.

[6] As taxes account for less than 10 % of total expenditure, businesses must include all relevant costs—including taxes—into their business models (Ranđelović and Đorđević 2012).

[7] One should bear in mind the fact that, in the minds of business people, the economic crisis can to a large extent be equated with issues of poor liquidity (and insolvency) faced by the corporate sector.

4.3.3 Inefficient Market Exit

The already-mentioned issue of poor efficiency and substantial liquidity shortages should lead to an orderly exit of businesses from the market, through either insolvency (bankruptcy) or voluntary liquidation. Reforms of the insolvency procedure have resulted in some progress, both in terms of the duration and cost of the proceedings and the number of insolvency cases (primarily owing to the application of 'automatic bankruptcy'), and have also brought about a major reduction in the number of insolvent businesses (i.e., businesses whose bank accounts have been frozen). Nevertheless, the late initiation of formal insolvency proceedings or the lack of such proceedings has made it possible for a number of debtors whose bank accounts have been frozen to continue operating, mainly in the informal sector. In mid-2012 the Constitutional Court declared the 'automatic bankruptcy' provisions of the Bankruptcy Law unconstitutional. This ruling will lead to a renewed increase in the number of businesses with illiquidity problems, some of which will be forced to continue operating in the informal sector.[8]

Another problem also present in Serbia is the so-called 'phoenix company' mechanism, where businesses keep their debts vested in the old business while their assets are transferred to a new business (or they temporarily move the business into the shadow economy) and then *de facto* wind the old business up. In practice this often takes place with no sanctions for the owner. 'Phoenix companies' most often do business with small and medium-sized businesses and cause them substantial liquidity problems. To be able to survive, the victims of 'phoenix companies' themselves rely on moving part of their operations into the shadow economy.

4.3.4 High Administrative Burden

A high administrative burden incentivises businesses and individuals to do business in the informal sector. Empirical findings show a substantial positive correlation between the regulatory burden imposed on the private sector and the extent of the shadow economy.[9] Some authors (e.g., Friedman et al. 2000) even believe that

[8] Provisions on automatic insolvency (as governed by the Bankruptcy Law, *Official Gazette of the Republic of Serbia* Nos. 104/2009, 99/2011—other law, and 71/2012—Constitutional Court ruling) have been repealed. This has made it possible for debtors whose accounts have been frozen due to non-payment for more than 1 year to continue operating.

[9] Johnson et al. (1998) showed that changes to the regulatory environment (as measured using the regulation index, which ranges between 1 and 5) have a major impact on the share of the shadow economy. A one-point change in the index will lead to an increase of 8.1 % in the share of the shadow economy. Enste (2010) used a comprehensive regulation index (comprising regulation of the labour and goods market, and the quality of institutions) to also analyse the relationship between the regulatory environment and the shadow economy. The findings, based on research into 25 OECD member countries, show that regulation is one of the main factors that determine the extent of the shadow economy, in addition to the tax wedge and tax morality.

Table 4.1 Comparison of administrative costs and extent of shadow economy

Country	Administrative costs (% of GDP)	Shadow economy (% of GDP)
Serbia (2010)	4.0	30.1
Denmark (2006)	2.2	17.0
Netherlands (2003)	3.6	13.3
Czech Republic (2005)	3.0	17.8
Austria (2006)	2.8	9.6

Sources: For the share of administrative costs in GDP in Serbia, see Radulović (2011b); for the Netherlands, see Netherlands Bureau for Economic Policy Analysis, CPB (2004), *Reducing the administrative burden in the European Union, CPB Memorandum*; for Denmark, see SCM Network (2006), *Information about the Danish SCM measurements*; for the Czech Republic, see Office of the Government of the Czech Republic (2006), *Regulatory Reform in the Czech Republic*. For the shadow economy, see Schneider et al. (2010), except for Serbia, for which see Chap. 4 of this study

entrepreneurs base their decision as to whether or not to enter the informal sector more on their desire to avoid bureaucracy (and corruption) than to evade paying taxes.[10] The administrative burden is considered to be one of the major causes of the shadow economy in Serbia. The administrative costs of doing business in Serbia—estimated between 3.8 and 4.2 % (Radulović 2011b)—put it at the top of the list of countries that have made similar measurements. Table 4.1 shows a comparison of the share of administrative costs and the shadow economy in GDP in selected countries.[11]

However, it is interesting that in the Survey on Conditions for Doing Business in Serbia, carried out for the purposes of this study, complex administrative procedures were ranked 'only' eighth in the list of causes of the shadow economy, behind macroeconomic and tax factors, as well as behind corruption and lack of trust in the state (Fig. 4.1). When analysing the findings of this study we should take into account the fact that the respondents came from businesses that operate, as a rule, mainly or even wholly in the formal economy. Hence, we cannot conclude that complex administrative procedures have ceased to be a major factor for those still remaining outside the formal market.

4.3.5 Poor Regulatory Environment and Legal Insecurity

In assessing the regulatory burden we should bear in mind the fact that it is not just the burden that matters (in terms of money and time spent on compliance, etc.): it is

[10] The findings of Friedman et al. (2000) indicate a substantial link between various indicators of the regulatory burden and the extent of the shadow economy: more regulation means a larger shadow economy.

[11] One should exercise caution when comparing these data, due to the different methodologies used to calculate administrative costs. The standard cost model is treated in greater detail and a comparison of methodologies by country is given in Radulović (2011a).

also the quality of the regulatory environment that is important.[12] Where the regulatory environment is poor, and the regulatory burden great, business entities will tend to shift at least part of their activities into the shadow economy. In this context, Enste (2010) cites the advantages of deregulation over other instruments aimed at reducing the extent of the informal economy. On the one hand, tax policy and the social security system are much more difficult to reform, due to the rigidity of the need to finance public goods and services and the political sensitivity of such reforms. On the other, deregulation does not bring about an increase in the budget deficit, while at the same time removing constraints and creating greater freedom of choice in how to do business, thereby directly contributing to the shadow economy becoming a less attractive option.

The findings of the survey show that "frequent legislative changes and imposition of unnecessary costs by the state" were cited by business entities as the second most important problem when doing business (a total of 41 %). As regulatory expenses are mainly fixed, they theoretically affect small businesses the most. There are multiple causes of the low quality of the regulatory environment and legal insecurity in Serbia, the most important being lateness in adopting bylaws, inadequate consultation with the private sector, and poor analysis and drafting process. One of the main causes of legal insecurity is lateness in adopting bylaws, which makes it impossible to implement the laws, while simultaneously old legislation lapses.[13] Faced with this legal vacuum, business entities are often forced to operate not knowing whether they are operating in accordance with the law or if their activities fall within the scope of the shadow economy. The second cause of the poor regulatory environment is the frequent lack of publicity and consultations with the private sector in designing new legislation. According to analyses carried out by Transparency Serbia (2012), statutory provisions governing public comment periods in Serbia are inadequate. Among other things, there is no pre-defined form of public debate, nor are there sanctions in the event that a public body fails to launch such a debate.[14] Non-compliance with the law by public authorities is compounded by the frequently passive stance of business entities. Businesses often lack the time and resources needed to take part, or simply do not feel that they can change anything. Besides, the frequent use of urgent law-making procedure in adopting legislation makes any kind of public participation difficult. In 2012 as many as 45 of the 55 laws affecting the business environment were adopted

[12] Loayza et al. (2006) state that "Countries with better institutions tend to create regulatory environments genuinely aimed to improve business conditions rather than privilege a few interest groups. They are also more likely to enforce regulation in a transparent and even-handed manner, limiting the regulator's margin for arbitrariness and corruption". Unfortunately, this does not apply to the Republic of Serbia.

[13] According to analysis carried out by NALED in 2012 (NALED 2012b), only three bylaws were adopted before the deadline, 33 were adopted after the deadline, and in 163 cases the deadline expired before the bylaws were adopted. Some bylaws were more than 2 years late.

[14] The last instance of a consultation process related to the package of tax laws adopted in late 2012.

under urgent procedure. The lack of transparency and abuse of urgent procedure often result in inadequate statutory provisions (of which the administrative costs mentioned above are just one part) that make it difficult or impossible for the private sector to operate normally. Finally, the very manner of analysing and drafting legislation is also often poor. Even when there are formal regulatory impact analysis (RIA) reports that are part of the explanatory notes accompanying a proposed piece of legislation, the quality of such analysis is often questionable, as it is not carried out simultaneously with the law drafting and, as a rule, does not contain any type of quantitative assessment of the impact (costs and benefits) on the private sector. The current manner of drafting and adopting legislation does not contain appropriate mechanisms to prevent the adoption of legislation containing unnecessary regulatory requirements, while criteria guiding the authorities tasked with appraising the adequacy of analyses and the regulatory impact on business are excessively mild.[15]

4.3.6 Construction Permit Issues for Existing Buildings ('Legalisation') and New Construction

According to a recent study entitled Assessment of Constraints on Construction Permits in Serbia (USAID 2012b), investors often face difficulties in establishing title to tracts of land due to complex and often unclear restitution, 'legalisation', and conversion procedures. Unclear and complex 'legalisation' of buildings (i.e., issuance of construction permits for buildings constructed without appropriate approval) hinders access to the formal sector and commencement of legal operations, which means that some resources are placed completely beyond the scope of legal transactions and use in the formal economy. This leads to the well-known consequences described in de Soto (1989, 2000). According to data made available by the Ministry of Construction and Urban Planning, there are more than 700,000 unpermitted buildings in Serbia. In addition to legalisation issues, market entry is also hindered by the very complex construction permit system that entails filing for approval with a large number of bodies.[16] The construction permit procedure is

[15] For instance, the Office of Regulatory Reform and Regulatory Impact Analysis received only 67 draft bills throughout 2012. Of these, the Office found that 24 contained impact analyses; 37 were provided with partial analyses; no analysis was required in three cases; while another three cases did not contain such analysis. Even the three bills missing RIAs were able to enter law-making procedure after the appropriate government committee so resolved. This means that 'filtering' legislation by quality does not function appropriately.

[16] According to the construction permitting study carried out by the USAID Business Enabling Project (BEP 2012b), 52 steps are typically needed to obtain a construction permit for an industrial company. Public businesses and other public authorities are in charge of as many as 90 % of these procedures; there are as many as 20 different bodies exercising public powers that take part in the procedure.

inefficient and lengthy; unable to obtain permits the proper way, a number of business entities start construction on their own initiative, thereby assuming a great deal of risk. In these circumstances they engage workers from the informal sector and businesses and entrepreneurs who do not report their work. The results of the survey carried out for the purposes of this study bear out the above conclusions. In addition to the pronounced extent of the shadow economy in the construction sector, this industry was also noted for a number of other responses (e.g., cost-cutting due to unfair competition is more pronounced in construction, as is operation without appropriate permits, etc.).

4.3.7 Quality of Public Services

Quality of public services correlates negatively with the extent of the shadow economy, with greater quality of public services implying greater readiness by the public to pay taxes, as those taxes go towards financing goods and services that meet their needs appropriately. Since relevant international studies show that the quality of general public services (healthcare, education, efficiency of public administration, efficiency of the justice system, etc.) is lower in Serbia than in most other European countries (World Bank 2009), the readiness of taxpayers to pay taxes in the manner and amounts set by law is also lower. The results of the survey show that the lack of trust in the state and public institutions is the second most important cause of the shadow economy in Serbia. Given that the degree of trust in the state reflects the degree of taxpayer satisfaction with the way that the state functions (and the quality of public goods it provides), it can be concluded that this is one of the major causes of the shadow economy in Serbia.

4.3.8 High Levels of Corruption

High levels of corruption disincentivise taxpayers from paying taxes, since the impression corruption creates is that those taxes will not be used to adequately finance the public sector, but will rather result in private gain by certain categories of people. Serbia has been ranked 86th (out of a total of 183 countries) in the global corruption perceptions index, indicating a high level of perceived corruption in society and, consequently, lower willingness of the public to pay their taxes. In addition, our survey found that respondents ranked corruption as the fourth most important cause of the shadow economy in Serbia.

4.3.9 High Tolerance for the Shadow Economy by the Government

Many forms of the shadow economy are visible and could be tackled with relative ease. However, for a multitude of reasons, the Serbian Government has been postponing measures aimed at doing so. Thus, for instance, new (unused) industrial products are generally sold in flea and farmers' markets where taxes are evaded partially or wholly. The government tolerates these activities, as it views them as social welfare of sorts, aimed at the unemployed. Non-taxation of property is motivated more by political than by social reasons (e.g., local authorities avoid realistically estimating market values of real estate for tax purposes or avoid taxing all real estate in their areas in order to gain the political support of the electorate).

4.3.10 Large Number of Small Business Entities

The large number of small business entities has an adverse impact on the extent of the shadow economy, as more taxpayers mean that the Tax Administration is less likely to audit any one of them, which serves as an incentive for tax evasion. Empirical research carried out worldwide, including in Serbia (see Chap. 6 of this study) shows that the shadow economy is at its most widespread with entrepreneurs and small and micro-businesses (Tedds 2010; Williams 2006). Although comparative data indicate that the structure of Serbia's economy, in terms of the number of small, medium-sized, and large businesses, is similar to that of EU member states, it has been estimated that the current ratio of Tax Administration staff effectively engaged in tax audit to the number of taxpayers is relatively unfavourable. This contributes to the relatively low perceived probability of the discovery of tax evasion (issues faced by the Tax Administration will be covered in greater detail in Chap. 8 of this study). The unfavourable ratio of tax inspectors to number of taxpayers potentially subject to audit is primarily the consequence of the poor staffing structure of the Tax Administration, where only slightly more than 10 % of staff are tasked with performing audits. In view of this, reorganising the Tax Administration to substantially increase the number of staff engaged in audits and improve their skills, while at the same time reducing the number of employees charged with administrative duties, would be an improvement of the current situation.

4.3.11 The Structure of the Population's Income

The structure of the population's income affects the extent of the shadow economy because of the differentiation in tax collection mechanisms by amount of income.

The structure of the population's income is closely linked to the relative significance of individual forms of incorporation in the economy: companies, entrepreneurs, and agricultural estates. Thus the level of evasion of tax on income from wage-employment is much lower in Serbia than that of the tax on income from self-employment (paid by farmers, entrepreneurs, etc.), since income from wage-employment is generally taxed at source by means of withholding a portion of income, while tax on income from self-employment is generally either self-assessed or payable when assessed by the Tax Authorities. In addition, states with a greater share of agriculture in GDP have greater volumes of the shadow economy on average, since the consumption of own products is not taxed.

4.3.12 A High Unemployment Rate

A high unemployment rate makes labour supply inelastic, meaning that the unemployed, with few opportunities to find employment in the formal labour market, consent to informal work that does not involve the payment of taxes and contributions on their wages (nor the rights arising from the payment of such dues). At 26.1 %, according to the Labour Force Survey, the unemployment rate in Serbia is among the highest in Europe (similarly high unemployment rates are seen only in Spain, Italy, Macedonia, and Greece). This factor has a major impact on the extent of the informal economy in Serbia, particularly in the field of employment.

4.3.13 Tax Morality

Tax morality defined as the readiness of a taxpayer to pay taxes in full and on time and thus pay in full for the public goods and services provided by the government, also has a substantial effect on the extent of the shadow economy. Hence, in countries with a low degree of trust in government institutions and their fairness and efficiency (such as Serbia) tax morality is also low, which adversely impacts the volume of the shadow economy. Low tax morality is also caused by the government's high tolerance for the shadow economy. However, the results of the survey show that 'just' 9 % of all respondents believe that operating informally is justified in full or to a large degree.

4.4 Incentives from the Financial Sector

The major factors that indirectly support the shadow economy within the system include the significant share of cash transactions in the total volume of payments, informal finance, and unregistered remittance inflows sent by migrants from abroad.

4.4.1 Cash Transactions

Cash represents a means that enables informal operations.[17] Cash transactions include off-account payments that often occur informally and in foreign currency (in dollarized economies). As a rule, countries where the use of electronic money is more widespread see substantially lower volumes of shadow economy. According to the findings of Schneider (2011a), a 10 % increase in the share of electronic payments will lead to a 5 % drop in the shadow economy. Payments in cash still account for a large portion of total payments made in Serbia, although they have been seeing a downward trend over the past 5 years. According to NBS data for Q3 2012, more than six million payment cards (debit, credit, and corporate cards) have been issued in Serbia, with the number of active cards (with at least one payment during the previous quarter) standing at 2.7 million. Between 2007 and 2011 an increase of 56 % in the number of transactions at cashpoints and points-of-sale involving cards issued in Serbia was recorded (a rise from 75 to 132 million transactions). However, of the total turnover of RSD 534 billion, as much as RSD 372.5 billion, or some 70 %, is accounted for by cash withdrawals.

Seen in this context, Serbia is characterised by an extremely high degree of euroisation (IMF 2011). According to the NBS report, in late March 2012 the degree of dinarisation of the Serbian financial system, measured as the share of dinar lending in total corporate and household lending, stood at 27.9 % (NBS 2012).[18] As the formal sector is euroised, a large number of transactions in the informal sector also take place in euros. It is quite common to pay for, say, more valuable services provided by tradesmen, or minor construction work etc., in euros. In addition to the fiscal motives discussed above, euroisation provides clear (non-fiscal) incentives for transactions to take place in the informal sector. Payments in foreign currency, instead of in dinars, in the informal sector avoid commission fees charged by banks and the differences in the exchange rates applied

[17] According to Schneider (2011b), "Countries with high levels of electronic payment usage, such as the United Kingdom and the Netherlands, have smaller shadow economies than those with minimal levels of electronic payments, such as Bulgaria and Romania."

[18] In addition to the fact that the share of the dinar measured in this way is less than one-third, it should be borne in mind that the bulk of dinar-denominated loans are actually those subsidised by the state.

by banks when buying and selling foreign currency (for instance, when a business entity issues a foreign currency sales order to the bank where it keeps its foreign currency assets, whereupon the bank pays the appropriate dinar amount to the payee's dinar-denominated account).[19]

4.4.2 Informal Finance

Informal finance is a phenomenon that accompanies the large extent of the shadow economy in developing countries. The reasons for its existence are poor local legislation and enforcement regulations, market entry barriers, expensive formal financing sources, lack of finance products that meet beneficiaries' needs, inappropriate tax legislation, and high tax rates (USAID 2005, 2012a). The consequences of informal finance are reflected in greater information asymmetries between market participants, lack of tax revenue derived from this area, and exclusion of formal financial intermediaries from the funds transfer process. This has a negative effect on the development of the financial sector and the efficient allocation of financial resources to recipients. Low efficiency, lack of transparency, and greater uncertainty reduce the trust of the participants in the system, which leads to less readiness to embark on new projects and invest: this in turn has adverse repercussions on the growth of the economy as a whole. Thus it is in the interest of economic policymakers to disincentivise informal financing channels in parallel with efforts aimed at tackling the informal economy, and to foster financing through existing formal channels and the development of new ones. This would reduce uncertainty, enhance the efficiency of allocation of funds received, boost employment, and increase tax revenues generated by formal activity. A greater finance supply should result in lower financing costs, which could increase the availability of these funds, primarily to entrepreneurs and small and medium-sized businesses, which are among the main drivers of new cycles of economic activity in developing countries. A major role in this process, in addition to the private sector, should be played by various forms of public-private partnership, as well as by special development institutions.

According to one of the initiatives announced by the Serbian Ministry of Finance and Economy, the state will acquire up to 25 % of the equity of a number of primarily export-oriented SMEs that cannot secure appropriate financing. Businesses with the best investment programmes will be eligible to apply for this support, while the Serbian Export Credit and Insurance Agency (AOFI) will be in charge of the technical arrangements. The key issue in determining the success of

[19] The Foreign Currency Operations Law (*Official Gazette of the Republic of Serbia*, Nos. 62/2006 and 31/2011) stipulates, among other things, that incoming and outgoing payments and transfers between residents and non-residents in Serbia must be made in dinars, save for particular cases listed in Article 34(2), in which foreign currency may be used.

this programme will certainly be the need to reduce the moral hazard risk involved in distributing the limited funds available in the budget.

Alternatively, Serbia could gradually shift to the globally accepted practice of establishing institutions providing micro-finance to entrepreneurs and SMEs that find traditional borrowing either inaccessible or too costly. Originally envisaged as non-profit entities owned by the very people most at risk and in need of financing to start their businesses, these institutions can take the form of either co-operatives or credit unions. They can also formally be incorporated as non-governmental organisations or savings banks, or can even be owned by the government as sector-oriented banks (e.g., agricultural development banks, rural banks, etc.). The key issue and precondition for establishing these specialised entities essentially remains similar to that for the proposal to establish a single Serbian Development Bank: it is necessary to design appropriate laws and bylaws to prevent corruption in allocating funds, and ensure professionalism and efficiency in managing the limited resources available to such an entity.

As shown by the survey of businesses and entrepreneurs in Serbia, one of the major constraints on doing business is access to formal financing, as well as weak purchasing power, frequent changes to legislation, high tax rates, inflation, and political instability. Most business entities are financed from net profits (92 %), while slightly more than one-quarter borrow from banks (24 %). Business entities tend to borrow either from banks or from their owners, while entrepreneurs rely on funds borrowed from individuals, friends, or family members. Another initiative of the Ministry of Finance and Economy current in 2013, which should facilitate access to liquid financing, is a programme of subsidised liquidity loans, which will be aimed at SMEs.

Slightly more than half of all business entities surveyed believe that financing in their sector of activity came in part from informal sources on which no tax is paid; the estimated share of informal investment was up to 50 % of the total investment. On the other hand, such financing was rarely admitted when respondents spoke about their own operations. Only one-fifth of all business entities stated that investment in their companies came in part from informal financing (with up to 30 % of the sum total of investments), while 66 % claimed that no such financing was invested in their company.

4.4.3 Unregistered Remittances Sent by Migrants from Abroad

These represent a particularly important source of foreign capital in developing countries, which in absolute amounts often exceeds other forms of capital inflow from both private and public sources (Adams and Page 2005; Irving et al. 2010; Abdih et al. 2009, 2012). As the greatest volume of remittances enters most developing countries mainly through informal channels, better knowledge of the features of these transfers is necessary if they are to be formalised and directed into productive activities in the recipient country.[20]

Remittances were undoubtedly the largest source of financial inflows into Serbia during and after the global crisis. According to data for the period 2007–2011, inflows of remittances reached €2.5–4 billion annually. The share of remittances in GDP is significant (7.6 % between 2007 and 2011) and they cover nearly 40 % of the trade deficit (the difference between the monetary value of imports and exports of goods and services) (Janković and Gligorić 2012).

According to some estimates, only between 10 and 50 % of remittances are actually transferred through formal channels (Giuliano and Ruiz-Arranz 2009). In some countries the actual volume of remittance flows not registered officially or transferred through informal channels is often considered much greater than the estimates made by the relevant institutions, which only serves to underline the importance of remittances as a possible external source of financing consumption and investment in developing countries (Chami et al. 2008, 2009). The inflow of remittances into Serbia is at present estimated on the basis of formal inflows, primarily through the banking sector, while informal inflows are approximated primarily using the volume of activity of foreign currency exchange services.

In spite of the dearth of responses, the findings of the Survey on Conditions for Doing Business in Serbia are significant, since this is one of the first studies to date on the possible impact of remittances on Serbia's economy.[21] All entrepreneurs whose households receive remittances from abroad claimed they did so via bank accounts. As expected, no informal channels were mentioned. Entrepreneurs who responded came predominantly from the trade and other services sectors, and primarily represented small businesses with up to 4 or between 5 and 19 employees. Although few entrepreneurs confirmed they did receive remittances from abroad, they claimed that they used the money mainly to start or carry on operations (77 % of all entrepreneurs' households that received remittances). Interestingly enough, only 34 % of the funds received had been used for consumption, while as much as 66 % had been employed in business. It is also important to note that funds from remittances have been used in business for some time now. Entrepreneurs who had employed such funds over the previous year made up 23 % of those who received remittances. A total of 32 % of respondents stated that they had been using

[20] The World Bank defines migrant remittances as the sum of workers' remittances, employee compensation, and migrants' transfers. Under the IMF *Balance of Payments Manual*, 6th Edition (IMF 2010), workers' remittances are defined as personal transfers of migrant workers residing in the country in which they work. Residence is assumed to be where a worker remains abroad for 1 year or more, while income earned during shorter stays abroad is categorised as employee compensation. Migrant transfers represent the net value of the assets of migrants transferred from one country to another during their migration for a period of at least 1 year. The recipients of these assets reside in their country of origin.

[21] An attempt was made by the Statistical Office of the Republic of Serbia to study and analyse the inflows of remittances into Serbia. This was an ad hoc survey into unregistered remittances carried out as part of a regional project aimed at assessing a portion of the unreported economy.

remittances in business for 6–10 years, while 15 % claimed that they had used remittances in business for more than 10 years. Remittances are most often used to purchase current assets, which is only logical in these activity sectors. These findings are particularly relevant since it is certain that a substantial portion of remittances is transferred through informal channels, which increases the amount of funds potentially available for investment, notwithstanding the fact that the respondents did not formally substantiate this assumption.

References

Abdih Y, Chami R, Gapen M, Mati A (2009) Fiscal sustainability in remittance dependent economies. IMF Working Paper WP/09/190. International Monetary Fund, Washington, DC

Abdih Y, Barajas A, Chami R, Ebeke C (2012) Remittance channels and fiscal impact in the Middle East, North Africa, and Central Asia. IMF Working Paper WP/12/104. International Monetary Fund, Washington, DC

Adams RH, Page J (2005) Do international migration and remittances reduce poverty in development countries? World Dev 33(10):1645–1699

Alm J, Jackson B, McKee M (1992) Estimating the determinants of taxpayer compliance with experimental data. Natl Tax J 45(1):107–114

Arandarenko M, Avlijaš S (2011) Behind the veil of statistics: Bringing to light structural weaknesses in Serbia. In: Schmidt V, Vaughan-Whitehead D (eds) The impact of the crisis on wages in South East Europe. ILO, Budapest

Arandarenko M, Stanić K (2006) Labor costs and labor taxes in Serbia. Background paper for World Bank report. Labor market assessment, Serbia

Arsić M, Ranđelović S, Pejić M (2012) Reform of the system of Quasi-Fiscal charges for the improvement of business conditions in Serbia. Quarterly Monitor, vol 29, April–June 2012

Chami R, Barajas A, Cosimano T, Fullenkamp C, Gapen M, Montiel P (2008) Macroeconomic consequences of remittances. IMF Occasional Paper No 259. International Monetary Fund, Washington, DC

Chami R, Barajas A, Gapen M, Fullenkamp C, Montiel P (2009) Do workers' remittances promote economic growth? IMF Working Paper WP/09/153. International Monetary Fund, Washington, DC

De Soto H (1989) The other path. Harper and Row, New York

De Soto H (2000) The mystery of capital: why capitalism triumphs in the west and fails everywhere else. Basic Books, New York

Enste DH (2010) Regulation and shadow economy: empirical evidence for 25 OECD-countries. Constit Polit Econ 21:231–248

Fiscal Council (2012) Predlog mera fiskalne konsolidacije 2012–2016

Friedman E, Johnson S, Kaufmann D, Zoido-Lobatón P (2000) Dodging the grabbing hand: the determinants of unofficial activity in 69 countries. J Public Econ 76:459–493

Giuliano P, Ruiz-Arranz M (2009) Remittances, financial development and growth. J Dev Econ 90 (1):144–152

GIZ (2010) Addressing tax evasion and tax avoidance in developing countries. Study prepared by GIZ and the German Federal Ministry of Economic Cooperation and Development

IMF (2010) Balance of payments manual, 6th edn. International Monetary Fund, Washington, DC

IMF (2011) Republic of Serbia: request for stand-by arrangement, IMF Country Report 11/311. International Monetary Fund, Washington, DC
Irving J, Mohapatra S, Ratha D (2010) Migrant remittance flows: findings from a global survey of central banks. Working Paper 94. The World Bank, Washington, DC
Janković I, Gligorić M (2012) Remittances as a stable source of foreign currency inflow in Serbia. In: Jovanović-Gavrilović B, Rakonjac Antić T, Stojanović Ž (eds) Thematic collection of papers "Economic Policy and Development". Faculty of Economics, Belgrade, pp 215–236
Johnson S, Kaufmann D, Zoido-Lobaton P (1998) Regulatory discretion and the unofficial economy. Am Econ Rev 88(2):387–392
Koettl J (2012) Does formal work pay in Serbia? The role of labor taxes and social benefit design in providing disincentives for formal work. In: Laderchi CR, Savastano S (eds) Poverty and exclusion in the Western Balkans. New directions in measurement and policy, vol 8. Springer
Kovtun D, Cirkel AM, Murgasova Z, Smith D, Tambunlertchai S (2014) Boosting job growth in the Western Balkans. IMF WP/14/16
Krstić G, Sanfey P (2011) Earnings inequality and the informal economy: evidence from Serbia. Econ Transit 19(1)
Loayza N, Oviedo AM, Serven L (2006) The impact of regulation on growth and informality, cross-country evidence. In: Guha-Khasnobis B, Kanbur R, Ostrom E (eds) Linking the formal and informal economy, concepts and policies. Oxford University Press, Oxford
NALED (2012a) Businesses can run, but they cannot hide – the system of non-tax and para-fiscal charges in Serbia: inventory, analysis of effects and recommendations for reform
NALED (2012b) Siva knjiga 5 - Preporuke za uklanjanje administrativnih prepreka za poslovanje u Srbiji 2012/2013
NBS (2012) Report on the Dinarisation of the Serbian financial system. www.nbs.rs
OECD (2008) Serbia – a labour market in transition. OECD, Paris
Radulović B (2011a) Merenje administrativnih troškova primenom modela standardnog troška – Kritički osvrt i moguća poboljšanja. u S. Tabaroši, ur. "Razvoj pravnog sistema Srbije i harmonizacija sa pravom EU". Pravni Fakultet, Beograd
Radulović B (2011b) Standard cost model – baseline measurement. Serbia, Mimeo
Ranđelović, S, Đorđević A (2012) Unapređenje performansi malih i srednjih preduzeća u Srbiji kroz reformu sistema oporezivanja. Istraživački rad pripremljen za potrebe Istraživačkog foruma Evropskog pokreta u Srbiji
Schneider F (eds) (2011a) Handbook on the shadow economy. Edward Elgar, Cheltenham
Schneider F (2011b) The shadow economy in Europe – using payment systems to combat the shadow economy. http://www.bblf.bg/uploads/files/file_378.pdf
Schneider F, Enste D (2000) Shadow economies: size, causes and consequences. J Econ Lit 38 (1):77–114
Schneider F, Buehn A, Montenegro CE (2010) New estimates for the shadow economies all over the world. Int Econ J 24(4):443–461
Tedds LM (2010) Keeping it off the books: an empirical investigation of firms that engage in tax evasion. Appl Econ 42(19):2459–2473
Transparency Serbia (2012) Public comment periods in the Republic of Serbia – analysis of the statutory framework and practice
USAID (2005) Removing barriers to formalization: the case for reform and emerging best practice
USAID (2012a) Financing the growth of small and medium-sized enterprises: critical issues and recommendations for Serbia
USAID Business Enabling Project (2012b) Assessment of constraints to construction permits in Serbia
Williams CC (2006) The hidden enterprise culture: entrepreneurship in the underground economy. Edward Elgar, Cheltenham
World Bank (2009) Serbia – doing more with less: addressing the fiscal crisis by increasing public sector productivity. Report no. 48620-YU, Washington, DC
World Bank (2011) Republic of Serbia – country economic memorandum: the road to prosperity: productivity and exports, vol 2, Report no. 65845-YF, Washington, DC

Chapter 5
What Is the Extent of the Shadow Economy in Serbia?

Friedrich Schneider, Gorana Krstić, Milojko Arsić, and Saša Ranđelović

5.1 Introduction

The last country study on the shadow economy in FR Yugoslavia/Serbia with policy recommendations dates from 1998 (Krstić et al. 1998). The size of the shadow economy is estimated at 34.5 % of registered GDP, using data from the special individual survey on the informal economy and applying the modified labour market supply approach suggested by Contini (1981, 1992).

Two multi-country studies that include estimates of the shadow economy for transition economies including Serbia are Schneider (2004) and Christie and Holzner (2004). Schneider's paper provides estimates of the shadow economy for countries from around the world using the MIMIC econometric approach. The size of the shadow economy in Serbia and Montenegro (still one country at that time) was estimated at 39.1 % of measured GDP in 2002/2003 and 41.4 % in 2006/2007 (Schneider 2007). Christie and Holzner (2004) analyze a range of South Eastern Europe (SEE), Central Eastern Europe, and Baltic (CEB) countries. They take a different approach from that of Schneider (2004) and focus instead on household tax compliance (HTC). They found a wider range of estimates compared to Schneider's results, with Serbia, perhaps surprisingly, estimated at just 19 % of GDP in 2001.

In this chapter, we will present estimates of the extent of the shadow economy based on three methods: (1) the MIMIC method, (2) the household tax compliance (HTC) method, and (3) the Survey on Conditions for Doing Business in Serbia. Estimates of the shadow economy for the period 2001–2010 using the MIMIC

F. Schneider (✉)
Department of Economics, University of Linz, Linz, Austria
e-mail: Friedrich.schneider@jku.at

G. Krstić • M. Arsić • S. Ranđelović
Faculty of Economics, University of Belgrade, Belgrade, Serbia
e-mail: gkrstic@ekof.bg.ac.rs; arsicm@ekof.bg.ac.rs; randjelovic@ekof.bg.ac.rs

G. Krstić, F. Schneider (eds.), *Formalizing the Shadow Economy in Serbia*, Contributions to Economics, DOI 10.1007/978-3-319-13437-6_5

method were made for Serbia and ten other Central and Eastern European countries: Bulgaria, the Czech Republic, Estonia, Lithuania, Latvia, Hungary, Poland, Romania, Slovenia, and Slovakia.

The estimate of the shadow economy using the HTC method was based on macroeconomic data on household consumption and income for 2010. The third estimate was made using the findings of the Survey on Conditions for Doing Business in Serbia. When comparing these assessments it is necessary to bear in mind that their coverage of the shadow economy differs, both in terms of institutional sectors (businesses, households, etc.) and informal activities (trade in goods, undeclared work, unreported property, fees, charges, etc.). The MIMIC method has the greatest coverage, since it comprises all institutional sectors and all forms of the shadow economy. The HTC method covers informal activities that can be identified in household income and consumption, but not those that are exclusively in the businesses. The Survey on Conditions for Doing Business in Serbia was the basis for estimating the extent of the shadow economy in the sector of businesses and entrepreneurs for the two main types of informal activity, illicit trade in goods and undeclared work. It is necessary to bear in mind that estimates of the shadow economy in the households sector (the HTC method) and the business and entrepreneur sector (the Survey) cannot be viewed as cumulative since they for the most part cover the same forms of informal activity (undeclared work, trade in goods), albeit with some minor differences in their coverage.

In addition to estimating the shadow economy, this chapter also provides estimates of the VAT gap, the personal income tax gap, and the social security contributions gap. Differences in coverage must be taken into account when interpreting and comparing these assessments, as must be the fact that all estimates of the shadow economy are only approximate.

Methodological differences between the methods and sources of data must also be considered, since they can affect the findings to some degree. Whilst the first method of estimating the shadow economy is based on modelling, the second is indirect in its approach, since the estimates are based on macroeconomic data obtained from national accounts. The third method is direct and is based on microeconomic data from the Survey on Conditions for Doing Business in Serbia.

5.2 Estimate of the Shadow Economy Using the MIMIC Method

5.2.1 Introduction

The size and development of the Central and Eastern European shadow economies have been measured since the late 1980s, starting with the work of Kaufmann and Kaliberda (1996), Johnson et al. (1997), and Lackó (1996). All these authors use the physical input (electricity) method and come up with quite large figures (from a macro perspective). In the work of Belev (2003) the above mentioned studies are critically evaluated, arguing that the estimated size of the shadow economies are to a large extent a historical phenomenon (due to the communist eras of all of these countries) and partly determined by institutional factors.[1]

Definition of the Shadow Economy

The shadow economy is defined as the ensemble of all market-based legal production activities that are deliberately concealed from public authorities for one or more reasons: to evade payment of income, value added, or other taxes; to evade payment of social security contributions; to evade certain legal labour market standards, such as minimum wages, maximum working hours, safety standards, etc.; and to evade certain administrative procedures, such as completing statistical questionnaires or administrative forms (Schneider et al. 2010). On average, the informal economy refers to legitimate goods rather than illegal goods. The macro estimates include smuggling of legitimate goods within the definition. Thus, smuggled goods/inputs that make their way into legitimate production are implicitly included in the definition of shadow economy.

In this section, we present the estimation procedure of the MIMIC method, and estimation results and their interpretation for the following countries over the period 2001–2010: Serbia, Bulgaria, the Czech Republic, Estonia, Latvia, Lithuania, Hungary, Poland, Romania, Slovenia, and Slovakia.

Based on the MIMIC method, we estimated that the extent of the shadow economy in Serbia declined from 33.2 % of GDP in 2001 to 30.1 % of GDP in 2010. When compared to other countries the shadow economy in Serbia was greater than the averages for the selected 11 countries throughout the period observed. Only Bulgaria recorded a more extensive shadow economy, in percentage of GDP, than Serbia (by 2.2 percentage points in 2010).

5.2.2 *The MIMIC Model Approach*

Most methods for estimating the size of the shadow economy so far consider just one indicator that captures all effects of the shadow economy. However, effects of the shadow economy show up simultaneously in the production, labour, and money markets. An even more important critique is that several causes that determine the size of the shadow economy are only taken into account in some of the monetary approach studies that usually consider one cause, the burden of taxation. The model

[1] For a critical evaluation of the various estimations and calibration methods see Schneider (2005), Feld and Schneider (2010), and Schneider (2010, 2011).

approach explicitly considers multiple causes of the existence and growth of the shadow economy, as well as the multiple effects of the shadow economy over time in several indicator variables. The empirical method is based on the statistical theory of unobserved variables, which considers multiple causes and multiple indicators of the phenomenon to be measured. For the estimation, a factor-analytic approach is used to measure the hidden economy as an unobserved variable over time. The unknown coefficients are estimated in a set of structural equations within which the 'unobserved' variable cannot be measured directly. The MIMIC (multiple-indicators multiple-causes) model consists in general of two parts, with the measurement model linking the unobserved variables to observed indicators.[2] The structural equations model specifies causal relationships between the unobserved variables. In this case there is one unobserved variable, the size of the shadow economy: this is assumed to be influenced by a set of indicators for the shadow economy's size, thus capturing the structural dependence of the shadow economy on variables that may be useful in predicting its movement and size in the future. The interaction over time between the causes Z_{it} ($i = 1, 2, \ldots, k$), the size of the shadow economy X_t, in time t, and the indicators Y_{jt} ($j = 1, 2, \ldots, p$) is shown in Fig. 5.1.

There is a large body of literature[3] on the possible causes and indicators of the shadow economy, which distinguishes four types of cause:

(1) The burden of direct and indirect taxation, both actual and perceived—an increasing tax burden is a strong incentive to work in the shadow economy.
(2) The burden of regulation as a proxy for all other state activities. It is assumed that increases in the burden of regulation are a strong incentive to enter the shadow economy.
(3) Tax morality (citizens' attitudes toward the state), which describes the readiness of individuals to leave their official occupations, at least partly, and enter the shadow economy: it is assumed that a declining tax morality increases the size of the shadow economy.[4]
(4) Institutional factors such as good governance or corruption and rule of law are also important.[5]

[2] Papers dealing extensively with the MIMIC approach, its development, and especially its weaknesses are by Dell'Anno (2003) as well as the studies by Giles and Tedds (2002), Breusch (2005a, b), Dell'Anno and Schneider (2009) and Schneider (2011).

[3] Thomas (1992), Schneider (1994, 1997, 2003, 2005, 2010, 2011), Pozo (1996), Johnson et al. (1998a, b), Giles (1997a, b, 1999a, b), Giles and Tedds (2002), Giles et al. (2002), Dell'Anno (2003), Dell'Anno and Schneider (2004), and Feld and Schneider (2010).

[4] When applying this approach to European countries, Frey and Weck-Hannemann (1984) had difficulty in obtaining reliable data for the cause series, as well as for the direct and indirect tax burdens. Hence, their study was criticized by Helberger and Knepel (1988), who argued that the results were unstable with respect to changing variables in the model and over the years.

[5] Compare here the survey of Feld and Schneider (2010).

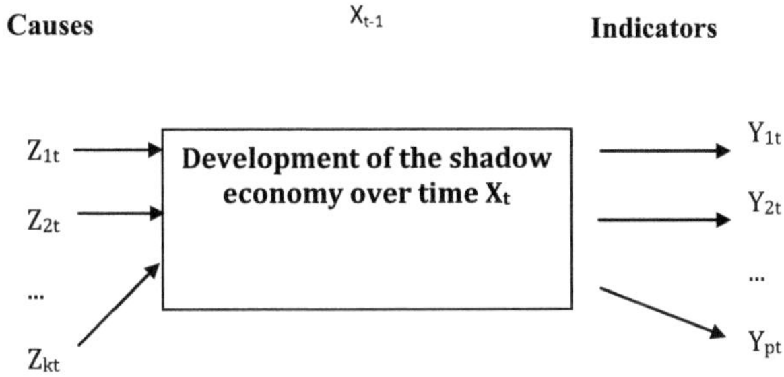

Fig. 5.1 Development of the shadow economy over time

A change in the size of the shadow economy is reflected in the following indicators:

(1) Development of monetary indicators. If activities in the shadow economy rise, additional monetary transactions are required.
(2) Development of the labour market. Increased participation of workers in the hidden sector results in a decrease in participation in the official economy. Similarly, increased activities in the hidden sector may be reflected in shorter working hours in the official economy.
(3) Development of the production market. An increase in the shadow economy means that inputs (especially labour) move out of the official economy (at least partly), and this displacement might have a depressing effect on the official growth rate of the economy.

The approach has been used e.g., by Giles (1999a, b) and by Giles et al. (2002), Giles and Tedds (2002) and Bajada and Schneider (2005), who obtain a time series index of the hidden/measured output of New Zealand, Canada, India, and Australia, and then estimate a separate 'cash-demand model' to obtain a benchmark for converting this index into percentage units. Unlike earlier empirical studies of the hidden economy, proper attention is directed at the non-stationary and possible co-integration of time series data. Again, this MIMIC model treats hidden output as a latent variable, and uses several (measurable) causal variables and indicator variables. The former include measures of the average and marginal tax rates, inflation, real income, and the degree of regulation in the economy. The latter include changes in the (male) labour force participation rate and in the cash/money supply ratio. In their cash-demand equation they allow for different velocities of currency circulation in the hidden and recorded economies. Their cash-demand equation is not used as an input to determine the variation in the hidden economy over time, but only to obtain the long-run average value of hidden/measured output, so that the index for this ratio predicted by the MIMIC model can be used to calculate the level and the percentage units of the shadow economy. Overall, this latest combination of the currency demand and MIMIC approach clearly shows that some progress in the estimation technique of the shadow economy has been achieved and a number of critical points have been overcome.

However, there are also objections to this method, as follows:

(1) instability in the estimated coefficients with respect to sample size changes,
(2) instability in the estimated coefficients with respect to alternative specifications,
(3) difficulty in obtaining reliable data on cause variables other than tax variables,
(4) the reliability of grouping the variables into "causes" and "indicators" in explaining the variability of the shadow economy, and
(5) the calibration method used to transform the relative estimates into absolute ones.

In spite of these objections, and knowing that all other methods also have severe weaknesses, the MIMIC procedure is used to estimate the shadow economies of 11 Eastern and Central European countries.

5.2.3 *Econometric Results and Their Interpretation*

In Table 5.1 the econometric estimation results using the MIMIC approach (latent estimation approach) is presented for the 11 Central and Eastern European countries over the period 2001–2010 (e.g. ten data points). As causal variables we can chose from the following:

i. Indirect taxation revenues in percent of GDP,
ii. Direct taxation revenues in percent of GDP,
iii. Marginal income tax burden in percent,
iv. Effective average tax rate in percent,
v. Regulatory quality index (World Bank indicator), which ranges from −2.5 (weak) to +2.5 (strong) governance performance,
vi. Rule of law (World Bank indicator), which ranges from −2.5 (weak) to +2.5 (strong) governance performance,
vii. Corruption Index, World Bank (=0 bad freedom from corruption and =100 most freedom from corruption),
viii. Self-employment in percent of total employment and
ix. Unemployment rate in percent.

As indicator variables we use:

i. Cash per capita growth,
ii. Employment rate in percent and
iii. GDP per capita.

If we interpret the econometric results shown in Table 5.1[6] we realize that indirect taxation has the expected positive sign and is highly statistically significant.

[6] We present three plausible and 'best' results: the stability of the econometric results is somewhat weak due to the dataset.

Table 5.1 MIMIC estimation of the shadow economies of 11 Central and Eastern Europe Countries, 2001–2010

Cause variables	Model 1	Model 2	Model 3
Indirect tax in % of GDP	0.54** (7.01)	0.51** (7.40)	0.15* (2.03)
Direct taxes in % of GDP	–	–	–
Marginal income tax burden in %	–	0.27** (3.25)	0.26** (2.93)
Effective average tax rate in %	0.21** (2.13)	–	–
Business freedom (Index = 0 least, = 100 most freedom)	0.03 (0.41)	0.07 (0.86)	−0.05 (−0.71)
Corruption (=0 least freedom from, =100 most freedom from corruption)	−0.68** (−6.13)	−0.63** (−6.59)	–
Self-employment in % of total employment	0.12 (1.61)	0.03 (0.49)	0.21** (2.61)
Unemployment rate in %	0.41** (5.72)	0.42** (6.37)	0.53** (7.12)
Rule of law (−2.5 weakest rule of law, 2.5 strongest rule of law)	–	–	−0.93** (−7.75)
Indicator variables			
Cash/M1 per capita growth	0.15 (1.41)	0.16 (1.49)	0.17 (1.48)
Employment rate in %	1.00	1.00	1.00
GDP per capita	−0.64** (−6.01)	−0.60** (−5.58)	−0.70** (−6.55)
RMSEA	0.29	0.22	0.19
Chi-squared	35.23	37.45	47.47
AGFI	0.82	0.81	0.91
N	64	64	64
D.F.	27	27	27

Source: Own calculations

Also, the variables measuring the direct income tax burden have the expected sign and are statistically significant. The business freedom index of the World Bank is not statistically significant, as opposed to the cause variable "rule of law". Self-employment has the expected positive sign but is not statistically significant; the unemployment rate again has the expected positive sign and is highly statistically significant. The corruption index has the expected negative sign and is highly statistically significant. If we switch to the indicator variables, the variable "cash per capita" has the expected positive sign but is not statistically significant. GDP per capita has the expected negative sign and is highly statistically significant.

In order to calculate the size and development of the shadow economy in these 11 Central and Eastern European countries we have to overcome the disadvantage of the MIMIC approach, which is that it gives only relative estimated sizes of the shadow economy and it is necessary to use another approach to get absolute figures.

Table 5.2 Size and development of the Serbian shadow economy and of other transition countries (in % of GDP)

Country	2001	2002	2003	2004	2005	2006	2007	2008	2009	2010	Average
Bulgaria	36.2	35.4	35.2	34.6	34.2	33.5	33.0	32.6	32.9	32.3	33.9
Czech Republic	18.4	18.0	17.6	17.3	17.0	16.4	16.1	15.6	15.9	15.2	16.8
Estonia	32.0	31.6	31.2	31.0	30.6	29.9	29.4	29.2	29.6	29.2	30.4
Hungary	24.3	24.0	23.7	23.4	23.0	22.6	22.4	22.0	22.6	22.1	23.0
Latvia	30.0	29.6	29.3	29.1	28.6	27.8	27.3	26.9	27.2	26.6	28.2
Lithuania	33.0	32.9	32.5	31.7	31.4	30.7	29.8	29.4	29.7	29.3	31.0
Poland	27.5	27.3	27.1	27.0	26.7	26.3	26.1	25.8	25.9	25.6	26.5
Romania	33.4	33.2	32.7	32.3	31.8	30.5	30.2	29.6	29.8	29.5	31.3
Serbia	**33.2**	**32.7**	**32.1**	**32.0**	**31.6**	**31.2**	**30.7**	**30.1**	**30.6**	**30.1**	**31.4**
Slovak Republic	18.8	18.5	18.3	18.0	17.7	17.2	16.6	16.3	16.9	16.2	17.5
Slovenia	26.6	26.2	26.1	26.0	25.7	25.3	24.8	24.3	24.6	24.1	25.4
Average per year of 11 countries	28.5	28.1	27.8	26.8	27.1	26.5	26.0	25.6	26.0	25.5	26.9

Source: Own calculations

In order to calculate absolute figures for the size of the shadow economies of these 11 countries from this MIMIC estimation result, we use already available information from the currency demand approach for Hungary, Poland, and Slovenia, and for the other countries from Schneider (2005) and Lackó (2000).

The results of the size and development of the shadow economies of these 11 Central and Eastern European countries are presented in Table 5.2 using Model 1. Table 5.2 clearly shows that in principle we have a declining trend in the size and development of these shadow economies in all 11 countries. As the table is self-reading, only the values for Serbia will explicitly be mentioned here.

The size of the Serbian shadow economy was 33.2 % in 2001 and declined to 30.1 % in 2008, increased in 2009 to 30.6 % and decreased again in 2010 to 30.1 %. A small increase in 2009 is observable for almost all of these 11 countries. The results show that the shadow economy declined in Serbia over the period of economic growth and then stayed almost unchanged after the beginning of the economic crisis. We can also see that over the whole period considered the shadow economy in Serbia is higher than the average values for the selected 11 countries. Only Bulgaria has a higher shadow economy in percent of GDP than Serbia (by 2.2 percentage points in 2010).

Another important result is that the size and development of the Serbian shadow economy between 2001 and 2010 show a strong (highly statistically significant) negative relationship between the size and development of the shadow economy and the size and development of official GDP. If the official GDP decreases by 1 percentage point the shadow economy increases between 0.60 and 0.70 percentage points, depending on the model used. Hence, if the official economy is in a severe recession the shadow economy greatly increases. This is an obvious result, which can be observed in a lot of other studies (compare e.g., Field and Schneider 2010 or Schneider 2011). If the official economy shrinks and if people have less opportunity to earn money in the official economy they will increase their activities in the shadow economy to compensate for the loss from the official economy or to earn extra.

5.3 Estimate of the Shadow Economy Using the Household Tax Compliance Approach[7]

The shadow economy can be estimated in other ways besides the MIMIC model. A frequently utilised approach is the HTC (Household Tax Compliance) method, based on data from macroeconomic accounts. This method estimates the extent of the shadow economy generated by activities in the household sector, and as such is narrower in its scope than the MIMIC model, which also includes other institutional sectors. Any estimate of the shadow economy obtained using the HTC approach is

[7] The methodology applied was described and used in Christie and Holzner (2004).

expected to be lower than that using the MIMIC method, since some informal activity takes place outside the household sector, i.e., in the corporate sector. So, for instance, taxpaying businesses and entrepreneurs can conceal part of their profits, under-report the value of taxable property, engage in trade without declaring VAT and excise duty (e.g., by setting up 'phantom companies'), etc.

The extent of the shadow economy in the household sector (SEHS), defined as the share of undeclared household income (UHI) in GDP, was calculated as the difference between the total taxable household income (THI) and the declared/taxed household income (DHI), expressed as their respective shares in GDP:

$$SEHS = \frac{UHI}{GDP} = \frac{THI}{GDP} - \frac{DHI}{GDP} = \beta_H - \beta_H \lambda_H = \beta_H (1 - \lambda_H) \tag{5.1}$$

where β_H is the share of total household income in GDP, while λ_H is the ratio of taxed to total i.e., taxable household income. Therefore, to estimate the shadow economy in the household sector, total taxable household income and taxed household income must be estimated first.

The estimate of the amount of taxable household income (THI) was based on the assumption that households can use their income for consumption (THC—total household consumption), savings (SAV), and taxes (TAX). Starting from the fact that data on total household savings are not known in advance for any given year, the amount of savings was estimated by multiplying the net household savings rate (σ) and total household income:

$$\begin{aligned} \mathrm{THI} &= \mathrm{THC} + \mathrm{SAV} + \mathrm{TAX} = \mathrm{THC} + \sigma \mathrm{THI} + \mathrm{TAX} \\ &= \frac{1}{1-\sigma}(THC + TAX) \end{aligned} \tag{5.2}$$

For the purposes of estimating the taxable income of Serbian households we used data on total household consumption presented in national accounts, as published by the Statistical Office of the Republic of Serbia.

The savings rate was calculated as the ratio between total current household savings and total household income. Total current household savings were estimated as the difference between total gross disposable income and total final household consumption,[8] plus the increase in household financial savings, and less net household liabilities with financial institutions (according to data published by the National Bank of Serbia). Although savings should include other non-financial types of savings, such as investment in durable consumer goods or increase in inventories of non-durable consumer goods, etc., for the purposes of this estimate we assumed, due to lack of data, that 2010 did not see any changes to non-financial household savings. Net savings estimated thus amounted to some

[8] According to data obtained from the UN database.

4.7 % of gross disposable household income.[9] Starting from the estimated net savings rate and official data of the Ministry of Finance and Economy on government revenue in the form of personal income tax and social security contributions, we estimated Serbia's total taxable household income (THI).

The estimate of the amount of taxed income was based on the assumption that total government revenue from taxes and contributions (TGR) is the product of total (declared) taxed household income (DHI) and the statutory household tax rate (SHTR), so that the relative extent of total taxed household income can be calculated in the following manner:

$$\frac{\mathrm{DHI}}{\mathrm{GDP}} = \frac{TGR/GDP}{SHTR} \tag{5.3}$$

Data on total government revenue from personal income tax and social security contributions were taken from official publications of the Ministry of Finance and Economy, while the statutory household tax rate needed to be estimated.

The statutory household tax rate depends on the average personal income tax rate (PITR), the rate of social security contributions payable by employees (SSCR), and the net household savings rate, as well as the average VAT rate (VATR), the average rate of excise duty (EXCR), and the rate of consumption of excise goods (RCEG). It is calculated in the following manner:

$$\begin{aligned} SHTR = PITR + SSCR + (1 - PITR - SSCR) \\ * (1 - \sigma)(VATR{+}RCEG{*}EXCR) \end{aligned} \tag{5.4}$$

The average rate of personal income tax was calculated as the weighted average of tax rates applicable to all types of household income, including: wages; pension income; social welfare payments; and income from agriculture, hunting, and fishing, remittances, property, capital gains, gifts, and other income, as well as income in kind and imputed housing rent. Of all these forms of income, tax is levied on wages, income from property, and other income, while other forms of income are non-taxable (i.e., neither income tax nor social security contributions are payable). The weight applied in calculating the average statutory tax rate was the share of particular forms of income in the total income of the population in Serbia. The same approach was used to calculate the average rate of mandatory social security contributions payable by employees.

The average VAT rate was calculated by taking into account the statutory general and reduced VAT rates, the structure of consumption (share of goods and services taxable at the general and reduced rate in total consumption, according to data from the Household Budget Survey), and types of consumption *de facto* not

[9] If net savings were estimated using data from the Household Consumption Survey, the net savings rate would stand at about 8.4 %, which is close to the figure obtained by CLDS (2012). However, due to the respondents' propensity to underestimate income in these surveys, we felt that more precise estimates could be obtained using macroeconomic accounts.

Table 5.3 Estimate of the shadow economy based on macroeconomic data—HTC method

	Shadow economy
As % of GDP	23.6
In RSD billion	680.3

Source: Own calculations

subject to VAT, such as consumption from own production. The average rate of excise duty was calculated by considering statutory excise rates and the structure of household consumption, where particular excise duties were converted into *ad valorem* rates, using typical excise goods as an example (e.g., starting from the price of an average packet of cigarettes).

Taking formula (5.1) and the relevant variables for 2010 as our starting points, we estimated the total extent of the shadow economy in Serbia at 23.6 % of GDP, or RSD 680.3 billion (Table 5.3). The detailed calculation is provided in the Appendix table. Since the official GDP figures for Serbia are underestimated for various reasons (which will be described in greater detail below), an increase in the GDP would cause a change in the absolute amount recorded in the shadow economy. Thus a nominal increase in registered GDP of 15 % (considered a realistic figure) would raise the shadow economy to RSD 782.5 billion, since the extent of the shadow economy in unregistered GDP is assumed to be nearly identical to that in registered GDP.

The estimated value of the shadow economy based on household consumption and income data was lower by about one-fifth, or some six percentage points of GDP, than that obtained by using the MIMIC method. This difference was primarily caused by the fact that the HTC method does not cover informal activities not reflected in household income and consumption, such as various types of informal activity in the sector of businesses and entrepreneurs. Furthermore, some of the divergence in the estimates can be accounted for by differences in methodology and data sources.

5.4 Estimate of the Shadow Economy Based on the Survey on Conditions for Doing

5.4.1 Business in Serbia

Microeconomic estimates of the shadow economy can be obtained by using data collected from taxpayers themselves or from the Tax Administration on detected evasion. Microeconomic methods are complementary with estimates of the shadow economy obtained through the use of macroeconomic methods. These methods may also provide additional information on which industries see the greatest extent of tax evasion, differences in perceptions of tax evasion depending on the number of employees in a business, type of business entity (enterprises/entrepreneurs), and the like. Surveys can provide information about taxpayers' views on the extent to which tax evasion jeopardises the equality of market participants, their value judgments and reasons for tax evasion, the efficiency of government bodies, the extent of corruption, etc. This chapter estimates the total volume of the shadow economy in trade in goods and employee wages in the business and entrepreneurial sectors, while Chap. 6 takes a closer look at other aspects of the shadow economy.

Microeconomic methods do, however, have certain drawbacks. The main potential weakness of surveys is the near certainty of respondents being biased downward and thus underestimating tax evasion in their own businesses. In addition, there is the objective issue of the reliability of answers on tax evasion, as they are made from memory and not based on any systematic records. Figures calculated using data on tax evasion uncovered by the Tax Administration are systematically underestimated, since it is clear that only a certain percentage of evasions are discovered.

5.4.2 Estimated Extent of the Shadow Economy in the Trade in Goods

Microeconomic estimates of the extent of the shadow economy in the trade in goods presented in this study are based on the Survey of Conditions for Doing Business in Serbia that covers businesses and entrepreneurs. The survey does not cover individuals, unregistered entrepreneurs, or businesses operating completely in the shadow economy (see Chap. 3). However, it is estimated that this segment of the shadow economy is indirectly included in the estimate of the total volume of informal trading; i.e., trading without the payment of taxes. It is likely that respondents from registered businesses and entrepreneurs included illicit trade with unregistered businesses when estimating the total volume of illicit trade.

As expected, the businesses and entrepreneurs surveyed underestimated the volume of informal trade engaged in by their own businesses. As little as 31 % of businesses and entrepreneurs surveyed responded that they made some payments in cash. The average volume of payments in cash estimated by the 31 % of respondents stood at some 32.1 %. However, if we extrapolate this percentage onto the total number of entities, we can see that cash payments account for about 11 % of all payments—a consequence of the fact that as many as 66.6 % of all respondents claimed that there were no cash payments at their businesses or shops. The next chapter takes a more detailed look at 'shadow trade' for the set of VAT payers, by features of business.

Obviously, regardless of the anonymity offered by the survey, the respondents were less than honest when replying to the question designed to capture the extent of cash transactions at their business/shop. An estimate of informal transactions can thus be obtained on the basis of respondents estimates on the participation of other businesses from the same sector and this estimate could be considered the upper limit of its likely extent (see Chap. 3). Based on the responses of the surveyed businesses and entrepreneurs, cash payments accounted for about 21.6 % of total payments in their sector of activity.[10]

The macroeconomic relevance of illicit trade in the business sector can be gauged on the basis of the share of corporate GDP in total GDP. According to 2010 data, corporate GDP accounted for some 53 % of total GDP (Statistical Office of the Republic of Serbia 2012). If we assume that the share of businesses in the trade in goods is approximately equal to their share in GDP, it follows that illicit trade of 21.6 % implies that the extent of the shadow economy in the trade in goods amounts to 11.6 % of GDP. When interpreting these figures, it must be noted that it reflects the amount of added value avoided, which serves as the VAT base, rather than the value of gross turnover avoided. If the shadow economy were to be estimated on the basis of gross turnover, rather than on added value, it would be taken into account multiple times, which is incorrect from the standpoint of methodology.[11] Besides, calculating the extent of the shadow economy based on gross turnover runs counter to the general idea of value added tax, which is designed so that added value, rather than gross turnover, is taken as its base.

5.4.3 Estimated Extent of the Shadow Economy in the Payment of Wages

One of the standard procedures for estimating the shadow economy in the field of taxing personal income is also based on carrying out a survey on a representative sample of taxpayers, although answers obtained in this manner have often been known to underestimate the amount of overall and untaxed income.[12] As employee wages are the dominant form of taxable household income in Serbia, and the taxes and contributions are paid by employers, the gap in personal income tax and contributions was estimated using data obtained in the Survey on Conditions for Doing Business in Serbia. Although this does not cover the portion of the household income shadow economy that is generated through working outside of regular working hours or outside of formal employment (e.g., private lessons given by teachers), the findings can nonetheless serve as an approximate indicator of the

[10] The average estimate of tax evasion was calculated using the weighted average, whereby estimates within an interval were replaced by the median of that interval. In calculating the average amount of tax evasion we excluded non-responses, i.e., respondents who claimed they did not know how much was evaded and those who refused to answer.

[11] Estimates of the shadow economy based on gross turnover are probably one of the most significant reasons why the shadow economy is overestimated in public debates in Serbia.

[12] The problem of bias inherent in answers to these questions has been partly resolved by posing implicit questions that relate to the entire sector of activity the respondent engages in, rather than on the respondent alone. However, this method also carries the risk of untruthful answers, or misunderstanding of the concept of sector of activity.

extent of the household income shadow economy, on condition that the extent of non-declaration of other forms of income is similar to that seen with wages.

The extent of the shadow economy in the field of household income is defined as the relative divergence between (total) taxable income and taxed (declared) income in relation to the amount of taxable income. The difference between taxable and taxed income has been defined in the survey as the wage paid to a worker in cash (rather than via a bank account) in the sector of activity in which the particular business entity operates. Thus, the extent of the shadow economy in the field of household income is an indicator of the ratio of undeclared to declared household income, and, as such, shows how widespread the shadow economy is in this field. As respondents were able to choose between intervals of figures for this rate for the sector of activity they operate in, the average weighted amount was calculated using the median of the intervals, as well as a weight based on the frequency of respondents selecting a particular interval.

As reported in the survey, the average extent of the shadow economy in wages (the ratio between undeclared and total actual income from labour) stands at 26.2 %.[13] On average, this is higher with entrepreneurs, i.e., wages paid by entrepreneurs, than with businesses (Fig. 5.2). When viewed by sector of activity, the extent of employee wages paid in the shadow economy is the highest in construction, catering, and transportation, much lower in production, and lowest in businesses engaging in trade. Moreover, the payment of wages in cash is the most widespread in micro-businesses and by entrepreneurs, and, as businesses grew, the extent of wages paid informally decreased. In addition, when the data are viewed by region, the results show that 'envelope wages' were more common among employers in Central Serbia than those based in Vojvodina or Belgrade. The Tax Administration should take into account this structure of informal employment when designing an audit system.

The share of gross wages in the sectors of businesses and entrepreneurs in GDP can be used to estimate the share of avoided wages paid by the business sector in GDP. Wages account for some 51 % of GDP, while wages paid by businesses make up some 70 % of all wages. When the 26.2 % rate of informal wages paid by businesses is applied to this figure, it can be estimated that the extent of the shadow economy in the payment of wages by businesses stands at 9.4 % of GDP.[14]

---

[13] According to data from the 2007 Living Standards Measurement Study, the rate of underreporting of income (% of unreported income in relation to reported income) stood at 26.9 % in Serbia, which underlines the robustness of estimates of the extent of the shadow economy in the field of household income (Ranđelović 2011).

[14] If we take into account the percentage of workers without formal employment contracts whose wages are paid wholly in cash (23.9 %), and assuming that the respondents did not include them in their estimates, but rather referred only to workers with a portion of wages paid in cash, the percentage of wages paid in cash rockets to 43.8 %. This means that the aggregate estimate of the shadow economy in the payment of wages also increases, to 15.6 % of GDP. A more detailed overview of the methodology used can be found in Putninš and Sauka (2011).

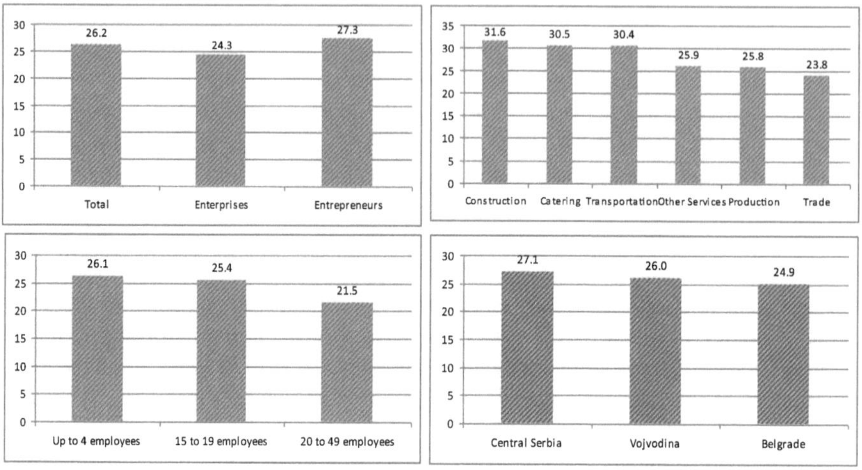

Fig. 5.2 Extent of the shadow economy in wages, based on the Survey on Conditions for Doing Business in Serbia. *Source*: Own calculations. Survey on Conditions for Doing Business in Serbia, FREN 2012

5.4.4 Summary Estimate of the Shadow Economy in the Sector of Businesses and Entrepreneurs

Based on the Survey of Conditions for Doing Business in Serbia, it is estimated that the extent of the shadow economy in the sector of businesses and entrepreneurs with respect to the trade in goods and the payment of wages stands at some 21.2 % of GDP (Table 5.4). This estimate covers the greatest portion of informal activity of businesses and entrepreneurs, but not all types of such activity. The other types of companies' informal activity, including the evasion of corporate income tax, property tax, and various fees and charges, probably collectively account for 10–15 % of the volume of informal activity in the trade in goods and payment of wages.

As expected, the extent of the shadow economy in the sector of businesses and entrepreneurs estimated using the findings of the survey was lower than that estimated using the MIMIC and HTC methods. This is because the MIMIC model takes into account all institutional sectors and all types of informal activity, while the survey only looks at the shadow economy among businesses and entrepreneurs (and not among households), and takes into account only the most important types of informal activity, illicit trade in goods and under-reporting of wages.

Table 5.4 Estimated extent of the shadow economy in the sector of businesses and entrepreneurs, based on the Survey on Conditions for Doing Business in Serbia

	As % of GDP
Total extent of shadow economy	21.2
Shadow economy in trade in goods	11.6
Shadow economy in payment of wages	9.6

Source: Own calculations

5.5 Estimate of the Tax Evasion Gap

5.5.1 Introduction

The tax gap is the difference between hypothetical (theoretical) tax revenue and taxes actually collected. Hypothetical tax revenues are sums that would be collected over a particular period of time provided that all taxpayers pay their taxes in full compliance with tax legislation. However, the tax gap is also made up of other elements in addition to tax evasion, for example, taxes declared but unpaid and tax revenue lost due to taxpayer insolvency, but their significance to the balance is mostly low. In the case of Serbia, taxes declared but unpaid may have a relatively large share due to widespread fiscal indiscipline, and also because of the tolerance of non-payment by some groups of taxpayers (businesses undergoing restructuring, poorer individuals, etc.). In this study we have focused on estimating the tax gap without going into whether it is caused by evasion or non-payment of declared taxes.

We have estimated the tax gap for the most important types of tax in Serbia: value added tax (VAT), social security contributions, and personal income tax. The share of these taxes in Serbia's total tax revenue is about 80 %. The tax gap was not estimated for another important tax, excise duty, which has a share of some 15 % in total tax revenues. Estimating this tax gap would have required detailed assessment by groups of excise product (oil products, cigarettes, alcoholic beverages, etc.), which would have gone beyond the scope of this survey.

The application of various methods resulted in an estimate of 7.5 % of GDP for the total VAT, personal income and social security contributions tax gap. Of this amount, the income tax and contributions gap amounted to some 5 % of GDP, while the VAT gap stood at about 2.5 % of GDP. Assuming that the extent of evasion was slightly lower for other taxes (excise duty, customs duty, corporate income tax, property tax, fees, charges, etc.), we estimate that the total tax gap stands at some 11 % of GDP, or, rather, that the sum total of taxes evaded and those declared but not paid amounts to about €3 billion per year.

5.5.2 Estimate of the VAT Gap

The VAT gap is the difference between the hypothetical (theoretical) VAT assessed and the amount actually collected. The VAT gap will be estimated using macroeconomic aggregates (with a top-to-bottom approach), as well as on the basis of microeconomic data obtained from a survey of VAT payers.

5.5.2.1 Estimating the VAT Gap Based on Macroeconomic Aggregates

Methodology for Estimating the VAT Gap

The macroeconomic estimate of the VAT gap was made using methodology applied to EU member states (Reckon 2009); other institutions use similar methodologies (HM Revenue & Customs 2011). According to this methodology, the starting point for estimating the VAT gap is the system of national accounts, as well as disaggregated data on the consumption of various products by household. Thus the reliability of such estimates is critically dependent on the quality of information found in the national accounts and the Household Consumption Survey. One advantage of estimating the VAT gap on the basis of macroeconomic accounts rather than other methods of assessment is that it includes VAT contained in all components of aggregate demand (household consumption, investment, other consumption) and across all institutional sectors (households, businesses, government). Under the macroeconomic approach the total hypothetical VAT is equal to the sum of the hypothetical VAT contained in household consumption, fixed investments, and other consumption. VAT figures obtained by these means are then adjusted for several factors, such as small taxpayers exempted from VAT, purchase of business car fleets and other goods not subject to a refund of input VAT, specific areas of taxation in some countries, etc.

The most important macroeconomic basis for calculating VAT is household consumption, which is financed from household income but also includes consumption funded by non-governmental organisations (such as the Red Cross, religious communities, and other NGOs). Hypothetical VAT contained in household consumption accounts for by far the largest portion of total hypothetical VAT in EU countries, averaging 64 %. The share of household consumption VAT in hypothetical VAT has been stable, both by year and by country. The coefficient of variation of the share of EU25 hypothetical VAT on household consumption in total EU25 VAT amounted to a mere 9.1 % between 2000 and 2006.[15]

Another significant macroeconomic base for VAT is made up of fixed investments. Although this is generally exempt from VAT, some of them contain substantial VAT. Most VAT is accounted for by investments made by non-VAT payer entities, such as private individuals, small-scale entrepreneurs, and the like.

[15] Calculation based on Reckon (2009).

The most important component within this group is investment in the construction and purchase of housing. In addition, in many countries (Serbia included) VAT payers are required to pay VAT on fixed assets that can be used for private purposes, such as cars, furniture, etc. The share of VAT contained in fixed investments in EU member states stood at 14.7 % on average between 2000 and 2006, but variations between individual countries were substantial, with the coefficient of variation standing at 32 % on average. Such relatively high variation was caused by both fluctuations in investment and the differing tax treatment of some investments, such as the purchase of cars or furniture by taxpayers.

The third significant macroeconomic base for VAT is other consumption. Within this factor the most significant areas are private household consumption provided by the state through transfers in kind, collective consumption, and financial services. Private consumption provided by the state in kind includes various types of service provided by the state to private individuals, the most important being healthcare, education, and social security, as well as sports and cultural needs, which are less significant. All of these services have the features of private goods, but the state provides them to the public for various reasons (goods egalitarianism, exogenous effects and information asymmetries, etc.). Collective consumption comprises public goods, such as defence, internal security, justice, etc. that the state also provides to citizens. Added value in the financial sector is not yet subject to VAT, but there have been calls to remove this exemption.

VAT is not charged on the added value of private goods provided by the state, collective consumption, and financial services, but VAT contained in the inputs is not deducted as input VAT. This means that VAT is not payable on education, healthcare, internal and external security, justice, and financial services; however, the costs of the delivery of these services include VAT payable on inputs such as fuel, medications, utilities, office supplies, etc. Hypothetical VAT contained in other consumption is a major component of overall hypothetical VAT, with an average share of 19.6 % in the EU25 between 2000 and 2006. However, the variation in the share of hypothetical VAT on other services in total hypothetical VAT is relatively high—the coefficient of variation amounts to 25 %.

Hypothetical VAT contained in each macroeconomic base (household consumption, fixed investment, and other consumption) is obtained by multiplying the tax base and the average weighted statutory tax rate for each tax base. As VAT is included in these bases in macroeconomic accounts and consumption data, recalculated statutory tax rates must be used instead of the original ones.[16]

[16] The general statutory rate in Serbia stood at 18 % at the time the analysis was carried out, while the recalculated statutory rate amounted to 15.2 % $= 18/(100 + 18) * 100$. All estimates were made using the statutory rates in force in 2011.

Estimation of the VAT Gap in Serbia

In estimating the VAT gap in Serbia in accordance with methodology applied in EU member states (Reckon 2009), particular attention was paid to estimating the hypothetical VAT contained in household consumption. This approach was both justified, since nearly two-thirds of total VAT is accounted for by household consumption, and feasible, as data on the detailed structure of household consumption are available, unlike those regarding the structure of investments and other consumption.

The starting point for estimating hypothetical VAT was the set of data on household consumption by product group (Radisavljević 2010) adjusted to household consumption data from national accounts, as well as the Law on VAT. This piece of legislation stipulates which products attract the standard rate or the reduced rate, and which activities are VAT exempted without credit (government services, financial services, etc.). The average statutory VAT rate was estimated on the basis of the Law on VAT and the structure of consumption for each product group. We obtained the value of the hypothetical VAT for each product group by multiplying the average statutory VAT rate for that product group (e.g., food and soft drinks) with the value of consumption for that group. In the case of food and soft drinks, we also took into account the fact that households obtain a portion of consumption from their own production: this is termed in-kind consumption. No VAT is payable on the added value of these products, but some VAT is contained in inputs (fuel, seeds, crop protection, cattle feed, etc.) used to produce these mainly agricultural products; we took this into account when estimating the average VAT rate applicable to this group of products. We assumed that imputed rent, which has a share of close to 11 % in personal consumption (Radisavljević 2010), did not contain any VAT, i.e. that the tax rate was equal to zero.

Hypothetical VAT on fixed investment was estimated on the basis of the share of fixed investment in Serbia's GDP and the average share of VAT contained in investment in new EU member states. This approach was used because there are no data for Serbia on the structure of investment by type of investor (VAT payers vs. others) or product (amounts of investment in products not exempt from VAT—cars or furniture purchased by VAT payers, etc.) that could be used to estimate the share of VAT in them.

Value added tax contained in other consumption (private and collective consumption provided by the state, financial services) was estimated under the assumption that the value of the inputs taxed amounted to 60 % of the added value in the respective sectors of activity. In addition, we have assumed that these activities used inputs taxed at an average VAT rate of 14 %.

Adding together the VAT contained in household consumption, fixed investment, and other consumption yields total hypothetical VAT. Total hypothetical VAT is then adjusted with the aim of correcting for standard exemptions and special tax regimes that are part of the VAT system. The most important adjustment is the reduction in total hypothetical VAT for VAT contained in the added value of entrepreneurs and businesses below the VAT entry threshold. These businesses and entrepreneurs do not pay VAT on their own added value, but are also unable to claim refunds of VAT paid on their inputs. The correction also takes into account the fact that businesses that purchase cars are not able to claim VAT refunds. As there are no data for Serbia that would make it possible to make these adjustments, we applied an average adjustment rate of 3.5 % of the total hypothetical VAT, which is slightly above the EU average.

The application of this procedure resulted in an estimate of the hypothetical VAT of Serbia between 2008 and 2011. We calculated the VAT gap by subtracting actually collected VAT from hypothetical VAT; this gap was made up mainly of evaded VAT, as well as VAT declared but not paid. Based on official statistics of macroeconomic aggregates and consumption and using the above methodology, the VAT gap in Serbia between 2008 and 2011 was found to range between 7.3 and 9.4 % of the hypothetical VAT, with an average value of 8.6 % (Table 5.5). The estimated VAT gap in Serbia amounted to just about 1 % of GDP.

The VAT gap calculated in this manner for Serbia was significantly lower than the EU25 VAT gap seen between 2000 and 2006, which stood at 13.5 % of the hypothetical VAT on average. The difference is even more marked in relation to the eight new Central and Eastern European member states, where the average VAT gap[17] was 19.3 % in 2000–2006.

The VAT Gap and Registered GDP

The fact that the VAT gap is much smaller in Serbia than in EU member states could be caused by an underestimated macroeconomic base (household consumption and investment) in Serbia, or by exceptionally low tax evasion and small amounts of tax declared but not paid. It is perfectly clear that the low VAT gap estimated in Serbia was caused by an underestimate of the GDP and its elements that are subject to VAT. Unlike EU member states, Serbia does not include a portion of the shadow economy in the calculation of its GDP. Yet another indication of the fact that underestimated GDP was the primary cause of the low VAT gap in Serbia can be gleaned by comparing the share of actually collected VAT in Serbia with that in EU member states. The share in Serbia was among the highest in Europe, although Serbia's VAT rate was among the lowest.

The hypothetical VAT in investments and other consumption was calculated using the appropriate parameters for EU member states.

The structure of the hypothetical VAT in Serbia differs from the EU average. VAT contained in household consumption has a relatively high share in the hypothetical VAT, while the share of VAT in investments and other consumption is lower than the EU average (Table 5.6). This difference is the consequence of the

[17] The average VAT gap for EU25 and the eight new CEE member states was calculated as the unweighted average of data obtained by Reckon (2009).

Table 5.5 Estimate of hypothetical VAT, in millions of RSD

	2008	2009	2010	2011
Hypothetical VAT, total	325,370	328,832	347,515	377,597
VAT in household consumption	227,973	238,396	253,978	276,866
VAT in fixed investments	41,107	33,165	33,299	35,290
VAT in other consumption	44,892	45,351	47,603	52,048
Net adjustment	11,399	11,920	12,635	13,393
Actual VAT	301,700	296,900	319,400	342,000
VAT gap, in millions of RSD	23,670	31,932	28,115	35,597
VAT gap, in % of hypothetical VAT	7.3	9.7	8.1	9.4

Source: Own calculations. Calculated using macroeconomic data, household consumption data, and Law on VAT

Table 5.6 Structure of hypothetical VAT, in %

	2008	2009	2010	2011
Hypothetical VAT, total	100.0	100.0	100.0	100.0
VAT in household consumption	70.1	72.5	73.1	73.3
VAT in fixed investments	12.6	10.1	9.6	9.3
VAT in other consumption	13.8	13.8	13.7	13.8
Net adjustment	3.5	3.6	3.6	3.5

Source: Own calculations

large share of personal consumption in Serbia's GDP relative to the EU average. In 2009, household consumption in Serbia had a share of 77 % of GDP, while on average this figure was 57 % in EU member states (Radisavljević 2010). The share of household consumption in GDP was greater in Serbia than in any EU member state, which was probably caused by specific factors; however, error cannot be ruled out when estimating GDP or some of its components, such as investments. Key factors affecting the high share of household consumption in GDP are the high share of wages, pensions, and remittances in GDP.

To obtain a more realistic assessment of the amount of hypothetical VAT, and thus of the VAT gap, while ensuring international comparability, official GDP data for Serbia must be adjusted in line with ESA 95 methodology. This entails increasing the official GDP by a portion of the shadow economy[18] etc. included in the GDP in countries that apply EU or United Nations methodology. According to the latest estimate of the unobserved economy carried out in Serbia by the Statistical Office of the Republic of Serbia for 2003–2005, the GDP would be greater than the official GDP by between 13.5 and 16.2 % if a portion of the shadow and unregistered economy were included, as is done in other countries.[19] Although the estimate of the unobserved economy relates to a period of nearly a

[18] For a more detailed discussion, see the overview of activities not included in GDP in developing countries in United Nations (2008).

[19] Website: http://www.stat.gov.rs/nacionalni_racuni.

decade ago, adjustments made to Serbia's official GDP will be based on it in the absence of newer research. The official GDP of Serbia, therefore, rose by 15 % between 2008 and 2011.

The increase in GDP by components of final use approach was differentiated: investments increased by 20 %, household consumption by 16 %, and other consumption by 5 %. The above-average adjustment in investments was caused by the great extent of the excluded shadow economy in the construction industry, encompassing businesses, entrepreneurs, and households equally. The adjustment in household consumption was slightly greater than the average adjustment of GDP, while other consumption saw a relatively modest adjustment, since it was dominated by consumption provided by the state. Individual forms of consumption recorded different levels of adjustment: above-average adjustment was seen in the consumption of clothing and shoes[20] and in the sectors of catering, personal services, and food; below-average adjustment, on the other hand, was recorded in the consumption of utilities, telecommunications services, etc. These differentiated adjustments of particular forms of household consumption are important, since various forms of consumption are taxed at different average weighted statutory tax rates.

The hypothetical VAT was estimated on the basis of adjusted household consumption, investments, and other consumption, using the methodology described above. As expected, based on the adjusted macroeconomic bases, it was found that the hypothetical VAT was greater by some 15 % in relation to the hypothetical VAT obtained on the basis of official VAT data. The estimated VAT gap between 2008 and 2011 amounted to 20.6 % on average (Table 5.7), which was much greater than the EU25 average, which stood at 13.5 % between 2000 and 2006.[21] However, it is more relevant to compare Serbia with similar EU member states,[22] where the VAT gap amounted to 18.1 % between 2000 and 2006. It is also pertinent to note that the VAT gap in these countries stood at 19.3 % in 2000–2003, before their accession to the EU (Reckon 2009).

The macroeconomic relevance of the estimated VAT gap can be assessed by its share in GDP. The use of adjusted GDP shows that the VAT gap in Serbia stood at, on average, 2.5 % of adjusted GDP (or 2.9 % of official GDP) between 2008 and 2011. The VAT gap estimated using adjusted GDP is nearly three times as high as that found using official GDP data.

According to the Survey on Conditions for Doing Business in Serbia, businesses and entrepreneurs estimated that the extent of informal transactions in their respective sectors of activity stood at some 22 % of the total volume of transactions. This

[20] These products are sold in large quantities at flea markets, or even in high-street shops, without VAT being paid. However, the products—mainly imported from abroad—may contain some VAT paid at the time of import, probably using an underestimated base.

[21] Calculated as the unweighted average of data from Reckon (2009).

[22] The Czech Republic, Poland, Slovakia, and Slovenia. An even more relevant comparison would involve Romania and Bulgaria, but data for these countries are not available.

Table 5.7 Estimate of hypothetical VAT using adjusted base, in millions of RSD

	2008	2009	2010	2011
Hypothetical VAT, total	374,389	377,527	399,979	434,538
VAT in household consumption	268,771	280,458	295,507	322,137
VAT in fixed investments	49,328	39,798	39,958	42,349
VAT in other consumption	44,892	45,351	49,983	546,499
Net adjustment	11,399	11,920	14,530	15,402
Actual VAT	301,700	296,900	319,400	342,000
VAT gap, in millions of RSD	72,689	80,627	80,579	92,538
VAT gap, in % of hypothetical VAT	19.4	21.4	20.1	21.3

Source: Own calculations. Calculated using macroeconomic data, household consumption data, and Law on VAT. Hypothetical VAT contained in investments and other consumption calculated using appropriate parameters for EU member states

estimate supports the estimate of the tax gap made on the basis of adjusted macroeconomic data, whereby the VAT gap in Serbia is seen to amount to some 21 % of hypothetical VAT.

5.5.3 *Estimated Personal Income Tax and Social Security Contributions Gap*

As has already been mentioned, the term 'tax gap' is narrower than 'shadow economy', since the shadow economy denotes income that is taxable by law but is not declared or taxed, while the tax gap denotes the amount of tax evaded expressed as a percentage of hypothetical tax revenue. The income tax and contributions gap is defined as the difference between the hypothetical amount of income tax and social security contributions that could be collected (if all income taxable under law were actually taxed) and the amount of income tax and contributions actually collected. The income tax and contributions gap can be estimated if we first estimate the extent of the shadow economy in the payment of wages, using data from the survey (the amount of income not taxed) and the statutory average rates of tax and contributions payable on such income. Since the survey covered exclusively income from labour, only such income was taken into account in calculating the statutory tax rate.

Starting from the extent of the shadow economy in the payment of wages estimated using the survey (26.2 %) and the total amount of gross wages earned by employees stated in the national accounts, we were able to estimate the total extent of the shadow economy in the area of income from labour (approximately 9.4 % of GDP, or some RSD 313 billion). By applying the average statutory tax rate for taxable income from labour to this figure, we arrived at a figure of 4.1 % of GDP (or RSD 135.7 billion) as an estimate of the personal income tax and social

Table 5.8 Estimated personal income tax and social contributions gap, based on the Survey on Conditions for Doing Business in Serbia

Income tax and contributions gap (as % of GDP)	4.1
Income tax and contributions gap (as % of hypothetical amount of income tax and contributions)	22.7

Source: Own calculations

contributions gap, or 22.7 % of the hypothetical revenue from personal income tax and all social security contributions (Table 5.8).

The total amount of the income tax and contributions gap is probably slightly higher than the estimated 4.1 % of GDP, since there are other types of informal activity in the area of labour income that contribute to the income tax gap which are not covered (e.g., self-employment after formal working hours such as private tuition by schoolteachers, etc.). Moreover, evasion is also present in taxation of income from capital (e.g., undeclared interest income from lending money informally, or dividends earned from unregistered corporate income, etc.) Since income from wage employment and self-employment dominated total personal income, the total personal income tax and social contributions gap is estimated to stand at about 5 % of GDP (or 27.7 % of the hypothetical amount of income tax and contributions).

Shadow Economy, Tax Evasion, and the Tax Gap

'Shadow economy', 'tax evasion', and 'tax gap' are related but distinct concepts, and as such are sometimes confused by the general public, which can lead to misunderstandings. The shadow economy, from the taxation standpoint, is the value of taxable activities (labour, trade, etc.) and rights (ownership of property, etc.) on which tax is not paid, although they are statutorily taxable. Tax evasion is the difference between the tax liabilities of a taxpayer under current laws, and their reported tax liabilities; in the case of total evasion, the tax liabilities reported equal zero. The tax gap is the difference between the tax evaded and the amount of statutory tax liabilities ('hypothetical tax').

We will present two hypothetical examples to clearly underline the distinction between shadow economy, tax evasion, and tax gap. If earned income amounting to RSD 100 is fully evaded, given a fiscal burden on labour of 40 %, the shadow economy amounts to 100 dinars, while the tax gap stands at RSD 40 (i.e. 100 % of the statutory tax liability). In the case of turnover of RSD 100, of which half was made informally, given a VAT rate of 20 %, the absolute amount of the shadow economy is RSD 50, the evaded tax amounts to RSD 10, while the tax gap stands at 50 %. As can be seen from these examples, the percentages of the shadow economy and the tax gap are identical, and stand at 100 and 50 %, respectively, but their absolute values differ greatly. The absolute value of the shadow economy is greater than the

(continued)

tax evaded by the amount of the reciprocal value of the tax rate, so that, for instance, given a VAT rate of 20 %, the shadow economy is five times greater than the tax evaded (1/0.2 = 5).

In the case of Serbia, the MIMIC method resulted in an estimate of 30 % of GDP for the shadow economy, or €10 billion, while the total tax gap in Serbia was estimated to stand at about 10 % of GDP, or about €3 billion. It follows from these estimates that the total implicit tax rate (the ratio of the tax gap to the shadow economy) stands at 33 % in the shadow economy in Serbia, slightly lower than the total tax rate in the formal sector, which amounts to between 37 and 38 %.

Appendix

Estimation of the shadow economy in household income, based on macroeconomic data (Household tax compliance method)

Description	Designation	2010 (RSD million, at current prices)
GDP at current prices	GDP_{MP}	2,881,891
Estimated total household income	**THI = THC + Savings + Paid taxes = THC +σ*THI + Paid Taxes**	
Total household income, National accounts		2,703,013
Total household consumption, National accounts	THC (total household consumption)	2,686,493
Total household income, HBS		2,703,013
Total household consumption, HBS		2,686,493
Change in household deposits (12/2010-12/2009)		165,141
Change in household liabilities (12/2010-12/2009)		101,859
Net household savings		79,802
Net Household Savings Rate	***SVR***	***0.03***
Taxes paid by households	Paid taxes	772,483
Income tax		*139,376*
Contributions		*161,507*
VAT		*319,400*
Excise duties		*152,200*
Total household income	**THI = (1 / (1 – SVR)) * (THC + Paid Taxes)**	**3,564,203**
Estimated statutory household tax rate	***SHTR = AIT + ESS + (1 – AIT–ESS) * 1 – SVR) * (VAT + ECR * AET)***	
Estimated income tax rate	AIT	0.046

(continued)

Description	Designation	2010 (RSD million, at current prices)
Average rate of contributions payable by employees	ESS	0.096
Average VAT rate	VAT	0.11
Average excise rate	AET	0.484
Rate of consumption of excise goods	ECR	0.087
Statutory household tax rate	**SHTR**	**0.27**
Statutory household tax rate (inc. employer SSC)		**0.363**
Total household tax revenues	**THTR = ITR + SSR + VAR + ETR**	772,483
Income tax	*ITR*	*139,376*
Contributions	*SSR*	*161,507*
VAT	*VAR*	*319,400*
Excise duties	*ETR*	*152,200*
Estimated shadow economy due to households		
Percentage of declared household income	λ_H = DHI / THI = THTR / (THI * SHTR)	0.81
Total household income (as % of GDP)	β_H = THI / GDP	1.24
Shadow economy in households sector (as % of GDP)	**SEIH = $\beta_H(1 - \lambda_H)$**	**23.6**
Volume of shadow economy in households sector (RSD million)		**782,443**
Estimated total tax gap		
Total tax gap (RSD million)		**284,348**
Total tax gap (% GDP)		**11.3**
Total tax gap (% of hypothetical tax revenues)		**23.3**

Source: Own calculations

References

Bajada C, Schneider F (eds) (2005) Size, causes and consequences of the underground economy: an international perspective. Ashgate, Aldershot

Belev B (2003) The informal economy in the EU accession countries: size, scope, trends and challenges to the process of EU enlargement. Center for Study of Democracy, Sofia

Breusch T (2005a) The Canadian Underground Economy: An Examination of Giles and Tedds. Can Tax J 53(2):367–391

Breusch T (2005b) Estimating the underground economy using MIMIC models. Working Paper. National University of Australia, Canberra

Centar za liberalno demokratske studije – CLDS (2012) Rast privatne domaće štednje u cilju ubrzanja privrednog rasta Srbije. Beograd
Christie E, Holzner M (2004) Household tax compliance and shadow economy in central and southeastern Europe. The WIIW Balkan Observatory Working Papers No. 038
Contini B (1981) The second economy of Italy. Taxing and Spending 3:17–24
Contini B (1992) The irregular economy in Italy: a survey of contributions, guide book to statistics on the hidden economy. United Nations, New York
Dell'Anno R (2003) Estimating the shadow economy in Italy: a structural equation approach. Working Paper 2003-7. Department of Economics, University of Aarhus, Aarhus, Denmark
Del'Anno R, Schneider F (2004) The shadow economy of Italy and other OECD countries: what do we know? Discussion Paper. Department of Economics, University of Linz, Linz, Austria
Dell'Anno R, Schneider F (2009) A complex approach to estimate shadow economy: the structural equation modelling. In: Faggnini M, Looks T (eds) Coping with the complexity of economics. Springer, Berlin, pp 110–130
Feld LP, Schneider F (2010) Survey on the shadow economy and undeclared earnings in OECD countries. German Econ Rev 11(2):109–149
Frey BS, Weck-Hannemann H (1984) The hidden economy as an unobserved variable. Eur Econ Rev 26(1):33–53
Giles DEA (1997a) Causality between the measured and underground economies in New Zealand. Appl Econ Lett 4(1):63–67
Giles DEA (1997b) Testing the asymmetry in the measured and underground business cycles in New Zealand. Econ Rec 71(2):225–232
Giles DEA (1999a) Measuring the hidden economy: implications for econometric modeling. Econ J 109(3):370–380
Giles DEA (1999b) Modeling the hidden economy in the tax gap in New Zealand. Empir Econ 24(4):621–640
Giles DEA, Tedds LM (2002) Taxes and the Canadian underground economy. Canadian Tax Paper, vol 106, Canadian Tax Foundation, Toronto
Giles DEA, Tedds LM, Werkneh E (2002) The Canadian underground and measured economics. Appl Econ 34(4):2347–2352
Helberger C, Knepel H (1988) How big is the shadow economy? A re-analysis of the unobserved-variable approach of B.S. Frey and H. Weck-Hannemann. Eur Econ Rev 32:965–976
HM Revenue & Customs (2011) Methodological annex for measuring tax gaps
Johnson S, Kaufmann D, Shleifer A (1997) The unofficial economy in transition, Brookings papers on economic activity. World Bank, Washington DC
Johnson S, Kaufmann D, Zoido-Lobaton P (1998a) Regulatory discretion and the unofficial economy. Am Econ Rev 88(2):387–392
Johnson S, Kaufmann D, Zoido-Lobatón P (1998b) Corruption, public finances and the unofficial economy. Research Paper. The World Bank, Washington, DC
Kaufmann D, Kaliberda A (1996) Integrating the unofficial economy into the dynamics of post socialist economies: a framework of analyses and evidence. In: Kaminski B (ed) Economic transition in Russia and the new states of Eurasia. M.E. Sharpe, London, pp 81–120
Krstić G et al (1998) Analysis of the grey economy in the FRY with estimates of its volume for 1997 and recommendations for its legalisation. Economics Institute Belgrade
Lackó M (1996) Hidden economy in East-European countries in international comparison. Working Paper. International Institute for Applied Systems Analysis (IIASA), Laxenburg (Austria)
Lackó M (2000) Hidden economy – an unknown quantity? Comparative analysis of hidden economies in transition countries, 1989–1995. Econ Transit 8(1):117–149
Pozo S (ed) (1996) Exploring the underground economy: studies of illegal and unreported activity. W.E. Upjohn, Institute for Employment Research, Michigan
Putninš TJ, Sauka A (2011) The size and determinants of shadow economies in the Baltic States. Baltic J Econ 11(2)

Radisavljević G (2010) Lična potrošnja u Republici Srbiji 2000–2009. Statistical Office of the Republic of Serbia
Ranđelović S (2011) Smanjenje sive ekonomije kao instrument fiskalne konsolidacije. Kvartalni monitor. FREN, Beograd, pp 25–26
Reckon (2009) Study to quantify and analyse the VAT gap in the EU-25 member states, London
Schneider F (1994) Measuring the size and development of the shadow economy: can the causes be found and the obstacles be overcome? In: Brandstaetter H, Güth W (eds) Essays on economic psychology. Springer, Berlin, pp 193–212
Schneider F (1997) The shadow economies of Western Europe. J Inst Econ Aff 17(3):42–48
Schneider F (2003) The shadow economy. In: Rowley CK, Schneider F (eds) Encyclopedia of public choice. Kluwer Academic Publishers, Dordrecht
Schneider F (2004) Shadow economies around the World: what do we really know? IAW-Diskussionspapiere 16
Schneider F (2005) Shadow economies around the World: what do we really know? Eur J Polit Econ 21(3):598–642
Schneider F (2007) Shadow economies and corruption all over the world: new estimates for 145 countries. Economics, 2007–2009 July
Schneider F (2010) The influence of public institutions on the shadow economy: an empirical investigation for OECD countries. Eur J Law Econ 6(3):441–468
Schneider F (eds) (2011) Handbook on the shadow economy. Edward Elgar, Cheltenham
Schneider F, Buehn A, Montenegro CE (2010) New estimates for the shadow economies all over the world. Int Econ J 24(4):443–461
Statistical Office of the Republic of Serbia (2012) Statistical Yearbook 2012
Thomas JJ (1992) Informal economic activity, LSE, handbooks in economics. Harvester Wheatsheaf, London
United Nations (2008) Non-observed economy in national accounts – survey country practices. United Nations Economics Commission for Europe, New York and Geneva

Chapter 6
Shadow Economy in the Business and Entrepreneurial Sectors

Gorana Krstić and Branko Radulović

6.1 Assessment of Main Types of the Shadow Economy and Their Characteristics

Research to date on the shadow economy in South Eastern Europe and beyond has mainly focused on macro assessments of this phenomenon or on the socio-economic characteristics of individuals involved in these activities. There have been far fewer studies analysing the characteristics of businesses engaged in the shadow economy and the factors that drive them to operating informally. Exceptions are research on the shadow economy in Bulgaria and the Baltic States (Estonia, Lithuania, and Latvia) based on data from the survey of businesses operating informally, and a study on the impact of the shadow economy on the operation and competitiveness of businesses in South Eastern Europe, based on data from the Business Environment and Enterprise Performance Study (BEEPS) (Kyle et al. 2001; Williams 2006; Tedds 2010; Putninš and Sauka 2011; Hudson et al. 2012).

G. Krstić (✉)
Faculty of Economics, University of Belgrade, Belgrade, Serbia
e-mail: gkrstic@ekof.bg.ac.rs

B. Radulović
Faculty of Law, University of Belgrade, Belgrade, Serbia
e-mail: bradulovic@ius.bg.ac.rs

G. Krstić, F. Schneider (eds.), *Formalizing the Shadow Economy in Serbia*,
Contributions to Economics, DOI 10.1007/978-3-319-13437-6_6

Definition of the Shadow Economy and Informal Employment in the Survey on Conditions for Doing Business in Serbia

Business entities engaged in the shadow economy are those that employ workers informally and/or make payments in cash as VAT payers. The term 'informally employed' refers to those workers who are either employed without a formal contract, or who do have a contract but only a portion of their wages is declared, meaning that they receive a portion of their pay in cash.

The findings of the Survey on Conditions for Doing Business in Serbia carried out for the purposes of this study show that 28 % of all business entities in Serbia engage in activities in the shadow economy (Table 6.1), while one-fifth of all business entities employ workers informally.

If we include the other two categories—workers employed through the youth employment agency and non-VAT payer entrepreneurs contracted to perform certain activities for a company instead of its regular permanent employees with the aim of cutting costs or securing cash (at a 10 % commission)—the percentage of businesses engaging in shadow economy activities would be substantially greater, reaching 32.2 %. Although these two categories most often represent informal practices, they are not included in our basic definition of the shadow economy, as the survey did not include questions we could use to estimate how informal they actually are. Thus, for the purposes of this analysis, we have used a narrower definition. Nonetheless, regardless of the definition we use, the ratio of business entities in the shadow economy to the total number of business entities is relatively high, particularly in light of the fact that this figure presents the lower limit of the observed phenomenon, due to respondents' inclination to disguise their informal activities.

Table 6.1 shows the share of business entities in the shadow economy in the total number of business entities by their basic characteristics. According to the findings of the survey, the share of business entities evading VAT is slightly higher (one-quarter of all VAT payers) than the share of those engaging in informal employment (one-fifth of the total number of business entities).

When the results are viewed by type of business entity, it can be seen that entrepreneurs are more involved in the shadow economy than businesses (30.7 % as against 23 %, respectively), since informal employment and VAT evasion are more frequent with entrepreneurs than with businesses. It is also evident that new businesses and entrepreneurs, i.e., those registered after 2009, are more likely to engage in the shadow economy than older businesses. This is primarily the result of their inclination to employ workers without formal contracts, or with contracts but without declaring their entire wages. On the other hand, no differences are visible when it comes to informal transactions. This type of employment can be explained by the fact that start-ups use it in an endeavour to cut their costs and improve competitiveness.

Table 6.1 Percentage of business entities involved in the shadow economy, by characteristics

	% of business entities in the shadow economy	% of business entities employing workers informally	% of VAT paying business entities making payments in cash	% of business entities engaging in both types of shadow economy
Total	28.4	20.5	24.5	5.7
Type of business entity				
Business	23.0	14.5	18.3	6.4
Entrepreneur	30.7	23.0	29.2	5.4
Age				
Start-up, 1–2 years	32.1	26.5	24.7	7.3
Others	27.9	19.6	24.8	5.5
Number of employees				
Up to 4	27.7	20.2	25.7	5.2
5–19	32.8	23.6	22.0	9.1
20–49	28.0	11.4	24.8	6.5
50–249	24.5	16.9	15.8	7.7
250 and above	31.4	31.4	0.0	0.0
Sector of activity				
Agriculture	33.8	20.0	25.3	3.4
Industry	27.5	20.2	24.8	7.3
Construction	42.9	32.7	42.3	11.6
Trade	24.9	15.0	20.8	6.3
Transportation	32.7	23.8	41.6	4.8
Catering	33.1	22.4	30.8	2.8
Other services	25.0	21.4	17.4	3.2
Region				
Vojvodina	25.6	19.8	18.8	4.3
Belgrade	24.7	16.2	20.2	3.8
Serbia excl. Belgrade	33.0	24.1	31.8	8.0

Source: Own calculations. Survey on Conditions for Doing Business in Serbia, FREN, 2012

When businesses are disaggregated by sector of economic activity, most business entities active in the shadow economy are seen to be operating in the construction sector (42.9 %), followed by agriculture (33.8 %), catering (33.1 %) and transportation (32.7 %). Similar results were obtained by Schneider (2011a), who studied six European countries (Turkey, Spain, Italy, Germany, Poland, and Romania and found that the shadow economy was at its most pronounced in the construction sector (about 30 % of the total number of sector employees), the wholesale and retail trade, catering, and transportation. A study of businesses in the Baltic States (Putninš and Sauka 2011) also found that the shadow economy was predominant in the construction sector, followed by services and retail trade, sectors of activity traditionally favourable for shadow economy activities.

Both components of the shadow economy—informal employment and transactions—are at their most pronounced in the construction sector. Approximately one-third of all business entities in the construction sector have informal workers, while 42.3 % of VAT payers engage in shadow transactions. If we consider all types of work, we can see that construction workers are most often engaged without a formal employment contract, through the intermediation of an entrepreneur, with a contract but with a portion of their wage undeclared, or under a temporary service agreement. All of these forms of work are present in construction to an above-average degree in relation to other sectors of activity. It is interesting to note that all construction businesses employing between 5 and 19 people included in our sample engaged in the shadow economy.

Underreporting of income is particularly noticeable in the construction sector, mainly in the sub-contracting process and in activities that are directly related to the population. In these activities, cash generated from the sale of a company's products can be used to pay suppliers, reducing both income derived from such sales and costs. Although the reduction in costs is not particularly useful, goods and services can be bought much more cheaply, as suppliers are able to evade paying VAT.

Many construction companies operate, on average, for very brief periods of time, up to two or three years, obtain some government contracts through public procurement procedures, and then vanish from the market. A significant number of these firms are actually intermediaries between the client and the sub-contractors, earning between 10 and 50 % of the contract price in commissions. These practices could be avoided if public procurement tenders were open only to companies with substantial references, an established number of permanent workers, and an annual turnover not lower than the value of the public procurement contract (Socio-Economic Council of the Republic of Serbia 2010).

After construction, the sectors with the highest proportion of activity in the shadow economy are agriculture, catering, and transportation (33.8, 33.1, and 32.7 %, respectively). According to Schneider (2011b), in these sectors, with the exception of agriculture, most income is under reported due to cash transactions.

The large percentage of business entities in the agriculture sector engaged in the shadow economy—mainly entrepreneurs with few employees—makes it impossible for these businesses to obtain government subsidies or to borrow to finance current operations or improve production. Most of them are smallholdings with low production volumes, and this means that they cannot develop their businesses and raise living standards.

Apart from catering, where a large shadow economy is expected, the shadow economy is also extensive in the transportation sector. There are several explanations for this. Transportation businesses are small compared to other sectors of economic activity, and are more able to operate informally. However, although transportation ranks second to construction in the share of businesses in the VAT system that make cash payments (41.6 %), it needs to be underlined that the amount of VAT actually evaded is minimal (Table 6.3), as the share of cash transactions in the total volume of payments is the lowest of any sector (a mere 4.8 %). Similarly, in catering the share of VAT payers engaged in cash transactions is above average

(30.8 %), while the percent of VAT avoided is below average. Finally, based on the results of the survey, it seems that transportation businesses are subject to less inspection than other sectors. However, businesses in trade are frequently subject to inspection, so part of the explanation for their lower share in the informal economy is due to a higher probability of detection. There are other explanations for the lower share of the shadow economy in trade: for example, the increasing share of large chains in the retail sector.

The typical link between the shadow economy and the size of the business, whereby businesses with fewer workers are more likely to engage in the shadow economy (Rice 1992; Hanlon et al. 2007; Tedds 2010; Williams 2006), is not as pronounced in Serbia. The shadow economy is mainly the domain of businesses with between 5 and 19 employees and large businesses with 250 or more employees. These businesses are over-represented as regards informal employment, while micro-businesses with up to five workers and medium-sized businesses (50–249 workers) are over-represented among VAT payers as regards cash payments.

Such substantial participation of business entities employing between 5 and 19 workers in the shadow economy can be explained by the large share of small construction firms and entrepreneurs who take part in the shadow economy (70 % of the total number of businesses in this group). Some 60 % of them employ workers informally; 45 % of them engage in cash payments. On the other hand, nearly one-third of all large businesses (with 250 or more staff) are involved in the shadow economy: their participation is manifested through informal employment, with above-average participation by state-owned businesses and below-average participation by private businesses (36 % and compared to 27 %, respectively).

When the data are viewed by region, business entities based in Central Serbia (excluding Belgrade) are the most likely to engage in the shadow economy, while those in Belgrade are least likely (33 % vs. 24.7 %). A similar difference can be observed when looking at type of shadow economy activity. Business entities from Central Serbia dominate in informal employment and informal transactions (VAT paying business entities making payments in cash) compared to businesses in Belgrade where informal employment is the least pronounced or to Vojvodina where informal payment is the least pronounced. We will see in next section, where we analyze the determinants of shadow economy participation, if these regional differences in shadow economy participation remain when the impact of business size, sector of economic activity, etc. is controlled for.

The last column of Table 6.1 shows that only 5.7 % of business entities practise both types of informal activities i.e., have informal workers and engage in informal transactions. This subset of the basic set of business entities involved in the shadow economy has similar features to the basic set. Businesses as opposed to entrepreneurs, business entities employing between 5 and 19 workers, start-ups, construction firms, and those based in Central Serbia are most likely to engage in both types of shadow economy.

We will analyse two additional indicators of the shadow economy. These are the share of informal workers in the total number of workers (both overall and by type),

Table 6.2 Comparison of respondents' views on the participation of their own and other businesses in the shadow economy

	Participation of businesses surveyed in the shadow economy	Respondents' subjective views on the participation of businesses from the same sector in the shadow economy
% of workers without formal contracts	1.9	23.9
% of workers with formal contracts but without fully declared wages	3.8	24.7
% of turnover in cash	11.3	21.6

Source: Own calculations. Survey on Conditions for Doing Business in Serbia, FREN, 2012

and the share of cash payments in total payments by basic characteristics of the business (Table 6.2).

The share of informally employed workers in the total number of workers is exceptionally low, amounting to 5.7 %, although one-fifth of all businesses claimed they had employed workers informally. This was caused by the respondents' twofold downward bias. Firstly, it can be assumed that a large number of respondents did not wish to admit they employed workers informally; secondly, one-quarter of those who did admit it did not wish to answer about the number of such workers and their earnings. Caution is thus needed when interpreting data about the share of informal employed in the total number of employed and their wages.

The share of employees whose wages are paid in cash (3.8 %) in the total number of those employed is greater than the share of those working without a formal contract (1.9 %). The share of workers paid 'envelope wages' was much lower in Serbia than in the five South Eastern European countries covered, along with other nations, in the 2007 Eurobarometer survey (Bulgaria, Cyprus, Greece, Romania, and Slovenia), where 16 % of all workers, on average, receive 'envelope wages' (EC 2007). Much of this difference can certainly be attributed to the fact that the respondents in the Eurobarometer survey were aged 15 and over, with fewer incentives to disguise the activities of their employers than the employers themselves who were surveyed in Serbia.

However, this picture becomes very different when respondents' views on their own shadow economy practice are compared to their views on the shadow economy participation of other firms from the same sector. They considered all forms of the shadow economy to be represented to a much greater degree at 'other' businesses in the same sector than in their own businesses. Thus, as we have already underlined in Chap. 3, we consider data obtained from biased answers made by owners/managers on the participation of their own companies in informal operations as the lower limit of the extent of the shadow economy, while taking data collected from their subjective opinions on the participation of other businesses in the same sector as the upper limit. We can therefore say that the share of workers employed without a formal contract ranges from 1.9 % (lower limit) to 23.9 % (upper limit); the share of

Table 6.3 Share of informal workers in total number of workers; share of cash payments in total payments, by company characteristics

	Informal employment in % of total employment	% of workers without formal contracts	% of workers with formal contracts but without fully declared wages	Cash payments as % of total payments made by VAT payers
Total	5.7	1.9	3.8	27.8
Type of business entity				
Business	3.5	1.0	2.5	22.6
Entrepreneur	12.5	4.8	7.7	30.3
Age				
Start-up, 1–2 years	10.8	4.8	6.0	27.7
Others	5.5	1.8	3.7	27.9
Number of employees				
Up to 4	9.7	4.3	5.4	28.3
5–19	12.4	3.7	8.7	28.8
20–49	2.5	1.0	1.5	3.8
50–249	1.0	0.2	0.8	1.8
250 and above	2.7	0.5	2.2	–
Sector of activity				
Agriculture	7.9	3.9	4.0	31.0
Industry	4.6	1.2	3.4	25.8
Construction	5.2	3.0	2.2	43.0
Trade	5.0	1.6	3.4	26.9
Transportation	4.9	0.6	4.3	4.5
Catering	8.4	1.5	6.9	13.8
Other services	8.0	3.3	4.7	21.7
Region				
Vojvodina	5.3	2.8	2.5	30.2
Belgrade	4.5	1.2	3.3	37.0
Serbia excl. Belgrade	6.6	2.0	4.6	22.0

Source: Own calculations. Survey on Conditions for Doing Business in Serbia, FREN, 2012

workers employed without their entire wages being declared ranges from 3.8 to 24.7 %; while the share of cash payments varies between 11.3 and 21.6 %.

According to the features of businesses (Table 6.3), the share of informal employment is greatest among entrepreneurs, start-ups one to two years old or less, companies employing between 5 and 19 workers, catering firms, other services, agriculture, and those based in Central Serbia. If we look at type of informal employment by sector of economic activity we see that agriculture, other services, and construction have the greatest share of those working without a formal contract, while the share of workers receiving 'envelope wages' is greatest in catering, other services, and transportation, which are also the sectors where it is easiest to sell goods and services for cash.

The share of cash payments in total payments made by VAT payers (both businesses and entrepreneurs) was 27.8 %. When disaggregated by business feature it is greater with entrepreneurs than with businesses; it is also the most pronounced in the smallest business entities, while no difference can be observed in terms of business age (Table 6.3). Cash payments are the most common in construction (43 %), where slightly less than half of all respondents (42.3 %) said they had made such payments (Table 6.1). Agriculture came next (31 %), with one-quarter of respondents reporting cash payments, followed by trade (26.9 %), where only six percent of all respondents reported having made payments in cash. When the data are viewed by region Belgrade is ahead of Vojvodina and Central Serbia with 37 % of all payments made in cash, although the share of business entities making cash payments was greatest in Central Serbia (excluding Belgrade). These results lead to the conclusion that there is no major causal link between these two indicators of informal transactions: the share of business entities making payments in cash and the share of cash payments in total volume of payment transactions.

However, Table 6.4 shows a marked correlation between the various types of informal activity as cited by the business entities surveyed: in other words, when a business entity is involved in informal cash transactions it also has undeclared workers and unreported wage payments.

Slightly over half of all respondents cited purchase of goods as the main reason for paying in cash, nearly one-quarter reported paying cash for services, while the remainder cited using cash to pay wages and rent (Table 6.5). Goods and services are most often procured from entrepreneurs (37.1 %) and small or medium-sized businesses (34.3 %), and less frequently from large businesses or friends/family members (Table 6.6).

For some two-thirds of all respondents the principal reason for making cash payments was that they cost less; far fewer respondents cited better quality and inability to procure the required goods or services in the formal market (Table 6.7).

Nearly two-thirds of all respondents reported making payments in cash once a month, slightly over one-quarter claimed they did so once a week, while far fewer said they did so every day or once a year (Table 6.8). Daily cash payments were most common in trade, transportation, and other services. On average cash payments accounted for 22.9 % of business entities' total costs/expenditure.

In view of these results, it can be concluded that the usual relationship between the shadow economy and the type, age, and sector of business exist in Serbia, with entrepreneurs, start-ups, and those in construction more likely to engage in shadow economy activity. However, the relationship between the shadow economy and business entity size whereby smaller businesses are more likely to participate in the shadow economy (Tedds 2010; Williams 2006) cannot be confirmed.

The wages of informal workers were lower than the wages of formal workers (those whose entire wage is paid via bank accounts). The wages of workers without formal contracts and workers who receive a portion of their wage in cash were lower than formal workers' wages by 51 and 28 % respectively (Table 6.9). When

Table 6.4 Correlation between types of informal activity

	% of undeclared workers	% of workers with formal contracts but without fully declared wages	% of wage paid in cash
% of workers with formal contracts but without fully declared wages	0.75		
% of wage paid in cash	0.74	0.72	
% of transactions carried out informally (i.e., in cash)	0.73	0.67	0.70

Source: Own calculations. Survey on Conditions for Doing Business in Serbia, FREN, 2012

Table 6.5 Most common reason for cash payments made by VAT payers

	Total (%)
Purchase of goods	52.4
Payment for services	23.6
Payment of employee wages	14.4
Payment of rent for premises	0.1
Purchase of foreign currency intended for payment abroad	9.6
Total	100.0

Source: Own calculations. Survey on Conditions for Doing Business in Serbia, FREN, 2012

Table 6.6 Who most often supplies the goods or services that you paid for in cash?

	Total (%)
Friends/family members	9.0
Other companies owned by respondent	1.3
Entrepreneurs	37.1
Small or medium-sized businesses	34.3
Large businesses	18.4
Total	100.0

Source: Own calculations. Survey on Conditions for Doing Business in Serbia, FREN, 2012

Table 6.7 Reasons for cash payments made by VAT payers

	Total (%)
Lower price	68.5
Better service	12.8
Better quality	4.3
Helping vulnerable social groups	1.1
Doing favours to friends and family members	4.4
Goods and services unavailable in the regular/formal market	9.0

Source: Own calculations. Survey on Conditions for Doing Business in Serbia, FREN, 2012

Table 6.8 Frequency of cash payments made by VAT payers

	Total (%)
Once every year	3.2
Once every month	62.4
Once every week	27.4
Every day	7.0
Total	100.0

Source: Own calculations. Survey on Conditions for Doing Business in Serbia, FREN, 2012

Table 6.9 Average net wages by type of work

Type of work	Net wage (RSD)
Open-ended employment contract (entire wage paid via bank account)	38,061
Open-ended employment contract (some money paid in cash in addition to portion of wage paid via bank account)	27,277
Employment pursuant to a temporary service agreement	25,752
Employment pursuant to a work for hire agreement	22,847
Employment through a 'youth employment agency'	16,160
Hiring an entrepreneur	23,401
Occasional/temporary work without a contract (trial work, training, volunteering)	19,261

Source: Own calculations. Survey on Conditions for Doing Business in Serbia, FREN, 2012

the cost of taxes and contributions for those in formal employment are added to wages, the difference in labour costs between formal and informal workers is enormous. These findings are similar to those found by earlier research on the informal economy based on the Living Standards Measurement Study (Krstić and Sanfey 2011), which found that informal workers earned 44 % less than formal workers, or 22 % less when other characteristics of the workers are controlled for. Although the definition of informal employment was not the same in these two studies, it is evident that workers in the informal sector remain at a major disadvantage compared to those working in the formal sector.

The distribution of wages by business characteristics differs significantly between employees whose entire wage is paid through a bank account and the two types of informal employment (Table 6.10). While formal workers' wages are higher when paid by entrepreneurs, start-ups (established one to two years ago), businesses with over 20 employees, businesses in the industrial sector, and businesses in Central Serbia, the wages of workers without formal contracts are highest when paid by businesses, entities established two or more years ago, businesses employing between 5 and 19 workers, businesses engaged in trade, and businesses based in Vojvodina.

Table 6.10 Average wages by type of work and business characteristics

	Permanent employees, entire wage paid via bank account	Permanent employees, portion of wage paid in cash	Employees with no formal contracts
Total	38,061	27,277	19,261
Type of business entity			
Business	35,441	27,572	39,527
Entrepreneur	39,337	27,187	16,953
Age			
Start-up, 1–2 years	65,054	36,060	15,904
Others	35,937	25,539	18,185
No. of employees			
Up to 4	37,879	26,759	16,118
5–19	33,787	28,830	21,542
20 and over	57,157	28,220	99,088
Sector of activity			
Agriculture	46,197	6,000	–
Industry	55,128	23,923	20,525
Construction	29,027	30,238	18,178
Trade	37,243	24,904	29,390
Transportation	29,353	24,210	20,000
Catering	21,848	22,740	15,579
Other services	35,781	35,470	14,585
Region			
Vojvodina	33,487	28,645	24,265
Belgrade	38,241	32,757	17,312
Serbia excl. Belgrade	40,890	23,339	17,753

Source: Own calculations. Survey on Conditions for Doing Business in Serbia, FREN, 2012

6.2 Determinants of Participation in the Shadow Economy

In the previous section descriptive statistics were used to show how shadow economy activities varied by key factors. In this section we use econometric analysis to identify specific factors that are statistically significant in a company's decision to take part in the shadow economy.

Tax evasion literature usually identifies two groups of factors that affect a business's (or entrepreneur's) decision to participate in the shadow economy.[1] The first group of factors relates to the model of the rational choice to engage in tax evasion. Entrepreneurs or businesses weigh the expected benefits and costs of

[1] For a concise recent survey of the literature on the informal economy and tax evasion, see Slemrod (2007).

tax evasion and participation in the shadow economy, or, rather, compare the savings they stand to achieve through tax evasion and the costs in case they are caught. The expected costs depend on the likelihood of getting caught, the amount and type of the penalty, the likelihood of that penalty actually being imposed, and their propensity to risk. These factors differ by region, industry, and size and age of the business entity, and other factors.

The reason why empirical studies usually find that the real level of tax evasion is significantly lower than forecasts made using the rational choice model is the existence of a second group of factors: attitudes and social norms. In tax evasion literature these factors include the perception of the fairness of the tax system—the attitudes on the equity of the tax burden and procedures. As our assessment deals with attitudes regarding participation in the shadow economy, we examine how the decision to participate in the shadow economy depends on social norms, or, rather, moral values (as well as any feelings of guilt and stigma that may arise if the tax evader is caught). Finally, participation in the shadow economy can be temporary and the result of short-term operating difficulties, especially given the current economic crisis, which must also be taken into consideration.

In both literature and empirical studies, sanction probability plays a very significant role in explaining the causes of tax evasion (shadow economy). According to the results of the Survey on Conditions for Doing Business in Serbia (Fig. 6.1), the estimated probability of companies that operate informally being discovered is generally low. As many as 67 % of the businesspeople surveyed believed that this probability was very low (i.e. that 50 % or fewer companies operating informally would be caught). Just 17 % of those surveyed thought that one in every two companies would be caught. Around 14 % of those surveyed believed that one in three companies would be discovered; 13 % thought that one in five businesses would be caught, while 14 % believed this would happen to one in every ten. Such expectations support the decision to take part in the shadow economy because doing so significantly reduces expected expenses.

Furthermore, business entities' expectations of receiving fines for operating in the shadow economy were even lower. The survey results show that they believed it was very unlikely for the company manager or entrepreneur to be penalised if caught operating informally. Two-thirds of all business entities surveyed thought that there was a 50 % or less chance of an entity or person operating in the shadow economy being penalised after getting caught, while 17 % thought that one in every ten managers would face sanctions. The total probability of anyone who gets caught facing any sanctions is even lower, since as many as two-thirds (67 %) of the businesspeople surveyed thought that the fine imposed would be paid in fewer than 50 % of all cases, while 17 % felt that only one in every ten fines would be paid. Thus the likelihood that those who get caught actually are fined and pay that fine is believed to be very low. There are various ways in which business entities avoid paying their dues. According to the results of the survey the most common means of avoiding payment of a fine is corruption (40 %), followed by shifting the company's business to a newly established entity (17 %), or simply waiting for charges to lapse due to the operation of the statute of limitations (18 %). However, in our

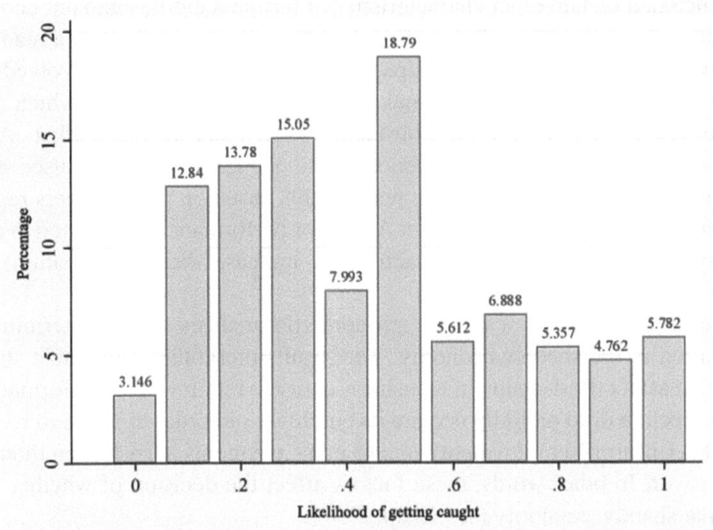

Fig. 6.1 Expectations of the likelihood of businesses not operating formally getting caught. *Source*: Own calculations. Survey on Conditions for Doing Business in Serbia, FREN, 2012

econometric analysis we focused on the simplest concept of expectations (how likely the respondents believed getting caught was if operating informally), mainly because some respondents may have misunderstood the question, which could mean that the calculation would result in unrealistically low expectations regarding the consequences of engaging in these activities.

Approximately two-thirds of all respondents thought that companies continued operating informally even after being fined for doing so. This result to some extent implies that the majority of respondents felt that fines were relatively mild. The majority of respondents (46 %) stated that fines for different types of informal operation should be increased. The attitude towards the severity of sanctions is very important for incentives, because if sanctions are perceived to be lax, business entities are more incentivised to take part in the shadow economy, or rather to evade taxes.

Finally, our analysis also examined attitudes toward the shadow economy itself; that is, whether the owners/managers considered informal operation to be justified. This factor can correlate with insincere answers, but we believe that it is still a good enough indicator of business entities' readiness to become active (or not) in the shadow economy in an environment where sanctions are less than likely. According to the results of the survey, over two-thirds (71 %) of all business entities thought that operating in this manner was unjustified. Just 17 % were neutral, while 9 % believed it to be justified. It is obvious that some business entities operating within the shadow economy were not being honest when they stated that informal operation was unjustified. The usual reasons cited when justifying informal operation were poor legal framework (46 %), competition from the informal sector (27 %), the great benefits of doing business in this manner (27 %), and the fact that almost all business entities engage in these practices (21 %).

We included certain other characteristics of business entities into our econometric analysis in addition to the factors already referred to. As has already been mentioned, nearly all recent start-ups are expected to be more involved in the shadow economy as tax evasion makes them more competitive, which is very important especially if they face obstacles when entering the market. Also, in order to consider the possible influence of the economic crisis, we used a proxy for the recent business results of the respondents based on their answers regarding trends in their total turnover (question A6). Poor performance is expected to affect a company's motivation to become active (or increase their participation) in the shadow economy.

Table 6.11 shows the results of econometric analysis of the determinants of participation in the shadow economy. The results presented in the table show the factors that affect the decision of a business entity to retain workers informally; that is, not to declare or to partially declare its employees in order to evade or reduce its tax burden (informal employment), and to make payments in cash even though it is a VAT payer. In other words, these factors affect the decision of whether to take part in the shadow economy (see Chap. 3).

Table 6.10 shows five logit models[2] where the dependent variable represents broadly defined participation in the shadow economy (dependent variable: entity engages in activities in the shadow economy [=1] or does not do so [=0]).[3] We divided independent variables into five groups. The first group consisted of business entities' characteristics: business/entrepreneur, VAT payer, privately held or otherwise, share of foreign equity (variables presented as dummy variables), company age, and number of employees (a natural log transformed continuous variables). The second group consists of regional dummy variables. The third group consists of sector dummy variables. The fourth group is variables related to business entities' expectations and attitudes: the likelihood of detection and attitudes regarding the amount of fines and justification of the shadow economy. This group of variables was obtained on the basis of the opinions voiced by the respondents. Finally, the fifth group is made up of only one variable, turnover decline in 2010, and is used to establish whether deterioration in the economic position of the business entity influences the decision whether to take part in the shadow economy.

All models are statistically significant, and we will focus our attention, based on selection criteria, on the last model (5). The total number of observations for that model was 830, fewer than for other models due to missing values. In the first group of independent variables, the binary variables of entrepreneur and VAT payer, as well as the logarithm (ln) of the number of employees (i.e., approximation of company size) are statistically significant. The other three variables—private

[2] Here we have shown the basic model only. The model does not contain interactions or other analysed variables.

[3] As the table shown contains different samples, we have not compared coefficients for the various models here (any explanation of the change in coefficients must also take into account the differences in sample size). For a detailed discussion, see Hosmer and Lemeshow (2000) and Long and Freese (2006).

Table 6.11 Determinants of participation in the shadow economy

	Model				
	(1)	(2)	(3)	(4)	(5)
Entrepreneur	2.398*** (3.91)	2.348*** (3.78)	2.417*** (3.77)	2.614*** (3.48)	2.611*** (3.46)
Business	*f*	*f*	*f*	*f*	*f*
VAT payer	1.949*** (3.31)	1.944*** (3.30)	2.317*** (3.91)	2.575*** (3.71)	2.639*** (3.76)
Non-VAT payer	*f*	*f*	*f*	*f*	*f*
Privately held	0.700 (−0.69)	0.683 (−0.73)	0.779 (−0.49)	0.507 (−1.05)	0.467 (−1.15)
Other	*f*	*f*	*f*	*f*	*f*
Foreign equity	0.649 (−0.63)	0.645 (−0.64)	0.650 (−0.69)	0.760 (−0.44)	0.453 (−1.02)
Non-foreign	*f*	*f*	*f*	*f*	*f*
ln(employees)	1.596*** (5.32)	1.588*** (5.23)	1.585*** (4.99)	1.674*** (5.06)	1.744*** (5.38)
ln(age)	0.960 (−0.38)	0.962 (−0.35)	0.985 (−0.14)	0.898 (−0.81)	0.868 (−1.03)
Belgrade		1.066 (0.28)	1.064 (0.26)	0.966 (−0.13)	0.959 (−0.16)
Central Serbia		1.204 (0.84)	1.253 (1.02)	1.169 (0.60)	1.124 (0.45)
Vojvodina		*f*	*f*	*f*	*f*
Agriculture			2.227 (1.15)	2.297 (1.26)	1.694 (0.72)
Industry			0.847 (−0.56)	0.892 (−0.33)	0.858 (−0.43)
Construction			1.944** (2.12)	1.969* (1.82)	1.887* (1.67)
Trade			0.696 (−1.53)	0.639 (−1.64)	0.611* (−1.81)
Transportation			1.675* (1.67)	1.839 (1.64)	1.745 (1.50)
Catering			1.042 (0.12)	1.144 (0.33)	1.091 (0.21)
Other services			*f*	*f*	*f*
Likelihood of getting caught				1.735 (1.50)	1.772 (1.56)
Attitude on shadow economy as a justified response				1.695*** (5.95)	1.656*** (5.73)
Attitude on penalties—penalties seen as mild (Q D8)				1.325 (1.35)	1.299 (1.25)
Turnover decline since 2010					1.213 (0.92)
Wald chi^2 (df)	62.01 (6)	62.49 (8)	79.97 (14)	105.8 (17)	108.5 (18)

(continued)

Table 6.11 (continued)

	Model				
	(1)	(2)	(3)	(4)	(5)
Pseudo R^2 [a]	0.0592	0.0601	0.0781	0.145	0.148
N	1,051	1,051	1,051	843	830
AIC	1,141.8	1,144.7	1,135.1	876.0	866.0
BIC	1,176.5	1,189.3	1,209.5	961.3	955.7

Source: Own calculations. Survey on Conditions for Doing Business in Serbia, FREN, 2012
Notes: f-reference variable. AIC is the Akaike information criterion for model selection; BIC is the Bayesian information criterion, where the lower the value, the better the model. $*p < 0.10$; $**p < 0.05$; $***p < 0.01$
[a]Pseudo R^2 or McFadden's likelihood ratio index compares the logarithm values of the likelihood functions for the intercept-only model and the model with the predictors (excluding all explanatory variables from the model). The value of this indicator ranges from 0 to 1; it resembles the linear model determination coefficient, but cannot be used as directly in interpreting results

ownership, foreign equity, and logarithm (ln) of company age—are not statistically significant, and for the sake of brevity will not be discussed further.[4]

We show results in terms of odds ratios. The odds ratio for entrepreneurs is 2.611.[5] We interpret this as the odds of the entrepreneurs taking part in the shadow economy vs. the odds of the business's chance of doing so (while other independent variables remain unchanged). These results are in accordance with the findings of other studies, according to which entrepreneurs are more engaged in the shadow economy than other types of business (Tedds 2010; Williams 2006). We can interpret the VAT-payer coefficient in a similar manner. Finally, the significant variable belonging to the first group (denoting company size as expressed by the number of its staff) can be interpreted as follows: the odds ratio of an entity's participation in the shadow economy increases by 1.75 for each standard deviation of the increase in the ln of total employment (with all other variables unchanged).[6] This finding is in accordance with the results of the descriptive analysis, which do not bear out the assumption that smaller companies are more prone to engaging in shadow economy activities. The difference from the usual result, according to

[4] As expected, the value of the coefficient for the age of company is smaller than one (with younger companies more likely to operate partially in the shadow economy). The same is true for the coefficient of business entities that operate wholly or in part with foreign equity.

[5] We can here consider the ratio of the chance of a business owner taking part in the shadow economy to the chance of a company doing so. To illustrate this, let us provide the example of the model of N = 1,000 businesses and entrepreneurs, with 100 businesses taking part in shadow economy and 300 not doing so, and with 300 entrepreneurs participating in the shadow economy and 300 not doing so. The ratio calculated for businesses would amount to (100/300)/(300/300) = 0.33. The ratio for entrepreneurs would amount to 3. It should be noted that a positive factor of 2 has the same effect size as a negative factor of 0.5. In other words, 2 is twice as great as 1, while 0.5 is twice as small as 1 (the effect size is 2 in both cases). Based on this, we can conclude that, for instance, a coefficient of 0.1 is such that it has a greater effect than a coefficient of 2.

[6] This result was obtained by using the listcoef command in Stata 11.1.

which small businesses are more likely to participate in the shadow economy, can be partially explained by the fact that the definition of the shadow economy was to a large extent dependent on whether businesses employ workers outside the formal sector. The second reason is the fact that other studies use the value of assets or turnover to approximate company size.[7]

Interestingly, in all models regional characteristics are not statistically significant. In the third group, consisting of seven sector dummy-variables, businesses in the construction sector are nearly twice as likely to engage in shadow economy activities compared to other service sectors (in line with our expectations), while the trade sector, also statistically significant, was nearly twice as unlikely to take part in the shadow economy than the other service sectors. We should note that the remaining sectors also had the expected signs, but were not statistically significant. In other words, major sectoral differences in the way businesses operate in the shadow economy described in the preceding section are lost (except in construction, and trade in model five) when the impact of other characteristics of the business—such as size, type of entity, ownership structure, etc.—are included in the model. This finding bears out the need for designing a strategy and specific measures to formalise the shadow economy that are mainly sector-neutral, apart from for construction.

As we have already presented the most important results in relation to activity sector and other features of business entities, we will now devote more attention to the fourth group: the perceptions and attitudes of business entities to taking part in the shadow economy. Attitudes towards operating in the shadow economy being/not being justified (a score ranging from 1, no justification, to 5, justified) are statistically significant. The business entities that think that engagement in the shadow economy is 'more justified' are more likely to be engaged in such activities. This is a significant result, as it not only indicates the presence of the view that operating in the shadow economy is perfectly normal for some business entities, but also plays an important role in explaining why entities take part in the informal economy when all other relevant factors are considered. Unlike the justification for operating in the shadow economy, the likelihood of being caught is borderline statistically significant (becoming significant only with a slight change in the specification of model 5, if attitudes on penalties are excluded) (Andrews et al. 2011). The one remaining variable in this group, the dummy variable describing respondents' attitudes to the severity of penalties, is not statistically significant. It is not entirely clear how this variable should affect the results. Companies that claimed penalties are mild do not operate in the shadow economy, but may expect additional protection from unfair competition through stricter sanctions. On the other hand a different interpretation is also possible: that it was the business entities participating in the shadow economy that claimed penalties were mild, which is certainly an incentive to do business in the shadow economy.

[7] The use of the logarithm value of turnover in the model did not change the result substantially. Many respondents refused to answer this question, which is why this variable was left out.

Finally, the economic crisis that hit most business entities is not statistically significant (while the values obtained were in line with expectations for the likelihood of taking part in a particular type of activity in the shadow economy). One possible explanation for its insignificance is the duration of the crisis. Another reason could be the fact that it is not only companies with declining turnovers but other businesses as well that turn to the shadow economy to either improve their cash flows or to secure additional sources of financing.

6.3 Effects of Competition from the Informal Sector

Competition in the formal sector creates incentives for economic efficiency and is the key driver of economic growth, since it motivates business entities to produce higher quality products at as-low-as-possible cost. On the other hand, as a rule competition between the formal and the informal sectors does not increase productivity and hurts progress in the economy (Perry et al. 2007). The relative cost advantage of business enterprises operating in the informal sector through tax evasion or non-compliance with regulatory requirements enables them to survive even at low levels of productivity. An exception to the adverse impact of competition from the informal sector is a situation where there are substantial barriers to entry, with the informal sector exerting competitive pressure without which the formal sector would face X-inefficiency and waste resources (Loayza et al. 2010). In Serbia, where small business entities are adversely affected by disproportionate tax and regulatory requirements, this positive effect of competition from the shadow economy should also be taken into account.

In this section we analyse the effects of competition from the informal sector due to lower relative costs in relation to business entities operating in the formal economy. In addition to the question of the extent to which informal operation by competitors hurts businesses in the formal sector, another question must be posed: who is hit the hardest, and why?

6.3.1 Competition from the Informal Sector

According to the results of the survey, competition from business entities that engage in at least one type of informal activity is extremely widespread. As many as 85.3 % of the business entities surveyed (of those who did respond) felt that there was competition from shadow economy within their sectors (Table 6.12). In some sectors such as transportation and construction nearly all of those surveyed said they faced some form of competition from the shadow economy; these sectors were also those where the majority of the surveyed admitted that they themselves took part in informal activities. Larger business entities, as well as the 'other services' sector, cited slightly lower levels of exposure to this type of competition.

Table 6.12 Informal sector as competition, obstacles to operation, and loss of revenue by the formal sector (share in number of respondents who answered)

	Loss of revenue (%)	Large or very large obstacle (%)	Presence of competition from shadow economy (%)
Total	27.8	34.4	85.3
Type of entity			
Entrepreneur	28.5	35.2	87.9
Business	26.2	32.1	79.1
VAT payer	25.0	28.6	85.5
Non-VAT payer	31.4	41.6	85.2
Number of employees			
Up to 4	28.7	35.3	85.6
5–19	24.8	30.6	85.4
20 and more	19.4	26.7	77.7
Participate in the shadow economy			
No	27.0	34.7	85.3
Yes	29.6	33.7	85.3
Sector of economic activity			
Agriculture	23.6	46.6	82.4
Industry	29.5	34.9	85.7
Construction	37.7	49.1	96.8
Trade	26.7	26.6	88.0
Transportation	36.0	53.8	94.2
Catering	24.7	24.0	86.8
Other services	22.5	31.2	73.8
Region			
Vojvodina	28.3	37.7	80.9
Belgrade	26.7	36.7	81.9
Central Serbia	28.3	31.0	90.8

Source: Own calculations. Survey on Conditions for Doing Business in Serbia, FREN, 2012

Both entrepreneurs and businesses can be considered competition. The findings of the survey show that entrepreneurs mainly compete with other entrepreneurs, while businesses generally do not differentiate between competition from businesses and from entrepreneurs.

6.3.2 Effects of Competition from the Informal Sector

Informal activities of competitors are no obstacle to doing business for only 12 % of business entities, while three times as many (34 %) respondents consider them a major obstacle. There is a large difference between different sectors (see Table 6.12), with informal activity particularly an issue in transportation,

Table 6.13 Informal sector as obstacle to operation

	Estimated coefficients
Entrepreneur	0.981 (−0.10)
Business	*f*
VAT payer	0.833 (−1.03)
Non-VAT payer	*f*
Private	0.636 (−0.57)
Other	*f*
Foreign equity	0.272** (−2.29)
Non-foreign	*f*
ln(employees)	0.870* (−1.73)
ln(age)	1.010 (0.97)
Belgrade	1.070 (0.31)
Central Serbia	0.825 (−0.99)
Vojvodina	*f*
Agriculture	3.837 (1.61)
Industry	1.180 (0.64)
Construction	2.348*** (2.76)
Trade	0.911 (−0.44)
Transportation	2.026** (2.48)
Catering	0.948 (−0.19)
Other services	*f*
Likelihood of detection	0.408*** (−2.75)
Prob > chi^2 (degree of freedom)	48.19 (15)
Pseudo R^2	0.0283
N (no. of observations)	825

Notes: *f*-reference variable; *$p < 0.10$; **$p < 0.05$; ***$p < 0.01$

agriculture, and construction. The results of an ordered logit model are presented in Table 6.13. We used a question (To what extent are practices of competitors from the informal sector an obstacle to the operation of your company?) as the dependent variable. The possible answers ranged from 1 (no obstacle) to 5 (very large obstacle).[8]

The importance accorded to competition from entities operating in the shadow economy is lower for companies with foreign equity, while the type of entity (entrepreneur and VAT payer), legal form, and ownership are not statistically significant. Small businesses (by number of workers) are aware of the existence and importance of informal activity to a greater degree. When viewed by sector of activity, construction and transportation are particularly exposed to competition from the shadow economy. The likelihood of detection is statistically significant: the easier these entities believe it is for informal operations to be detected, the smaller the extent of such competition.[9] It should be noted that these results are similar to those obtained for South Eastern Europe using the Business Environment and Enterprise Performance Study (BEEPS) database by Hudson et al. (2012).

Some research has concluded that the greatest concerns about corruption from the informal sector are voiced by those entities that most resemble the informal sector. These are small businesses faced with financial constraints that are oriented towards smaller clients, have under-utilised capacities, and operate in a market with low entry costs.[10] The only part of this conclusion that seems to be applicable in Serbia is that which refers to small businesses, while the greatest problems are present in activities with high entry costs and large participation of unskilled labour. In other words, operating savings—and, consequently, the pressure of competition from the informal sector—are greater in sectors where regulatory obstacles to formalisation are more substantial and where it is more difficult to control workers.

Similarly to the small number of those who believed informal operation was not an issue, a mere 17.8 % of all respondents claimed that unfair competition did not bring about a decline in their annual revenue. On average, lost revenue amounted to 27.8 %, affecting particularly the sectors of construction and transportation. In most cases lost revenue amounted to between 10 and 50 % (for about 70 % of all business entities), while 11.6 % of entities estimated that their revenues had been reduced by more than 50 % due to informal competition. It is interesting to note that the estimated loss in revenue (27.8 %) does not deviate significantly from the estimated share of the shadow economy in GDP as shown in Chap. 5.

In addition to the financial effects reflected in the estimated loss of revenue, we can also cite other consequences of competition from the shadow economy. Respondents primarily mentioned lower turnover and greater difficulty in selling

[8] For a similar approach, see Hudson et al. (2012).

[9] We can obtain similar results when using a dummy variable with the value of 1 in cases where business entities feel that competition from the informal economy is a large or very large obstacle. The key difference lies in the fact that the variable describing whether or not the entity is a VAT payer becomes statistically significant, while the presence of foreign equity and size (measured by number of workers) cease being statistically significant variables.

[10] The findings of the study on the impact of competition from the informal sector in Latin America indicate that sectors with low entry costs cite informal competition as a substantial obstacle (Gonzalez and Lamanna 2007).

products (52 % of all respondents), lower product prices (41 %), and less investment into technological development due to lower revenue (14 %). When the data are viewed by sector of activity, price cutting due to unfair competition is slightly more common in construction (64 %), while lower turnover and greater difficulty in selling products is at its most widespread in trade (60 %).

6.3.3 Types of Informal Operation

The relative cost advantage of business entities in the shadow economy stems from various types of informal operation. Business entities estimate that these types of operation (including not declaring workers, paying wages in cash, and making and receiving informal payments) are represented in their respective sectors of activity to a substantial degree. Thus, only one-quarter of all business entities felt that the practice of not declaring employees is absent from their sector of activity; the same percentage believed that no entities in their sector formally declared lower wages than those actually paid. About half of all respondents felt that up to 50 % of all workers in their sector of activity were either employed informally (without a contract) or declared lower wages (although most respondents believed that the portion of the wage paid in cash generally did not exceed 50 % of the total wage). Finally, about two-thirds of business entities felt that some transactions—up to 50 % of the total—in their sector of activity were made informally (i.e., without paying tax).

In addition to informal operation by registered businesses and entrepreneurs, competition also comes from entities that are not officially registered. The findings of the survey show that about half (46 %) of all respondents knew of unregistered entities operating in their sector of activity. This view was slightly more common among entrepreneurs than businesses (55 % relative to 37 %, respectively) and in the transportation (78 %) and construction (67 %) sectors.

References

Andrews D, Caldera Sánchez A, Johansson Å (2011) Towards a better understanding of the informal economy. OECD Economics Department Working Papers, No. 873. OECD Publishing

European Commission (2007) Undeclared work in the European Union, Special Eurobarometer

Gonzalez AS, Lamanna F (2007) Who fears competition from informal firms? Evidence from Latin America. Policy Research Working Paper Series 4316. The World Bank

Hanlon M, Mills L, Slemrod J (2007) An empirical examination of corporate tax noncompliance. In: Auerbach A, Hines JR, Slemrod J (eds) Taxing corporate income in the 21st century. Cambridge University Press, Cambridge, pp 140–162
Hosmer D, Lemeshow S (2000) Applied logistic regression, 2nd edn. Wiley, New York
Hudson J, Williams C, Orviska M, Nadin S (2012) Evaluating the impact of the informal economy on businesses in South East Europe: Some lessons from the 2009 World Bank Enterprise Survey. South East Eur J Econ Bus 7(1):99–110
Krstić G, Sanfey P (2011) Earnings inequality and the informal economy: evidence from Serbia. Econ Transit 19(1)
Kyle S et al (2001) The shadow economy in Bulgaria. Harvard University, Agency for Economic Analysis and Forecasting and Institute for Market Economics
Loayza V, Serven L, Sugawara N (2010) Informality in Latin America and the Caribbean. World Bank Policy Research Working Paper Series 4888
Long JS, Freese J (2006) Regression models for categorical dependent variables using Stata, 2nd edn. Stata Press, College Station
Perry G, Maloney W, Arias O, Fajnzylber P, Mason A, Saavedra-Chanduvi J (2007) Informality: exit and exclusion. World Bank, Washington
Putninš TJ, Sauka A (2011) The size and determinants of shadow economies in the Baltic States. Baltic J Econ 11(2)
Rice E (1992) The corporate tax gap: evidence on tax compliance by small corporations. In: Slemrod J (ed) Why people pay taxes: tax compliance and enforcement. University of Michigan Press, Ann Arbor, pp 24–39
Schneider F (eds) (2011a) Handbook on the shadow economy. Edward Elgar, Cheltenham
Schneider F (2011b) The shadow economy in Europe – using payment systems to combat the shadow economy. http://www.bblf.bg/uploads/files/file_378.pdf
Slemrod J (2007) Cheating ourselves: the economics of tax evasion. J Econ Perspect 21(1):25–48
Socio-Economic Council of the Republic of Serbia (2010) Efikasno suzbijanje sive ekonomije, Beograd
Tedds LM (2010) Keeping it off the books: an empirical investigation of firms that engage in tax evasion. Appl Econ 42(19):2459–2473
Williams CC (2006) The hidden enterprise culture: entrepreneurship in the underground economy. Edward Elgar, Cheltenham

Chapter 7
Effects of Formalisation of the Shadow Economy

Milojko Arsić and Gorana Krstić

7.1 Fiscal Implications of Formalisation of Shadow Economy

7.1.1 Estimate of Possible Fiscal Effects with Respect to VAT

As tax evasion is by far the largest component of the VAT gap, the question that needs to be asked is to what extent VAT revenue could be increased by ensuring better tax collection over the medium and the long term, all other considerations being equal.[1] Over the medium term a realistic aim for Serbia would be to reduce the VAT gap to the average level seen in the five new Central European EU member states before their EU accession. This means that in the next several years a realistic aim would be to cut the VAT gap from its current level of 21 % to 18–19 %, as experienced by Central European EU member states. Cutting the VAT gap by 2–3 percentage points would result in an increase in the Serbian budget revenues of between 0.2 and 0.5 % of GDP. In the long run, say within 10 years, Serbia could aim to reduce the VAT gap to the EU average of 13.5 %. Cutting the VAT gap to this level, all other conditions being equal, would increase budget revenue by 1 % of GDP. Hypothetically, if Serbia's VAT gap were reduced to the level seen by the

[1] It is important to bear in mind that other factors, such as a re-orientation of the economy towards exports (not subject to VAT) and greater investment (subject to lower VAT rates), will have an impact on the reduction of both hypothetical and actual VAT revenue. In this context any estimate of additional revenues due to a reduction in the VAT gap should be treated as a hypothetical estimate, all other conditions being equal, rather than as a realistic one. Closing the VAT gap is therefore a necessary precondition for preventing, or at least reducing, any future decline in the ratio of VAT revenue to GDP.

M. Arsić (✉) • G. Krstić
Faculty of Economics, University of Belgrade, Belgrade, Serbia
e-mail: arsicm@ekof.bg.ac.rs; gkrstic@ekof.bg.ac.rs

G. Krstić, F. Schneider (eds.), *Formalizing the Shadow Economy in Serbia*,
Contributions to Economics, DOI 10.1007/978-3-319-13437-6_7

five most efficient EU members (Finland, Sweden, Ireland, Luxembourg, and France), where it stands at a mere 5 %, the additional revenue would be 2 % of GDP.

All of the above estimates were made using current VAT rates as of 2011; we therefore ought to determine the effect on these estimates of the increase in the general VAT rate from 18 to 20 % that took effect in late 2012. The rise in the general tax rate by 2 percentage points, as well as other changes to the VAT system, will result in an increase in the potential VAT revenues of some RSD 33 billion at current prices, which equals about 1 % of GDP. However, given the existing tax gap (i.e. if the shadow economy remains unchanged), actual VAT revenues will increase by about RSD 25 billion, or about 0.8 % of GDP (Fiscal Council 2012).[2]

7.1.2 Estimate of Possible Fiscal Effects with Respect to Personal Income Tax and Social Contributions

Although the overall personal income tax and social contributions gap is relatively significant, as we have seen in Chap. 5, potential additional public revenues that could be generated through the efficient implementation of measures for reducing the shadow economy are far lower. Even with the efficient use of well-designed measures to combat the shadow economy, and given an effective institutional framework, the shadow economy cannot be reduced to zero—as is borne out by the fact that it is not insignificant even in the most developed countries. According to 2011 estimates the total extent of the shadow economy in EU countries is 19.7 % of GDP (Schneider 2011). Although separate estimates of the shadow economy in household income and consumption are not provided, theoretical and empirical studies have shown that the extent of the shadow economy is greater in income than in consumption. We can accordingly assume that the shadow economy in household income is more widespread than the EU average. Starting from the assumption that the estimated level of the shadow economy in household income in Serbia is 24.4 % of GDP, measures aimed at tackling the shadow economy could reduce this level by some 10–15 %, with a similar reduction in the relevant tax gap. The government would then see an increase of at most 0.6–0.9 % of GDP in income tax and social contributions revenue (0.6 % of GDP in the medium term and slightly more in the long run, assuming systemic measures are implemented consistently).

Taking into account VAT, income tax, and social contributions, reducing the shadow economy to the level present in other Central and Eastern European countries—an outcome that can be achieved in a relatively short span of time (1–3 years), assuming the adoption and consistent implementation of systemic

[2] These estimates differ from those made by the Fiscal Council because the impact on liquidity of the shift to VAT payment upon collection of accounts receivable for small and medium-sized businesses has been ignored, as this is a short-term effect.

Table 7.1 Estimate of the fiscal effects of formalising the informal economy in Serbia (in % of GDP)

	Short and medium term (1–3 years)	Long term (7–10 years)
VAT	0.2–0.5	1.0
Income tax and contributions	0.6	0.9
Total	0.8–1.1	1.9

Source: Own calculations

measures—could result in an increase in public revenue of between 0.8 and 1.1 % of GDP (Table 7.1). Reducing the shadow economy to the EU average would take longer (between 7 and 10 years) and require not only institutional measures, but also other structural changes to the Serbian economic system. It could, however, ensure additional public revenue of up to 1.9 % of GDP.

In interpreting the above estimates we must bear in mind that they reflect only the isolated impact of the formalisation of the shadow economy, and not the impact of other factors on the collection of tax revenue. In this sense the estimates presented in Table 7.1 are not a forecast of changes in tax revenue in relation to GDP. Other factors that will affect tax collection include long-term macroeconomic trends such as movements in domestic demand and GDP and changes to the employment rate. Thus, when estimating actual tax revenues, other factors need to be taken into account in addition to the possible formalisation of the shadow economy. The reduction in the difference between domestic demand and GDP, which is necessary to avoid a balance of payments crisis, will cause a substantial drop in VAT revenue in relation to GDP. A 5 percentage point drop in the ratio of domestic demand to GDP would cause a corresponding fall in VAT revenue of about 1 % of GDP. In this context, tackling the shadow economy can be interpreted as a necessary activity to prevent a drop in VAT revenue in relation to GDP, rather than as a possible source of additional tax revenue. In other words, if the shadow economy is not formalised VAT revenue will decline by about 1 percentage point in relation to GDP over the coming several years. Similarly, movements in the actual levels of tax and social contribution revenues in relation to GDP will be affected by changes in the employment rate. The number of employed might decline in 2013, which could, all other things being equal, bring a drop in social contributions and income tax revenue. However, employment in Serbia could increase in the medium and the long term, which would generate additional income tax and social contributions revenue.

7.2 Effects of Formalising the Shadow Economy on Economic Growth

The preceding section estimated the possible fiscal effects given certain assumptions of a possible reduction in the shadow economy. This section will attempt to consider how formalising the shadow economy can affect economic growth. This question is far more difficult to answer, as although there is a large body of empirical research on the impact of the shadow economy on economic growth, there are still no unequivocal empirical and theoretical findings (Schneider and Enste 2000). The basic question is this: Is the shadow economy, from an economic point of view, a positive phenomenon; in other words, does it make a positive contribution to economic growth? The answer to this question will result in two possible avenues of approach for government policy on the shadow economy: tolerance or active suppression.

We can generally distinguish between three situations:

- Shadow and formal economies are substitutes for one another: any increase in the shadow economy leads to a reduction in the volume of the formal economy;
- The volume of the formal economy is a given (i.e., fixed): the shadow economy increases the total economic activity of a country; and
- The shadow economy contributes to the growth of the formal sector: its effect is multiplicative.

The first view is the conventional one, based on a simple neoclassical model, that the total volume of economic activity in a country is a given, based on the assumption of full factor employment, so that the shadow economy may grow only at the expense of economic activity in the formal sector. According to this position, an entity chooses whether to take part in the shadow or the formal economy; not doing business (being unemployed) is not an option. In this case total GDP will even decrease, as operating efficiency is lower in the shadow than in the formal economy (less capital-intensive technologies, greater uncertainty, poorer protection of owners' rights, etc.). Loayza (1996) showed how, under certain conditions and using the example of Latin American countries, excessive tax burden and over-regulation encourage the growth of the informal sector, which has a negative impact on the pace of overall economic growth.

In the second case, given an unfavourable institutional environment, the volume of activity in the formal economy may be a given; i.e., adverse circumstances may preclude full-factor employment in this sector. For example, prohibitive laws, poor economic policies, sanctions, or wars may constrain growth, as was the case with Serbia in the 1990s. In this situation growth in the shadow economy does not affect the formal sector but rather leads to an increase in the total economic activity.

Finally, in the third case, the shadow economy can have a positive impact on economic activity in the formal sector through the interaction of the two sectors. According to empirical research carried out by Schneider (1999), two-thirds of income earned in the shadow economy in Germany and Austria is spent on consumption in the formal economy (where value-added tax is payable), thus boosting formal sector growth. The UK also saw a similar stimulating effect of the informal economy on consumption in the formal sector (Bhattacharyya 1999).

An answer to the question of whether the shadow economy is useful or not and how it affects economic growth can be found by using econometric models which will be presented below. However, in real life various models and factors can act together, usually in opposing directions, and have different impacts on the final result.

It can be posited that any major reduction in the shadow economy leads to a major increase in tax revenue, which leads to more and better public goods and services, which in turn boosts economic growth. This hypothesis was empirically confirmed by, among others, Loayza (1996), whose research covered Latin America. He established that any growth in the relative volume of the shadow economy (in percent of GDP) contributes to a reduction in the growth of official GDP in countries where (a) the statutory tax burden is greater than the optimum and where (b) enforcement of compliance is too weak. This negative impact on GDP can be explained by (a) reduced availability of public services in the formal sector and (b) lower efficiency of the use of existing public services. The foundations of this model have been criticised (Asea 1996), while the assumption that the shadow economy hurts economic growth has failed to find widespread acceptance.

In the case of transition countries, Kaufmann and Kaliberda (1996) estimated that the shadow economy has cushioned the drop in registered GDP, particularly in countries that faced major declines in their GDP levels. Over half of the decline in registered GDP carried over into the drop in overall economic activity, while the other half was absorbed by the growing shadow economy. Using Ordinary Least Squares regression, they concluded that the share of the shadow economy in overall GDP increased by nearly 4 % for each 10 % of cumulative decline in registered GDP.

Eilat and Zinnes (2000) came to a very important conclusion applicable to transition economies, showing that there is an inertia effect in the creation of the shadow economy, as well as a hysteresis effect in its destruction. If overall economic activity is on the decline, a drop in GDP of one dollar is linked to an increase in the shadow economy by 31 cents, meaning that the shadow economy cushions the fall of registered GDP. On the other hand, if overall economic activity is on the increase, a one-dollar rise in GDP leads to a reduction of just 25 cents in the shadow economy. These findings indicate that caution is necessary when estimating the effects of formalising the shadow economy on economic growth.

According to Schneider (2004), the shadow economy hurts economic growth in developing countries while having a positive effect on economic growth in developed countries. The results of this econometric analysis, which covered 21 OECD member states and 89 developing and transition countries, show that in developed economies an increase in the shadow economy of 1 percentage point of GDP leads to an increase in registered GDP of 7.7 %. On the other hand, in developing countries 1-percentage-point growth in the shadow economy leads to a 4.9 % drop in registered GDP, all other model variables being equal (openness of the economy, inflation, government spending, capital accumulation rate, population). One explanation for these results is that growth in the shadow economy in developed countries may stimulate the formal economy by generating additional income that boosts formal-sector consumption. On the other hand, in developing countries a greater volume of the shadow economy leads to a substantial erosion of the tax base, which results in lower availability of public infrastructure and basic public services (such as an efficient legal system), in turn causing lower economic growth. We believe that both of these explanations can be relevant to developing and developed countries, but their final effect on economic growth depends on which group of factors dominates.

However, a study carried out by USAID (2005) shows that there is no correlation between the GDP growth rate and the shadow economy, and concludes that no empirical confirmation can be found of the hypothesis that a reduction in the shadow economy automatically leads to economic growth, and vice versa. Although countries with higher GDP per capita have smaller shadow economies, it cannot be determined whether formalisation is the cause or consequence of the higher level of development. The authors also state that the available series of data on changes to the shadow economy are not long enough to confirm or deny the assumption that countries with high rates of economic growth are able to reduce their shadow economy levels faster than those with lower growth rates. When viewed from a theoretical standpoint the shadow economy limits business growth, as it denies companies access to critical services and the opportunity to separate their business and personal assets, which increases risk and constrains growth.

Serbia's experience over a lengthy period of time shows the predominance of distorting and negative effects of the shadow economy on balanced economic growth, particularly in times of economic crisis. In the crisis conditions that Serbia has faced since 2008 the shadow economy has become part of a vicious circle, where one consequence of recession is flight from the formal to the shadow economy, thus reducing tax revenue and thereby the availability of public services and increasing the fiscal deficit. The growing deficit must then be compensated for by greater tax rates, which drive companies and workers into the shadow economy or out of the economy altogether. This downward spiral keeps repeating itself, always at a lower level of GDP and employment. The state receives ever-lower amounts of money to pursue appropriate development policies and finance public services, leading to poorer public services and the continuation of the vicious circle where companies are increasingly less ready to pay taxes. Government bodies are thus faced with the task of adjusting how institutions operate and calibrating economic policies so that the reduction in the shadow economy is accomplished by shifting business from the informal to the formal sector, and so that there is neither a decline in activity nor a drop in GDP.

Results of the study conducted using the MIMIC method in Serbia and the other 10 Central and Eastern European countries shown in Chap. 5 indicate that the impact of the shadow economy on official GDP is statistically highly significant, and has the expected negative sign. Depending on the model used, the value of the GDP per capita coefficient varies between -0.60 and -0.70, meaning that if GDP per capita declines by 1 percentage point, the shadow economy will grow by between 0.6 and 0.7 percentage points. In other words, if GDP declines in the future the shadow economy will grow as business entities attempt to off-set the limited opportunities for doing business in the formal sector by becoming active in the shadow economy.

References

Asea P (1996) The informal sector: baby or bath water? Carnegie-Rochester Conference Series on Public Policy. 45: 163–171

Bhattacharyya DK (1999) On the economic rationale of estimating the hidden economy. Econ J 109(456):348–359

Eilat Y, Zinnes C (2000) The evolution of the shadow economy in transition countries: consequences for economic growth and donor assistance. CAER II Discussion Paper, No. 83

Fiscal Council (2012) Ocena predloga Zakona o budžetu za 2013. godinu

Kaufmann D, Kaliberda A (1996) Integrating the unofficial economy into the dynamics of post socialist economies: a framework of analyses and evidence. In: Kaminski B (ed) Economic transition in Russia and the new states of Eurasia. M.E. Sharpe, London, pp 81–120

Loayza NV (1996) The economics of the informal sector: a simple model and some empirical evidence from Latin America, vol 45. Carnegie–Rochester Conference Series on Public Policy, Washington, DC, pp 129–162

Schneider F (1999) Der Sozialstaat zwischen Markt und Hedeonismus? In: Lamnek S, Luedtke J (Hrsg.) Otto-von-Freising-Tagungen der Katholischen Universität Eichstätt. Leske Budrich, Opladen

Schneider F (2004) Shadow economies around the World: what do we really know? IAW-Diskussionspapiere 16

Schneider F (eds) (2011) Handbook on the shadow economy. Edward Elgar, Cheltenham

Schneider F, Enste D (2000) Shadow economies: size, causes and consequences. J Econ Lit 38(1):77–114

USAID (2005) Removing barriers to formalization: the case for reform and emerging best practice

Chapter 8
Analysis of the Administrative Capacity of the Institutions in Charge of Overseeing the Operations of Business Entities

Mihail Arandarenko

8.1 Introduction

According to the results of the survey, the respondents' negative views of inspection bodies were caused predominantly by corruption (32 %), inconsistency in implementing regulations (20 %), strictness in implementing regulations (12 %) and lack of regulation implementation (9 %). Nearly one-half of all respondents (46 %) felt that bribery of inspectors was common or very common; 30 % believed it took place sporadically, and only 6 % believed it never happened. The lack of a consistent, predictable relationship with taxpayers is a common feature of these findings.

About two-thirds of all business entities visited by oversight bodies stated that visits had happened only once, while about another one-fifth stated that they had received two visits. Visits generally took one day (in about 70 % of all cases).

Figure 8.1 shows the frequency of inspection visits tasked with oversight of corporate operations by sector of activity. Half or less of all respondents stated that they had been visited by these inspectors: 53 % cited Labour Inspection, 43 % mentioned Market Inspection, while 38 cited the Tax Authority. Audits by government bodies were much more rare for business entities in sectors most affected by the shadow economy such as construction, agriculture, and transportation. The only exception to this rule was catering, where inspection audits were more frequent than the average.

M. Arandarenko (✉)
Faculty of Economics, University of Belgrade, Belgrade, Serbia
e-mail: arandarenko@ekof.bg.ac.rs

G. Krstić, F. Schneider (eds.), *Formalizing the Shadow Economy in Serbia*,
Contributions to Economics, DOI 10.1007/978-3-319-13437-6_8

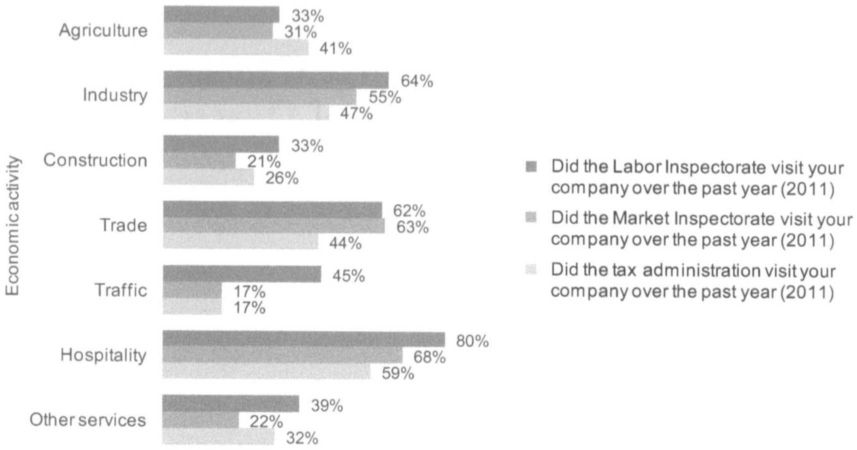

Fig. 8.1 Frequency of audit by sector of activity. *Source*: Own calculations. Survey on Conditions for Doing Business in Serbia, FREN, 2012

8.2 Tax Administration

According to 2011 data the Republic of Serbia Tax Administration employed 6,165 staff, which is less than optimal given the number of taxpayers and international standards. This problem is compounded by the inadequate structure of current staff by age, education, and organisation. Thus, of the total number, only 55 % have university degrees and the average age of employees is 49. In addition, many staff are tasked with receiving and technically processing tax filings, while the number of people effectively carrying out tax audits is lower than necessary.

The relatively low degree of efficiency in uncovering tax evasion is the consequence of the lack of human and financial resources available to the Tax Administration, the inadequate structure of Tax Administration staff, the lack of systemic exchange of information with other government bodies that could be used to discover tax evasion, etc. The total budget of the Tax Administration is lower than is required; as a result, employee salaries are rather low, which incentivises younger staff to leave after gaining experience in tax audits, which in turn has an adverse impact on the quality of audits and the overall efficiency of the Tax Administration. In addition, rigid public sector remuneration rules mean that the Tax Administration is unable to adequately pay professionals that are most in demand (e.g., IT experts or auditors). Many of its current employees are not sufficiently trained to do their jobs as those jobs are defined at present.

Lack of automation of business processes, lack of an organised cross-checking system to compare data from other government bodies (e.g., Real Estate Cadastre, Pension and Disability Insurance Fund, local Public Revenue Administrations, the police, etc.), and sub-optimal mechanisms used to select taxpayers for audit, together with inadequate staff structure have all resulted in the relatively low likelihood of uncovering tax evasion, which has served as an incentive for operating in the informal sector. The current IT platform used by the Tax Administration does not satisfy the needs of a modern public revenue authority. It needs replacing, and transitional solutions must be found in the meantime. Too many tax administration processes, including debt collection, rely on manual intervention. This substantially decreases the efficiency of the Tax Administration. There is a major gap between hardware and software: although multiple independent applications have been developed to solve various issues they do not function as a whole, with some posing their own problems. There are no business analysts in the Tax Administration who can appropriately define its business needs. An entire new system is necessary, which requires a great deal of financial resources and time.

Changes to the Law on Tax Procedure and Tax Administration have meant that the Tax Administration has become responsible for auditing entities engaged in unregistered activity. Placing these powers within the remit of the Tax Administration is justified, but, to achieve an appropriate level of efficiency, this broadening of authority should be accompanied by major reforms to how the Tax Administration operates. Given the current number of tax inspectors (some 600 covering all of Serbia), any new powers can be exercised only formally, since capacities to do so are constrained. To resolve this issue the structure of Tax Administration staff must be substantially changed: the number of employees tasked with administrative work (receipt, certification, and registration of tax returns) should be reduced and the staff effectively engaged in oversight increased. A switch to mandatory e-filing of tax returns would reduce the need for the several hundred Tax Administration staff estimated to be employed in administrative jobs, which would in turn enable part of them (particularly the younger, better-educated staff) to be shifted to oversight tasks after undergoing intensive training. Since many of these employees will nevertheless prove to be under-qualified for oversight tasks, the option of hiring well-educated employees to deal exclusively with oversight should be considered. Continuing improvements to the Tax Administration's remuneration system is a necessary precondition for retaining staff that already have the appropriate skills and knowledge of tax audit procedures and for attracting young high-quality employees.

Statutory, Institutional, and Organisational Framework The current framework imposed by tax legislation poses numerous obstacles to efficient revenue administration. The Tax Administration has no influence on how penalties are defined in statute, nor can it get involved with actual sanctions practice, as this is the domain of the courts. In addition, the threshold amount for tax fraud is much lower than in most other countries, which shifts the focus away from major tax offenders and means that tackling larger forms of evasion is less efficient.

The Tax Administration is formally a division of the Ministry of Finance, but communication between the two does not flow both ways. The Tax Administration is not sufficiently involved in providing support to the Ministry in its efforts to design taxation policy, which is partly due to the weakness of the Tax Administration. Interpreting legislation and decision-making are currently within the remit of the Ministry of Finance rather than the Tax Administration, while in international practice the reverse is often true. The current system in Serbia leads to substantial delays in advice on the treatment of taxpayers, even by the Tax Administration, which increases uncertainty among taxpayers.

The current organisational structure of the Serbian Tax Administration does not reflect current organisational approaches in modern public revenue administration. A strong central core is needed to design business processes, oversee their implementation, set operational goals, and oversee their realisation. At present the High Taxpayer Unit does not have sufficient resources at its disposal to manage its client base. The Education and Communication Division is in charge of training, rather than the Human Resources Division, which would be more appropriate. Human resources are under-utilised. For instance, more staff than necessary deal with desk review and processing of tax filings while other more important tasks are neglected. The number of branch offices is too large for an organisation the size of the Serbian Tax Authority.

Since findings of empirical research (Alm et al. 1992) show that an increase in the likelihood of tax evasion detection is a more efficient deterrent than other mechanisms (such as reducing the tax burden or increasing penalties), there is much room for tackling the shadow economy in Serbia by improving the efficiency of the Tax Administration.

The Tax Administration should strive to ensure that its activities are aimed at areas most at risk, that taxpayers who wish to comply with the law are able to do so quickly and easily, and that enforcement is directed at repeated non-compliers. To improve compliance the Tax Administration should particularly improve the validation of taxpayers and maintenance of taxpayer records by developing strategies and programmes for a taxpayer service and increasing the standards of services provided. In order to maintain compliance levels a greater focus on self-assessment is needed and an overhaul of basic business procedures: development of a collection strategy and a filing strategy (with various requirements for different types of filing, and an emphasis on electronic filing and the removal of unnecessary forms); improvement of oversight and collection of mandatory social security contributions and payroll taxes; review of rules on handling requests for refunds/exemptions; improvement of tax accounting; and review of penalties and their administration.

The relatively low efficiency of the Serbian Tax Administration in collecting taxes has been borne out by the views of taxpayers voiced in the Survey on Conditions for Doing Business in Serbia, where equal portion of respondents (46 % each) believed that the Tax Administration was either mainly unsuccessful in tackling tax evasion or mainly successful, which can hardly be considered a good result.

8.3 Labour Inspection

Tackling informal employment (colloquially known as 'working in the shadow') is the primary task of the Labour Inspectorate, a separate division of the Ministry of Labour, Employment, and Social Policy. The Labour Inspectorate is also charged with carrying out other activities related to the implementation of the Labour Law, the Health and Safety Law, and other labour legislation. The strategic aims of the Labour Inspectorate are to minimise risks employees face at work, tackle undeclared work, and combat breaches of rights arising from employment or collective agreements. The Inspectorate is entitled to audit registered companies: where it detects breaches of law—including work without a written employment contract—it can require any deficiencies to be eliminated within a short period of time. The Inspectorate employs some 260 inspectors, mainly lawyers, with a number of engineers specialising in various fields, and operates in each of the 25 administrative districts and in Belgrade.

Labour inspectors are authorised to inspect a business's internal bylaws and individual contracts, as well as any and all other documents. They may take statements from corporate officers and other interested parties, and may also inspect offices, production plants, and other premises. The inspectors are also entitled to launch audits based on reports made by members of the public, workers, or any other interested parties. An integrated inspection oversight concept has been in place in Serbia since early 2010, meaning that all labour inspectors undertake comprehensive inspection actions: employment issues are not kept separate from those related to health and safety.

A priority task of the Inspectorate has always been to verify whether workers have formal employment contracts. People in informal employment are not protected by workers' rights, face greater risk of injury, are not entitled to healthcare, and are denied unemployment benefits and old age pensions due to the fact they are not registered for mandatory social security when in work. From the point of view of safeguarding public interest, non-declaration of employees entails tax evasion and a number of safety hazards, as well as other issues. Due to all of the above, labour inspectors' main task is to oversee the implementation of statutory provisions governing "entering into labour relations": i.e., uncovering informally employed workers and formalising their status.

When workers without employment contracts are discovered at a business the employer is given a deadline for either signing contracts with those employees or letting them go. The employer must notify the Inspectorate of the steps taken within 8 days; inspectors will then visit the employer again to verify that the issue has been resolved. Although this procedure is clearly aimed at protecting workers without contracts its preventive role can be disputed, since there is no credible threat of sanctions to prevent future non-compliance (Arandarenko 2012).

The effective power of labour inspectors is further constrained by two factors. Firstly, although the law stipulates harsh fines, only courts can impose them. To impose mass penalties in order to discourage the widespread non-compliance the

Labour Inspectorate would have to become involved in a large number of individual court cases, which is unrealistic as the procedure for proving allegations of this type is demanding.

In performing oversight, labour inspectors establish whether people found on the premises of a business entity have employment contracts. Inspectors can base their official accounts of inspection visits on workers' statements and conclude those workers are employed informally (i.e., without a written employment contract, or not declared for social insurance purposes), but employers can circumvent sanctions by subsequently presenting employment contracts antedated to seem as if they were entered into a day or two previous to the audit, and claim that the workers will be declared for social insurance purposes by the statutory deadline—which, as a rule, does take place.

In cases where an audit establishes that an employer is not paying taxes, mandatory pension and disability insurance contributions, healthcare contributions, and unemployment insurance contributions (payable for every month by the 30th day of the next month, as required under Article 51 of the Law on Contributions for Mandatory Social Insurance), labour inspectors cannot act independently but have to report to the Tax Administration, the body in charge of implementing this particular law. This procedure illustrates the shortcomings of the current fragmented inspection system compared to the integrated inspection approach used by most European countries.

Secondly, wholly unregistered 'phantom firms', typically located in private homes and with all workers employed informally, are allowed by law to deny labour inspectors access to their premises, since the Labour Inspectorate does not have jurisdiction over them (unlike Market and Tourism Inspectorates). Audits have detected many cases where employers have organised production in basements, garages, and private homes, even though this is not easy to detect. The buildings are unmarked and entrances are guarded by dogs and secured by cameras and intercoms. Inspectors have found that these premises are most often venues for sewing, shoemaking, carpentry, or other small-scale production, and the workers are employed informally. Services, such as hairdressers or beauty parlours, may also operate in this way. In these cases inspectors are expected to call in the police, who generally lack enthusiasm for assisting since breaches of the Labour Law are, from their perspective, relatively minor offences. Thus the worst infringements of labour legislation remain almost completely beyond the reach of statutory sanction.

Articles 273 and 274 of the Labour Law envisage fines of RSD 1 million (about €9,000 at the current exchange rate) for businesses employing workers without appropriate contracts, not paying social security contributions, not paying wages, paying wages below the statutory minimum, or paying wages partly 'cash in hand'. Fines for entrepreneurs are also high and amount to half the amount applicable to businesses. Yet, in order for these fines actually to be imposed, inspectors must bring and argue each case in court, which happens only rarely—until recently, in only some 2 % of all cases. Of late there has been an increased number of employment contracts entered into and workers registered for social insurance after inspection visits. In addition to a stricter penal policy the way inspectors operate has changed, with visits now also being made outside of regular working hours.

Misdemeanour judges often claim that the amounts of fines for infringement of labour laws and health and safety regulations are unrealistic, given the current state of the Serbian economy, which is why they have trouble handing down fines. Nonetheless, penal policy applied by misdemeanour courts has become much stricter over the past several years, with judges now, as a rule, handing down fines that lie within the statutory range, rather than below the statutory minimum. The Labour Inspectorate has contributed to this trend: inspectors have been appealing judgments that only impose reprimands instead of fines or hand down fines below the statutory minimum; they have also been contesting rulings suspending proceedings for lack of evidence. In addition, court cases are still liable to lapse due to statutes of limitation. Labour inspectors have also been complaining that they must testify in nearly every misdemeanour proceeding and face defendants on multiple occasions, which is a large burden on their time.

Labour inspectors generally find that employers justify informal employment by citing 'trial employment periods', claiming they need to assess the performance of prospective employees before entering into employment contracts and registering workers for social insurance. They also attempt to justify shadow employment by claiming employees are reluctant to enter into formal contracts and wish to receive higher wages resulting from employers not paying taxes.

Inspectors also cite instances where informally employed workers refuse to enter into formal employment after inspectors intervene, instead leaving the employer in order to be able to retain other statutory rights or benefits. This particularly important consideration points to an often-overlooked cause of informal employment: the interests of the workers themselves, who might, when formally employed, lose the right to social benefits, child support, unemployment benefits, or other payments that are either de jure or de facto conditioned by the lack of any registered income.

The Labour Inspectorate (Annual Report 2011) has found that informal employment is most common in trade, construction, industry, tourism and catering, crafts and home repair, and personal services. Some activities record an increase in informal workers over the same periods of each year, which is a particular hallmark of catering and construction. Catering sees this trend in the summer, while in construction it is evident towards the end of the building season as employers strive to meet deadlines. However, enhanced inspection oversight is employed in the construction sector throughout the year due to the possible health and safety risk. Shadow employment in the construction sector is fostered by high employee turnover, frequent shifts from one construction site to another, and brief periods of employment, as workers remain on site only until a particular job is finished.

Inspectors have also discovered that unregistered employers in the shadow economy mainly hire young unskilled labourers, with at most secondary school diplomas; they also employ workers without permanent incomes, the unemployed over 40 years of age, beneficiaries of various types of assistance or social security, etc. In most cases there is agreement between these employees and their employers and no direct coercion.

The status of workers found on the premises of a business is also controlled through integrated inspection oversight. There were a total of 40,757 Labour Inspectorate audits in 2011 (including integrated audits), which found a total of 171,264 people at places of work, among them 6,230 people without employment contracts (that is, in shadow employment). After inspectors intervened, employers entered into contracts with a total of 4,622 people (or 74.2 %). The sectors of activity with the most frequent incidence of undeclared work were wholesale and retail trade, catering, construction, and food production. Of the total number of people found not to have employment contracts, 23 % were engaged in trade, 16 % in catering, 15.5 % in construction, and 8.7 % in food production.

Table 8.1 provides an overview of the overall results of inspection oversight of shadow employment in Serbia between 2007 and 2011.

As can be seen from Table 8.1, the Inspectorate carried out some 40,000 audits per year; this figure followed a downward trend, with 2011 seeing one-third fewer audits than 2007. At the same time, however, the total number of employees covered by these audits nearly doubled, which means that the focus of oversight shifted onto larger businesses with more employees: the average number of workers at a business or with an entrepreneur increased from six to more than 15 over the observed period. At the same time the number of people found to be working in the shadow economy nearly halved (from 10,448 to 5,744), as did the number of those employed following audits (from 7,517 to 4,314). Nonetheless, the efficiency of oversight remained high or even increased, given that nearly three-quarters of all workers found to be employed informally were admitted into formal employment following an audit.

The fact that far more undeclared workers were found in the 'boom years' of 2007 and 2008, and that the number continually declined from 2009 to 2011 after the crisis, is consistent with the findings of the successive Labour Force Surveys from 2008 to the present. It is, however, part of a longer-term trend that can be followed back in time to 2005. Starting in that year the number of workers without a valid employment contract discovered by inspectors has constantly been on the decline, while the degree of their subjective formalisation has remained relatively stable.[1]

Therefore, judging by the data collected by the Labour Inspectorate since 2005, we could conclude that tackling undeclared work at registered businesses has been very successful, and that the number of cases of such work uncovered has been reduced to one-quarter of the initial figure in just seven years. This would also match to a large extent the declining rate of informal employment, especially outside the agriculture sector, found by household surveys (admittedly from

[1] A total of 28,735 people were identified as illicit workers in 2005, while 21,563 of them went on to gain formal contracts. In 2006 the number of undeclared workers was 16,205, of which 11,324 were subsequently employed formally.

Table 8.1 Overview of overall results of inspection oversight of shadow employment in Serbia, 2007–2011

	Total number of audits	Number of people covered by audits	Number of people found in shadow employment	Number of people formally employed following audits
2007	48,255	268,682	10,448	7,517
2008	42,595	306,416	9,054	6,394
2009	40,222	357,498	5,734	4,178
2010	37,747	558,536	5,228	3,925
2011	33,920	503,613	5,744	4,314

Source: Labour Inspectorate, Annual Report 2011

different sources: the Living Standards Measurement Study for 2002, 2003, and 2007, and the Labour Force Survey conducted using indirect methodology in 2005 and direct methodology since 2008). Estimates made by respondents in the Survey on Conditions for Doing Business in Serbia of the extent, types, features, and desirability of shadow employment can neither definitely confirm nor deny data found in Labour Inspectorate reports.

The number of instances of oversight (audits) reported by respondents generally bears out the assumption that the focus of oversight was businesses and entrepreneurs employing five or more workers, with audits taking place at two-thirds of such entities; conversely, one in every two entities with four or less workers was audited (Table 8.2). When data are viewed by sector of activity, most audits were of catering businesses (80 %), followed by industry and trade (64 and 62 %, respectively); while far fewer audits were made of construction businesses where informal employment is most common—only one in three construction firms from the sample were audited by the Inspectorate in 2011. The greatest number of audits, proportionally, took place in Central Serbia (65 %), followed by Belgrade (50 %), while Vojvodina saw the fewest audits (39 %).

While companies taking part in the Survey on Conditions for Doing Business in Serbia believed that the extent of informal employment and undeclared wages was relatively high, a fairly low score was awarded to the Labour Inspectorate's efforts at uncovering workers without contracts and other types of informal employment (Fig. 8.2). A generally positive score was given by 42 % of respondents, while 51 % viewed the Inspectorate's work in a generally negative light.

8.4 Market Inspection

The Market Inspectorate is a separate division of the Ministry of Foreign and Internal Trade and Telecommunications. The division is made up of two sections: the Section for Co-Ordination Oversight of Trade in Goods and the Section for Co-Ordination of Oversight of Services, Prevention of Unfair Competition, and Oversight Support. The Market Inspectorate's headquarters are at the Ministry and

Table 8.2 Labour and Market Inspectorates audits by features of business entities

	Labour Inspectorate	Market Inspectorate
Total	52.7	42.7
Type of entity		
Business	49.0	38.0
Entrepreneur	54.0	45.0
Number of employees		
Up to 4	50.0	41.0
5–19	68.0	54.0
20 and more	64.0	44.0
Sector of economic activity		
Agriculture	33.0	31.0
Industry	64.0	55.0
Construction	33.0	21.0
Trade	62.0	63.0
Transportation	45.0	17.0
Catering	80.0	68.0
Other services	39.0	22.0
Region		
Vojvodina	50.0	43.0
Belgrade	39.0	29.0
Central Serbia	65.0	52.0

Source: Own calculations. Survey on Conditions for Doing Business in Serbia, FREN 2012

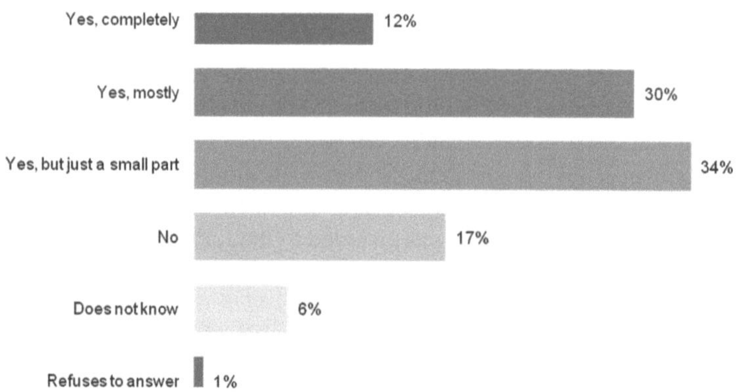

Fig. 8.2 How successful is the Labour Inspectorate in uncovering workers without employment contracts or in other types of informal employment? *Source*: Own calculations. Survey on Conditions for Doing Business in Serbia, FREN 2012

it has 24 territorial units and 4 specialised branches in Belgrade, Novi Sad, Niš, and Kragujevac.

The Market Inspectorate's remit is very broad and is governed by a myriad of laws and bylaws, which clearly impedes its efficiency and often leads to overlapping with other inspection services. However, it can be said that the primary task of this service is to ensure the application of the Law on Trade and, as part of that effort, prevent various types of informal trade. The principal legislative framework for the operation of the Market Inspectorate is the 2010 Law on Trade, a piece of legislation that provided a unified structure for issues hitherto regulated by three separate laws—the old Law on Trade, the Law on Conditions for Trading in Goods and Providing Services Related to Trade in Goods and on Inspection Oversight, and the Law on Prices. However, the remit of the Market Inspectorate goes beyond the scope of the Law on Trade and covers a total of 27 laws, including those governing consumer protection, prevention of money laundering, wholesale and retail trade in tobacco products, product safety, advertising, copyright protection, anti-smoking measures, etc.

The Market Inspectorate engages in various forms of oversight that differ in scope, methods, areas audited, and aims. Oversight may be pursued *ex officio*, pursuant to an official order, or pursuant to a report of an infringement. Any interested legal entity or individual may contact the Inspectorate; reports of infringements may also be filed online.

In the course of an audit a market inspector is authorised to inspect the premises of a business entity or the premises where its business is conducted; inspect ledgers, records, official documents, and any and all other documents both in paper form and stored by electronic means that relate to the trading engaged in; inspect personal identity papers of persons engaging in trade; extract oral and written statements on issues of importance for the audit; photograph or film premises where trading is engaged in, or the goods or other items being audited; inspect vehicles used in the course of trading; sample goods and other items; seek court warrants for searching homes or ancillary buildings in the event of suspecting them to be used for illicit trading; and seek assistance by the police or municipal police. In performing oversight the Market Inspection Division adheres to principles of administrative proceedings as governed by the Law on General Administrative Proceedings, which include the right of parties to lodge complaints against rulings issued by market inspectors.

In the event that the Market Inspectorate establishes that an infringement has taken place, it cannot impose a fine directly, but can only file criminal charges, charges for economic crime, or misdemeanour charges. It may also report the offender to a professional tribunal (the Court of Honour). However, if a law has been infringed, a market inspector is authorised to issue a ruling requiring the infringement be remedied, temporarily ban trading in particular goods or provision of particular services, temporarily close down a retail or wholesale outlet, or call for goods to be confiscated.

Article 54 of the Law on Trade has conferred some powers previously held by the Market Inspectorate onto the Municipal Inspectorate, particularly those relating to trade outside of formal shops and ensuring adherence to working hours. It is important to note that the Municipal Inspectorate has the same powers in exercising these functions as the Market Inspectorate.

The manifestations of the informal economy faced by market inspectors are many and varied. Firstly, market participants such as illicit traders or entrepreneurs and people who engage in illegal activity may be completely invisible to public registries. Secondly, business entities may be registered with a public registry but may pursue part of their activities in an illicit manner, without registration or the required permits. In trade sector, legal traders may sell smuggled or illicit goods; in catering, a legal café may quickly turn into an illegal nightclub, etc. A survey carried out by the Serbian Association of Employers (Socio-Economic Council of the Republic of Serbia 2010) showed that in the informal sector goods are most often sold through personal advertisements, in markets, in undeclared stores or craftsmen's shops held by self-employed persons, from improvised roadside stalls, at illegal distribution centres, through illegal door-to-door sales, through illicit sales in otherwise legal outlets, and through illegal commission sales at legal entities' premises.

In 2011 the Market Inspectorate employed 487 staff, nearly all of them with university degrees. The majority of staff had backgrounds in economics (44 %) and law (24 %). The standard of equipment is good, with all employees provided with laptop computers, portable 3G modems for accessing the Inspectorate's intranet, and mobile telephones. On average, there is one official vehicle for every two inspectors. The Inspectorate has developed software applications to improve the records of inspection activities, provide information on unsafe products ('NEPRO'), record actions taken to protect copyright, and to record goods confiscated during audits.

The Survey on Conditions for Doing Business in Serbia found that the Market Inspectorate had visited 43 % of all respondents (Table 8.2), of which one-third were audited more than once a year. Audits did not take more than one day in 73 % of cases and took more than 3 days in 9 % of cases. As expected, most audits were in the catering and trade sectors (68 % of all catering establishments and 63 % of all trading businesses and shops were audited). Above-average numbers of audit were also seen in production (55 % of entities visited), while other sectors recorded below-average levels of oversight. Greater incidence of oversight was seen by entrepreneurs than by businesses (45 % vs. 38 %, respectively); similarly, businesses with between 5 and 19 workers were audited more than those with less than five employees or those with more than 20 workers (54, 41, and 44 %, respectively). Most audits were made in Central Serbia, with oversight in Vojvodina being at the level of the national average, and Belgrade seeing a below-average incidence of oversight.

Respondents mainly viewed the Market Inspectorate in a positive light: 52 % gave it a score of 4 or 5 on a scale of one to five, while 13 % of respondents assessed its performance negatively (1 or 2 on the same scale). These scores were slightly lower than those awarded to the two other public services, the Labour Inspectorate and the Tax Administration. This is borne out by the average scores: 3.5 for the Market Inspectorate and 3.6 for both the Labour Inspectorate and the Tax Administration.

References

Alm J, Jackson B, McKee M (1992) Estimating the determinants of taxpayer compliance with experimental data. Natl Tax J 45(1):107–114

Arandarenko M (2012) How to make informal work less normal in Serbia. In: Mutual learning programme peer review on tackling undeclared work: developing an effective system for inspection and prevention, 4–5 October 2012, Prague (Czech Republic)

Labour Inspectorate (2011) Annual Report

Socio-Economic Council of the Republic of Serbia (2010) Efikasno suzbijanje sive ekonomije, Beograd

Chapter 9
Main Findings and Recommendations

Gorana Krstić, Friedrich Schneider, Mihail Arandarenko, Milojko Arsić, Branko Radulović, Saša Ranđelović, and Irena Janković

9.1 Main Findings

In this section we will summarise the findings presented in the previous chapters on the key causes of the shadow economy in Serbia and the mechanisms that contribute to its development. We will also present the results of an estimate of the extent of the shadow economy in relation to GDP, estimates of various forms of the shadow economy in the sectors of businesses and entrepreneurs and their characteristics, and an estimate of the effects that formalising the shadow economy can have on the government budget and economic growth. Finally, we will summarise findings that relate to the administrative and institutional capacity of government institutions tasked with overseeing the operation of business entities.

9.1.1 Causes of the Shadow Economy

Some of the fiscal causes of the shadow economy are the relatively high fiscal burden on labour, complex and expensive tax procedures, a complex and opaque tax system, the lack of organisation, training, and equipment at the Tax

G. Krstić (✉) • M. Arandarenko • M. Arsić • S. Ranđelović • I. Janković
Faculty of Economics, University of Belgrade, Belgrade, Serbia
e-mail: gkrstic@ekof.bg.ac.rs; arandarenko@ekof.bg.ac.rs; arsicm@ekof.bg.ac.rs; randjelovic@ekof.bg.ac.rs; irenaj@ekof.bg.ac.rs

F. Schneider
Department of Economics, University of Linz, Linz, Austria
e-mail: Friedrich.schneider@jku.at

B. Radulović
Faculty of Law, University of Belgrade, Belgrade, Serbia
e-mail: bradulovic@ius.bg.ac.rs

G. Krstić, F. Schneider (eds.), *Formalizing the Shadow Economy in Serbia*, Contributions to Economics, DOI 10.1007/978-3-319-13437-6_9

Administration, the low quality of public-sector services, and high tolerance of the shadow economy.

We have singled out the following features of the labour market that have a bearing on the growth of the shadow economy: taxation of labour; minimum wage; social benefits system; employment protection legislation; minimum wage regulation; unemployment benefits; and retirement rules. The most significant of these are the rules for taxing labour, primarily the high tax burden on lower-paid work caused by the low tax-exempt allowance, high contribution rates, and minimum contribution base. Since the natural zone for formalising the informal economy is around the amount of the minimum wage, a high burden on minimum wages implies high costs of formalisation, and thereby discourages it. This effect is compounded by the high minimum wage, which currently stands at around 50 % of the average wage, exceeding the recommended level by some 10 percentage points. The minimum contribution base makes part-time employment contracts unpopular, and also effectively prevents the introduction of special contractual arrangements at more favourable tax rates such as the 'mini jobs' and 'midi jobs' that have successfully contributed to the flexibility of the labour market in some European countries.

Apart from causes in the tax system and features of the labour market, other factors of particular importance in Serbia have to do with the unfavourable economic and regulatory environment. Of the economic conditions we can single out low productivity and widespread liquidity issues, especially pronounced in times of crisis. While low productivity forces business entities to shift at least part of their operations into the informal sector to be viable in the market, the lack of liquidity affects the taxpayer's decision to evade taxes and so preserve funds needed to pay suppliers. Regulatory constraints particularly include high administrative costs and legal insecurity. In addition there are many other factors that are the consequences of weak institutions and a chaotic system, such as issues with construction permits, inefficient market exit, and frequent abuses using 'phoenix companies'. The poor institutional framework is also reflected in a high degree of tolerance for the shadow economy on the part of the state and the high level of corruption. These two factors, coupled with the low quality of public services, further disincentivise taxpayers from paying their taxes.

Some of the major factors favourable to the shadow economy that are found in the financial sector are the major share of cash transactions in the total volume of payments, informal financing, and unregistered remittances sent by migrants residing abroad. Cash payments continue to account for a major portion of total payments in Serbia, although they have seen a downward trend of late. These circumstances have been further complicated by the fact that the high level of euroisation has stimulated moral hazard behaviour by transactors, while transactions have been made primarily in foreign currency and outside legal channels. Moreover, the volume of informal finance has grown with the shadow economy. The causes behind the use of informal sources of finance are poor local regulations and contract enforcement mechanisms, barriers to market entry, expensive formal finance, lack of financial products appropriate to consumer needs, inadequate tax regulations, and high tax burdens. Informal financing causes greater information asymmetries between market participants, lack of tax revenues from these activities, and exclusion of formal financial intermediaries from the transfer of funds. This adversely impacts the development of the financial sector and the efficient allocation of finance. Finally, remittances from migrants abroad are a particularly significant source of foreign capital in Serbia, as their post-crisis amounts in absolute terms exceed all other categories of capital inflows from private and public sources. The vast majority of remittances enter the country through informal channels and are often not invested in productive activity; this has negative effects on economic growth and development.

9.1.2 *Estimates of the Extent of the Shadow Economy and Tax Gap*

The extent of the shadow economy in Serbia was estimated using three methods: MIMIC, Household Tax Compliance (HTC), and the Survey on Conditions for Doing Business in Serbia. The application of the MIMIC method found that across all sectors in Serbia the shadow economy stood at some 30 % of official GDP in 2010. Data for the same year resulted in an estimate of 23.6 % of GDP for the shadow economy, identified on the basis of household income and consumption (the HTC method). According to the Survey on Conditions for Doing Business in Serbia, the shadow economy in the business sector stood at some 21 % of GDP for the two major types of informal activity (illicit trade and undeclared work). Based on these results we can conclude that the total extent of the shadow economy in Serbia was 30 % of GDP, and that this was for the most part accounted for by trade in goods and undeclared work.

The study also estimated the tax gap in the collection of VAT, personal income tax, and social security contributions. The VAT gap was estimated at 2.5 % of GDP, while the gap in personal income tax and social security contributions was put at about 5 % of GDP. We believe that the estimates of tax gaps for the key forms of taxation are relatively reliable. By extrapolating these estimates we arrived at an approximate estimate of the total tax gap in Serbia, which we put at about 10 % of GDP. A similar figure was also obtained using the HTC method, which indirectly supports the above estimate.

9.1.3 *The Shadow Economy in the Business and Entrepreneur Sector*

We analysed the shadow economy in the business and entrepreneur sector by using data from the Survey on Conditions for Doing Business in Serbia based on three indicators. These were: (1) the share of business entities engaged in the shadow economy in the total number of business entities; (2) the share of informal workers in the total number of workers, both overall and by type; and (3) the share of cash payments in the total volume of payments.

The Survey on Conditions for Doing Business in Serbia asked respondents whether their own business was engaged in the shadow economy, and found that 28 % of all business entities in Serbia did so. These businesses and entrepreneurs employed workers informally and/or made payments in cash even though they were VAT payers. The term 'informal worker' is used to describe workers employed without a contract, or those who do have contracts but only part of whose wage is officially declared, with the remainder paid in cash. The findings showed that there was a link between the shadow economy and the type and age of the business entity: entrepreneurs and new start-ups were more likely to engage in the shadow economy, while the common relationship between the shadow economy and the size of business entities, whereby smaller businesses are more likely to work in the shadow economy, could not be confirmed. Most business entities operating informally were in construction (42.9 %), as is also evidenced by most empirical research; this sector was followed by agriculture (33.8 %), catering (33.1 %) and transportation (32.7 %). According to region, business entities located in Central Serbia (excluding Belgrade) were the most prone to operate in the shadow economy, while those in Belgrade were least likely to do so (33 % versus 24.7 %).

A further two indicators of the shadow economy were based on respondents' views on the participation of their own businesses compared to their opinions on how active other businesses from the same sector were. All types of shadow economy were represented to a much greater extent in 'other' businesses in the same sector than in the respondents' own businesses. We therefore considered data obtained from owners/managers' biased responses regarding their own business activity in the shadow economy as the lower limit of the shadow economy, while figures obtained on the basis of their subjective views on the participation of other businesses from the same sector were deemed to denote the upper limit. Hence, the share of employees working without formal contracts ranged from 1.9 % (lower limit) to 23.9 % (upper limit) of the total number of employees; the share of workers whose total wages were not declared varied between 3.8 and 24.7 %; while the share of turnover in cash ranged between 11.3 and 21.6 % of the total volume of turnover.

The results of econometric analysis based on the survey data show that several variables are statistically significant and represent important determinants for making decisions on whether or not to join the shadow economy. They confirm the findings of similar studies that entrepreneurs are more likely to operate informally. In addition, we found that size (as measured by the number of employees) and the VAT status of entity are significant. Doing business in particular sectors of economic activity, (construction) is statistically significant, while according to some specifications the transportation sector increases and the trade sector decreases the probability of participation in the shadow economy. Regional variables are not statistically significant. Finally, the business attitude towards justification of the shadow economy is also statistically significant, which leads to the conclusion that measures aimed at changing opinions about the shadow economy should play a more pronounced role.

There is widespread competition from business entities operating in the informal sector. On average, entities claimed they lost nearly 28 % of their income from this competition, while almost 35 % stated that the shadow economy was a large or very large obstacle to doing business. This is particularly evident in the sectors of transportation and construction, where nearly all respondents said they were exposed to some type of competition from the shadow economy. Our analysis also found that competition from the informal sector was felt less by companies with foreign equity, as well as when informal activities are more likely to be detected. We found significant correlation between the various types of informal activity, so that making and receiving cash payments was often accompanied by employing undeclared workers and paying wages in cash.

9.1.4 Estimated Impact of Formalising the Shadow Economy

Based on our assessment of the tax gap, we estimate that a decrease in the extent of the shadow economy could, over a period of up to 3 years, result in additional revenues of between 0.8 and 1.1 % of GDP, while over a decade additional revenues of close to 2 % of GDP could be expected. When viewed in a broader fiscal context, additional revenues resulting from less informal activity will not make it possible to reduce tax rates, nor will they allow discretionary increases in public spending. The shadow economy must be addressed to compensate for the drop in revenues collected from consumption taxes that will occur due to the necessary reduction in the absorption gap. The current absorption gap, characterised by a balance of payments deficit of some 10 % of GDP, is unsustainable in the long run since it leads to continual growth of foreign debt and net foreign assets. A reduction of the absorption gap by some 5 percentage points of GDP is estimated to have an autonomous impact on the decline in VAT revenues of about 1 % of GDP. Moreover, autonomous growth of public expenditure can be expected in the long run as the population ages; it would thus be more favourable to ensure that additional expenditures can be met through better collection of existing taxes, rather than by increasing tax rates. If addressing the shadow economy generates additional revenue it should be used to reduce the fiscal deficit rather than to reduce tax rates or increase taxes in a discretionary manner.

Even though there has been a lot of empirical research on the effects of formalising the informal economy on economic growth, there are still no clear and unambiguous empirical or theoretical findings that indicate whether the shadow economy has a positive or a negative impact or what the direction of causality is (Schneider and Enste 2000). According to the findings of the survey carried out in Serbia and ten other Central and Eastern European countries for the period 2001–2010 using the MIMIC method, the effect of the shadow economy on official GDP is statistically highly significant and has the expected negative sign. The GDP per capita coefficient indicates that if GDP per capita declines by 1 percentage point, the shadow economy will grow by between 0.6 and 0.7 percentage points, depending on the model used. In other words, if GDP declines in the future the shadow economy will increase as business entities seek to compensate for fewer opportunities in the formal sector. This result is evidence of the importance of maintaining macroeconomic stability and creating conditions for future economic growth, as these are major components of successful strategies designed to formalise the informal economy.

9.1.5 The Administrative Capacity of Institutions Tasked with Overseeing Business: Labour Inspectorate, Market Inspectorate, and Tax Administration

The Labour Inspectorate is charged with tackling informal employment, or 'working in the shadow'. When workers without employment contracts are discovered at a business the employer is given a deadline for either signing contracts with those employees or letting them go. The employer has a brief window to notify the Inspectorate of the steps taken. Although this procedure is clearly aimed at protecting workers without contracts, its preventive role can be disputed since there is no credible threat of sanctions to prevent future non-compliance. Even though the law provides for substantial fines for these offences they can only be handed down by the courts, and the procedure for proving breaches of the law is very demanding. The Inspectorate is even more constrained in its oversight of completely unregistered businesses or 'phantom firms', since access to their premises needs police assistance. Respondents' estimates of the extent of informal employment made in the Survey on Conditions for Doing Business in Serbia are relatively high, especially in the sectors of construction, catering, trade, and industry. Similarly, estimates of the extent of the practice of paying a portion of wages while evading taxes and contributions for formally declared workers were also high. It comes as no surprise, therefore, that respondents had mixed views regarding the efficiency of the Labour Inspectorate. Nonetheless, this service was ranked slightly higher than both the Tax Administration and the Market Inspectorate, which corresponds to the finding that the principal issue does not lie with the capacities of the staff and the organisation of the Labour Inspectorate: rather it is prevented from being more effective in tackling informal employment and undeclared earnings by lack of resources and an inadequate statutory framework.

The primary task of the Market Inspectorate is to ensure the implementation of the Law on Trade and, in doing so, prevent various forms of illicit trade. Goods are most often sold in the informal sector through personal advertisements, in markets, in undeclared stores or self-employed craftsmen's shops, from improvised roadside stalls, and at illegal distribution centres. When the Market Inspectorate establishes that an infringement has taken place it cannot impose a fine but must bring proceedings in court. Market inspectors may issue rulings that require the infringement to be remedied, temporarily ban trading in particular goods or provision of particular services and temporarily close down a retail or wholesale outlet, or call for goods to be confiscated. The Market Inspectorate's remit is very broad and is governed by myriad laws and bylaws, which clearly impedes its efficiency and often leads to overlapping with other sectoral inspection services, including the Municipal Inspectorate. As regards its organisation, the Inspectorate is very fragmented, both horizontally and vertically, which hinders its effectiveness. Even though respondents in the Survey on Conditions for Doing Business in Serbia generally viewed it in a positive light, the Market Inspectorate scored slightly lower than both the Labour Inspectorate and the Tax Administration.

The Tax Administration was also less than efficient when uncovering tax evasion, which is the consequence of its lack of human and financial resources, inadequate staff structure, and systemic exchange of data with other government bodies aimed at discovering tax evasion. According to 2011 data the Republic of Serbia Tax Administration employed 6,165 staff, which is less than optimal given the number of taxpayers and international standards. Of the total number only 55 % have university degrees and the average age of employees is 49. In addition, many staff are tasked with receiving and technically processing tax filings, while the number of people carrying out tax audits is inadequate. The total budget of the Tax Administration is lower than necessary, and as a result salaries are low, which incentivises younger staff to leave after gaining experience in tax audit, which in turn has an adverse impact on audit quality and overall Tax Administration efficiency. The fact that business processes are not automated, that there is no cross-checking system to access and compare data from other government bodies (e.g., Real Estate Cadastre, Pension and Disability Insurance Fund, local Public Revenue Administrations, the police, etc.), that the mechanisms used to select taxpayers for audit are sub-optimal, and that the staff structure is inadequate, all result in a low likelihood of uncovering tax evasion, which serves as an incentive to operate in the informal sector.

9.2 Recommendations for Formalising the Shadow Economy

9.2.1 Strategy for Formalising the Shadow Economy

A successful policy to formalise the shadow economy must reduce the entry of new participants and foster the formalisation of existing participants by moving their activities from the shadow to the formal economy. This requires a strategy that addresses the root causes and mechanisms that contribute to its development: excessive tax burden, over-regulation of economic activity, and weak and ineffective government bodies. The causes of the shadow economy are many and varied and multiple methods are needed to reintegrate it with formal channels. Policies designed to reduce the shadow economy can be divided into general reforms that address the shadow economy by building a favourable environment for doing business in the formal sector, incentives directly aimed at the shadow economy, and building the administrative capacity of the state.

Business entities decide how to operate on the basis of their assessment of the costs and benefits associated with doing business in either the formal or the shadow economy. Therefore any policy aimed at formalising the shadow economy should change the cost-benefit ratio for both the shadow and the formal economies.

There have been frequent attempts to change this cost-benefit ratio in the shadow economy by increasing administrative repression (i.e., through better detection and greater penalties). The policy for reducing the extent of the shadow economy pursued by most European countries up until 2000 was founded on exactly these repressive measures (Williams et al. 2008). However, the experiences of these countries, as well as of Serbia and Yugoslavia since the 1990s, show that this is neither the only nor the best avenue of approach, since relying solely on repressive methods without tackling the underlying causes of the shadow economy decreases economic activity by reducing the shadow economy without a corresponding increase in the formal economy (Krstić et al. 1998; Williams 2005). The use of repressive measures does, however, yield good results when the aim is to prevent entities joining the informal economy or to close down businesses already operating in the shadow economy, rather than to move business entities from the shadow to the formal economy.

Another means of changing the cost-benefit ratio in the shadow economy is to use various measures to reduce the benefits enjoyed by entities operating in it. This can be accomplished primarily by cutting costs (reducing the burden of taxes and business regulations) and increasing the benefits in the formal economy (e.g. by providing access to incentives and loans) in order to make operating in this sector more attractive. This can be achieved through preventive measures and incentives. Preventive measures can prevent the emergence of the shadow economy by reducing the tax burden and allowing new types of formal work. Preventive measures are directly aimed at participants in the shadow economy and are intended to induce them to formalise their operation. They include amnesties at the individual or general level for those wishing to join the formal sector, business advisory and support services, and targeted direct and indirect tax breaks for employing declared workers.

The practical task and key challenge for economic policy in Serbia is to develop a well-balanced combination of incentives and sanctions that will maximise the formalisation of participants in the shadow economy—businesses, entrepreneurs, and workers—and result in the loss of as little GDP or overall employment as possible. Ideally, the admixture of these incentives and penalties should comprise incentives aimed at incorporating those population groups that are excluded from the formal economy and re-integrating businesses and entrepreneurs that have left the formal economy due to high taxes, rigid regulations, or the economic crisis; and sanctions designed to discourage voluntary, opportunistic use of the shadow economy to generate excessive profits through illegal cost-cutting.

The key prerequisite for a successful strategy to formalise the shadow economy is to complete transition and stabilise the legal and institutional structures of society, and then achieve and maintain macroeconomic stability and create preconditions for economic growth. The impact of these factors on the shadow economy is just one of their many desirable effects. The econometric findings presented in Chap. 6 indicate that an increase in registered GDP leads to a drop in the extent of the shadow economy. In other words, if GDP were to decline in the future the shadow economy would increase, since business entities would endeavour to compensate for fewer business opportunities in the formal sector by working in the shadow economy. In these circumstances the measures proposed will not be fully effective.

The econometric analysis shows that there are no statistically significant differences in the involvement of individual sectors in the shadow economy, except for in construction and trade. Thus the proposed measures for formalising the shadow economy are mainly sector-neutral; i.e., address all sectors equally. An exception to this is measures aimed at the construction sector and some services.

We propose a set of preventive measures and incentives aimed at formalising the shadow economy that cover tax policy and regulation, labour market institutions, and the financial sector. The recommendations that entail building the administrative capacity of government bodies relate primarily to the institutions that oversee businesses with informal employees and/or that make and receive cash payments: the Tax Authority, the Labour Inspectorate, and the Market Inspectorate. These recommendations are based on the analysis of the operation of these institutions presented in the preceding chapter. Table 9.1 at the end of this chapter shows the key recommendations for formalising the shadow economy for each of these areas, their sectoral coverage, the institutions responsible for conducting such measures, and the expected outcomes of their implementation.

9.2.2 Fiscal Policy Measures

Fiscal policy includes tax policy, public expenditures policy, and public debt management. The main factors affecting the formalization of the shadow economy are the characteristics of the tax and public expenditures system, while public debt policy does not have a substantial bearing on the informal sector.

The key measures that can be applied to combat the shadow economy within the framework of tax policy are:

- Reducing distortions introduced by taxes;
- Reducing tax compliance costs;
- Reducing the return to tax evasion, and
- Reducing tolerance of the shadow economy.

Table 9.1 Recommendations for formalising the shadow economy

Fiscal policy			
Measure	Sectoral coverage	Institutions	Expected outcome
Reduce fiscal burden on labour (see section on features of the labour market)	All sectors	Ministry of Finance and Economy	Lower extent of shadow economy in employment and medium-term increase in rate of registered employment
Remove tax breaks for corporate income tax and harmonise taxation of property of both individuals and legal entities	All sectors	Ministry of Finance and Economy	Less distortion generated by tax system and legal tax avoidance. Slight increase in public revenue
Reduce and simplify tax procedures	All sectors	Ministry of Finance and Economy/Tax Administration	Lower cost of administering taxes and greater readiness of taxpayers to pay taxes
Increase number of Tax Administration staff engaged in audits, improve their qualifications, and improve methodology used in selecting entities to be audited	All sectors	Ministry of Finance and Economy/Tax Administration	Greater cost of tax evasion and, consequently, less evasion
Improve consistency of implementation of statutory penalties for tax evasion	All sectors	Ministry of Finance and Economy/Tax Administration/courts	Greater cost of tax evasion and, consequently, less evasion
Ban sale of new industrial products in flea markets, farmers' markets, and roadside stalls	All sectors	Municipal Police	Reduction in volume of shadow economy in trade in goods
Register unregistered buildings for tax purposes	All sectors	Ministry of Finance and Economy/Local Tax Authorities/Cadastre	Fewer untaxed buildings
Reassign Tax Administration staff from administrative tasks to uncovering visible tax evasion (online, at catering establishments, etc.)	All sectors	Ministry of Finance and Economy/Tax Administration	Reduction in volume of shadow economy in trade in goods/services
Broaden application of statutory provisions for cross-checking property and income	All sectors	Ministry of Finance and Economy/Tax Administration	Less evasion of income tax

(continued)

Table 9.1 (continued)

Fiscal policy			
Measure	Sectoral coverage	Institutions	Expected outcome
Improve co-ordination between Tax Administration and other government bodies (police, social security funds, cadastre, local tax authorities, Business Registries Agency, Central Securities Depository, etc.), particularly in exchange of information	All sectors	Ministry of Finance and Economy/Tax Administration/Police/Cadastre/Central Securities Depository/Business Registries Agency	Greater probability of detecting unreported income and property
Improve activity by government in collecting taxes on reported income	All sectors	Ministry of Finance and Economy	Less reported and uncollected taxes
Credible commitment by state to abandoning practice of writing off interest on back taxes	All sectors	Ministry of Finance and Economy	Greater readiness of taxpayers to settle tax liabilities on time
Educate the public about the importance and value of services provided by the government and the drawbacks of the shadow economy through the public education system and the media	All sectors	Government of Serbia/Ministry of Education and Science/Ministry of Culture and Information	Greater tax morality
Invest effort in systematically improving the quality of public services (education, healthcare, administrative procedures, etc.)	Public services	Government of Serbia/all Ministries	Greater readiness of taxpayers to pay taxes
Features of the labour market			
Measure	Sectoral coverage	Institutions	Expected outcome
Lower fiscal burden on lower-paid work by increasing of tax-exempt allowance to level of minimum wage	All sectors	Ministry of Finance and Economy	Greater formal employment of lower-qualified workers, particularly in labour-intensive sectors
Remove minimum base for social insurance contributions	All sectors	Ministry of Finance and Economy	Greater formal employment of part-time workers, particularly those earning less

(continued)

Table 9.1 (continued)

Fiscal policy			
Measure	Sectoral coverage	Institutions	Expected outcome
Introduce more favourable tax treatment for 'mini' and 'midi' jobs	All sectors	Ministry of Finance and Economy	Greater formal employment of part-time workers, particularly those earning less
Introduce more favourable tax treatment for seasonal workers in agriculture, catering, tourism and construction	Agriculture, catering, tourism, construction	Ministry of Finance and Economy	Greater registered employment in seasonal jobs
Consider introduction of different contribution rates by sector or progressive social security contributions	Not defined	Research institutions	Based on findings of study
Reduce minimum wage from current level of 50 % of average wage to around or under 40 %	All sectors	Social and Economic Council	Increase in formal employment of minimum-wage earners
Reduce increased hourly rates for overtime work	All sectors	Ministry of Labour, Employment and Social Policy	Increase in formal hours worked by employees
Link severance payments to years of service with last employer rather than total years of service	All sectors	Ministry of Labour, Employment and Social Policy	Increase in formal employment of older workforce
Extend maximum duration of fixed-term contracts to 3 years	All sectors	Ministry of Labour, Employment and Social Policy	Increase in formal employment of younger workforce
Increase retirement age threshold, introduce actuarial adjustment of pensions to reflect expected use of retirement payments	All sectors	Ministry of Labour, Employment and Social Policy	Increase in formal employment of older workforce
Introduce in-work benefits	All sectors	Ministry of Labour, Employment and Social Policy	Greater activity and formal employment of beneficiaries of social welfare payments and other transfers
Support formal self-employment through grants and start-up loans	All sectors	Ministry of Labour, Employment and Social Policy and National Employment Service	Shift from informal employment into formal self-employment

(continued)

Table 9.1 (continued)

Fiscal policy			
Measure	Sectoral coverage	Institutions	Expected outcome
Introduce micro-lending facilities	All sectors	Ministry of Finance and Economy and National Bank of Serbia	Shift from informal employment into formal self-employment; increase in self-employment
Increase powers of Labour and Market Inspectorates, including entitling inspectors to audit unregistered businesses and impose penalties	All sectors, particularly those with major presence of informal activities	Ministry of Labour, Employment and Social Policy, Ministry of Trade and Telecommunications, and Ministry of Justice	Less informal employment in both formal and informal businesses
Introduce risk assessment and risk management system in inspection oversight	All sectors, particularly those with major presence of informal activity	Ministry of Labour, Employment and Social Policy, Ministry of Trade and Telecommunications	Less informal employment in both formal and informal businesses
Financial sector			
Measure	Sectoral coverage	Institutions	Expected outcome
Curb transactions in cash and incentivise cashless payments (incentives vs. repressive measures)	Services, hospitality, construction, transportation, trade	Ministry of Finance and Economy, NBS, commercial banks	Less concealment of portions of income generated in cash; substantial decrease in informal cash payments
Reduce extent of informal finance	All sectors	Ministry of Finance and Economy, NBS, commercial banks and other financial intermediaries	Less uncertainty, efficient allocation of funds, greater employment and more fiscal revenue from formal activity. Greater supply of finance would affect its cost and availability
Formalise remittances from abroad transferred through informal channels	Trade, other services, hospitality, construction, and potentially other sectors	NBS, Ministry of Finance and Economy, commercial banks and other financial intermediaries	Greater competition and lower costs of formal money transfers would stimulate migrant interest in transferring remittances through formal channels. This should foster domestic saving and new investment

(continued)

Table 9.1 (continued)

Fiscal policy			
Measure	Sectoral coverage	Institutions	Expected outcome
Business environment			
Measure	Sectoral coverage	Institutions	Expected outcome
Resolve issue of 'phoenix companies' (and consider establishing registry of bans imposed on business owners and managers in criminal or other proceedings)	All sectors	Ministry of Finance and Economy/Business Registries Agency/ Courts	Tax evasion and non-payment of commercial liabilities prevented
Introduce SME Test and Standard Cost Model	All sectors	Government of Serbia/ Regulatory Reform Office	Undue increases of administrative costs and obstacles to doing business in formal sector prevented
Simplify regulatory (administrative) requirements	All sectors	Government of Serbia/ Regulatory Reform Office	Lower administrative burden; constraints to business operations removed
Improve regulatory framework to enable relevant stakeholders to take part in the consultation process	All sectors	Government of Serbia	Private sector participates in consultation and law drafting process; constraints to doing business and incentives for shadow economy reduced
Adopt bylaws in a timely fashion	All sectors	Government of Serbia	Legal insecurity removed
Reduce unfair competition	All sectors	Ministry of Foreign and Internal Trade and Telecommunications	Lower share of shadow economy in trade in goods
Establish an e-portal for licences, permits, approvals, and consents	All sectors	Government of Serbia	Lower start-up costs
Remove barriers to entry to particular sectors	Multiple sectors	Multiple regulatory bodies	Lower start-up costs and fewer barriers to entry
Establish a publicly accessible electronic legislation registry	All sectors	Government of Serbia	Lower cost of doing business
Improve construction permitting process	Construction	Ministry of Construction and Urban Planning/local authorities	Easier start-ups; less employment of workers and businesses from informal sector

(continued)

Table 9.1 (continued)

Fiscal policy			
Measure	Sectoral coverage	Institutions	Expected outcome
'Legalise' buildings without permits	All sectors	Ministry of Construction and Urban Planning	Making assets tradable, fungible and wholly available for legal transactions
Outreach	All sectors	Government of Serbia	Less tax evasion; or more incentive to shift from shadow to formal economy

Reducing Distortions Introduced by Taxes

The extent of distortions introduced by taxes stands in proportion to the square of the tax rate, meaning that higher tax rates also introduce higher distortions. Tax rates in Serbia are generally relatively low, and so the distortions are not substantial. An exception to this rule is the total fiscal burden on labour, which stands at some 39 % in Serbia, slightly lower than in developed EU member states but greater than in countries at similar levels of development (Arsić et al. 2010). Therefore total taxes on labour in Serbia are high and create incentives for tax evasion. The high tax burden is a particular constraint on labour-intensive sectors of activity such as the textile industry and services. A major reduction in the fiscal burden on labour would have a positive impact on the readiness of taxpayers to actually pay their taxes. Detailed recommendations on the taxation of labour are presented in the following section, which deals with measures aimed at the labour market.

In addition to the high fiscal burden on labour, the highest marginal rate[1] of the regular annual property tax, standing at 2 %, is considered to be relatively high and serves to foster various forms of tax evasion. Any reform of property tax, assuming this type of taxation remains progressive, should therefore limit the top marginal tax rate to 1 %. This change would not have much significance for the budget, but would be justified from the point of view of both reducing the shadow economy and enhancing efficiency and equity.

Distortions introduced by taxes also depend on the number of tax rates, breaks, and exemptions for each type of tax, special tax regimes, etc. The more rates there are for each personal income tax, the greater the opportunities for tax evasion. In general, the Serbian tax system is well designed in this respect and does not offer much incentive for tax evasion. It would, however, be desirable for future reforms of the VAT framework to gradually introduce a single tax rate, as this would reduce the scope for tax evasion. The most tax breaks and exemptions apply to corporate

[1] The marginal tax rate is calculated by dividing the increase in tax by the increase in the tax base.

income tax. Although these breaks for the most part do not contribute to the shadow economy, they nonetheless facilitate tax avoidance and tax fraud, and as such should be gradually abolished.

Reduce Tax Compliance Costs

Greater costs associated with administering taxes encourage taxpayers to evade them. The tax compliance costs grow larger as the number of taxes in the system increase, become more complicated, as the number of payments per year increases, and as e-filing opportunities become more limited. The tax compliance costs are particularly relevant for small taxpayers (e.g., small and micro-businesses, entrepreneurs) whose incomes are low. One of the main measures to reduce tax compliance costs is continual re-examination of the justification for numerous fiscal and quasi-fiscal charges. Complicated and unclear tax regulations increase tax compliance costs and facilitate accidental or deliberate tax evasion. However, the assessment of some taxes—such as the corporate income tax—is not aligned with international accounting standards, which increases compliance costs, particularly for foreign companies doing business in Serbia. Although the divergence of accounting standards from international practice is probably not a major cause of the shadow economy, bringing them into line with global standards is important in improving general conditions for doing business in Serbia.

Simplifying tax procedures to cut the number of tax payments each year would increase e-payment options, reduce tax compliance costs, and increase the readiness of taxpayers to pay their taxes voluntarily.

Reforming the system of quasi-fiscal charges is an important precondition for improving the business environment and reducing the costs of doing business. The reform process begun in 2012 with the removal of 138 individual dues is an important step towards improving the business environment; it has resulted in the abolishment of many unjustified charges and the definition of statutory procedures for the introduction of new dues; moreover, all charges are now paid into the national budget. Besides removing the remaining unjustified charges, future efforts should focus on combining similar fees and appropriately naming and categorising them. It is particularly important to improve the parameters used in defining the charges that are justified: these include adjusting the tax burden to the financial strength of each taxpayer, aligning fees with the expenses associated with the provision of a service by the government, and bringing the amounts of charges into line with the benefits enjoyed or damage caused by the payer. Systemic limitations need to be introduced to avoid a return to an economically distorting and unfair system of quasi-fiscal charges. With this in mind, it is important to again apply the gross budget principle consistently, as well as to introduce any fiscal and quasi-fiscal dues exclusively by law.

Reduce the Return to Tax Evasion

Tax evasion can be viewed as a rational choice on the part of taxpayers that depends on the cost-benefit ratio of evading taxes. Hence, to reduce tax evasion its benefits must be reduced and its costs increased. An increase in the costs of tax evasion can be brought about by increasing the probability of detection, as well as by increasing penalties in the case of evasion. Empirical research shows that increasing the probability of detection is a greater deterrent to evasion than imposing harsher penalties. Reforming the Tax Administration is the one decisive precondition for increasing the probability of detecting tax evasion: this means carrying out more frequent audits, while the probability of a taxpayer being audited should be based on the risk of that taxpayer actually committing tax evasion.

In addition, the probability of prosecuting tax evasion needs to be increased. For this to happen, systematic measures must be taken to tackle corruption at the Tax Administration, as well as to improve co-operation between the Tax Administration and other government bodies. Efficient prosecution of tax evasion cases also depends on changes to criminal legislation, training of judiciary bodies, and combating corruption within the judiciary.

Increase Tax Morals

The readiness of taxpayers to engage in evasion does not depend only on the cost-benefit ration, but also on their moral views of tax evasion. Moral views of how justified tax evasion is depend on numerous factors, such as tradition, how other taxpayers behave, the existence of privileged taxpayers, government tolerance of tax evasion, the quality of public services, etc. There are many ways in which governments can encourage taxpayers to regard evasion as immoral, such as incorporating anti-evasion messages into the education system and media campaigns. The readiness of individuals to pay taxes depends on the behaviour of other individuals and their estimated readiness to pay their taxes. If the government is consistent and unselective in tackling tax evasion, taxpayers will be more certain that others will pay and will be more willing to pay themselves.

Reduce Tolerance for the Shadow Economy

Tax evasion is more or less tolerated in most democratic societies, and the shadow economy is often treated as an activity that contributes to the social security of the less well-off. However, the high tolerance of the shadow economy in Serbia does not extend only to vulnerable groups. Reducing tolerance for the shadow economy in Serbia is necessary to reduce the extent of informal operations. This primarily entails consistently and unselectively banning activities that result in visible and noticeable tax evasion. Specifically, in the case of Serbia, this would entail:

- Introducing a ban on the sale of new industrial products in flea markets, farmers' markets, and roadside stalls.
- The fact that there are many untaxed buildings sends a clear message that the government tolerates the shadow economy.[2] A major increase in the reach of taxation of real property would clearly indicate that the government is becoming less tolerant of the shadow economy. To this end, national authorities could provide technical support to local bodies and introduce a system of incentives and penalties for local authorities dependant on their degree of success in increasing the reach of taxation and property tax collection.
- Many forms of shadow activity are openly engaged in via the Internet, classified ads in newspapers, etc. These could be prevented relatively easily, but this is not done due to the passive stance of the Tax Administration, which does not monitor new channels of tax evasion. Particularly significant in this respect is the widespread practice of catering establishments (restaurants, coffee bars, etc.) not issuing fiscal receipts or not assessing and paying VAT, although added value is high in this sector. This type of tax evasion can be uncovered without a great deal of additional training for tax inspectors, since evasion is obvious and easy to discover. Therefore, since the introduction of e-filing will release many Tax Administration staff from their current technical and administrative duties (receiving and certifying tax filings, entering data into the database, etc.), it is recommended that they be reassigned to audits of sectors where tax evasion is obviously taking place.
- Over the past several decades there have been clear discrepancies between the amount of property owned by many Serbian nationals and income reported to the Tax Administration. The absence of any reaction from the Tax Administration is a form of tolerance for tax evasion—and for tax evasion that has nothing to do with social security. Regulations on cross-checking property and income must be implemented without delay, and those individuals whose assets far exceed their declared income must be subject to ex-post income tax. The government's decision to finally implement statutory provisions allowing the cross-checking of property and reported income is a major step forward in tackling the shadow economy. That said, it is crucial to ensure that the Tax Administration continues to cross-check property and income rather than for this effort to be a one-off exercise. For these measures to succeed fully, the Tax Administration needs to co-operate with other government bodies in order to increase its capacity for uncovering the real owners of property in Serbia. Establishing sound co-operation with foreign tax authorities is also necessary to identify and appraise the assets that Serbian nationals hold abroad.

[2] According to Tax Administration estimates, some 15 % of flats in residential buildings, as well as office buildings, are untaxed; for individual houses, the figure stands at over 20 % (Arsić and Ranđelović 2012).

Encourage Taxpayers to Settle Reported Tax Liabilities Fully and on Time

The practice of companies making tax filings and then failing to pay is widespread in Serbia. The reason for this is in the poor liquidity of companies, which is often actually insolvency in disguise. The Tax Administration often tolerates this behaviour to avoid forcing taxpayers into formal insolvency, which generally ends in many workers losing their jobs. This indicates that non-payment of taxes in Serbia, even when not formally the result of the shadow economy, is a significant type of financial indiscipline that results in both lower fiscal revenues and less equality for business entities. Statutory limitations on payment deadlines in commercial transactions are a major step forward in establishing financial discipline. An advantage of the proposed measure is that the deadlines are the shortest in cases where the government owes money. Yet the reach of this measure is relatively constrained by the fact that financial indiscipline is primarily caused by the presence of insolvent businesses in the market. The decisive factor in establishing financial discipline, therefore, would be the efficient and non-selective implementation of bankruptcy procedures, which would remove insolvent entities from the market. In that context, the suspension of automatic insolvency by the Constitutional Court is a step backward. To establish financial discipline it is also important to raise prices charged by infrastructure operators so that they cover costs.

Abandon the Practice of Writing off Interest for Late Payment of Taxes

In addition to being the consequence of tolerating a large number of insolvent companies active in the market, fiscal indiscipline is also partly caused by the periodical reductions in and write-offs of back taxes. Over the past two decades Serbia has, from time to time (generally just before or after a general elections), written off interest on corporate back taxes. Given the high inflation rate in Serbia, when interest is written off, so is part of the principal that has decreased in value due to inflation. When inflation is taken into account, a zero interest rate on tax liabilities actually becomes a negative interest rate. So, for instance, if interest on 3-year-old back taxes is written off, assuming inflation stands at 10 % per year, the principal of the tax debt will lose 27 % of its value. By writing off interest on back taxes the government systematically rewards non-conscientious taxpayers and directly encourages moral hazard. This means that some taxpayers who are eminently able to pay their taxes choose to wait for interest to be written off and their tax debt reduced. Writing off interest on tax debts hurts the level playing field for all participants in the market and fosters negative selection, whereby undisciplined taxpayers are rewarded and disciplined ones are not.

The adoption of a new Law on the Write-Off of Interest for Late Payment of Taxes will temporarily improve liquidity in the economy, as well as the inflow of funds to the budget. However, the long-term effects of this law on financial discipline will be markedly negative, since it represents the continuation of the practice of periodically rewarding undisciplined taxpayers by writing off a portion of the real value of their principal debt along with nominal interest. Thus the practice of writing off interest on back taxes should be discontinued, since it rewards non-compliance and enables insolvent companies to remain in the market.

Improve the Quality of Services Provided by the Government

Taxes are the price that the public pays for services provided by the government. Thus the readiness of the public to pay taxes depends on the actual volume and quality of public services, and on individual perceptions of the provided services. Low quality of public services, unproductive expenditure, and corruption affect the readiness of the public to pay their taxes. Improving the efficiency of the government by enhancing the quality and availability of its services (from security and justice to education and healthcare) is important for tackling the shadow economy.

Educate the Public About the Importance and Value of Services Provided by the Government

In addition to improving the quality of government services it is necessary for the government to work on the perception of the public regarding the value of those services. The public often underestimate the value of the services provided by the government: a year of elementary school, certain forms of healthcare, social security, agricultural subsidies, etc. This bias creates a widespread conviction among the public that the taxes they pay are much greater than the value of the services provided by the government. This belief, which is partly true, increases the willingness of people to not pay their taxes. It would be beneficial, therefore, for brochures to be periodically mailed to all households (modelled after the 'citizen's budget' prepared in many developed EU member states) explaining in clear and easily understandable language how much the government spends for what purpose and why it is important for individuals and businesses to pay their taxes regularly.

9.2.3 *Measures Relating to Features of the Labour Market*

Taxation of Labour

The most important recommendation in the field of labour taxation pertains to the need to substantially reduce labour costs for lower-paying jobs. Any kind of reform of labour taxation (or, in a broader sense, of the taxation of income derived from work) should ideally entail an increase in the tax-exempt personal allowance to the level of the minimum wage. Most European countries employ this practice.

Tax allowances for family dependents in Serbia are available only to annual income tax payers, i.e., the richest 1 % of the population. Introducing a tax-exempt allowance for dependents would reduce the tax burden of employees with an unemployed spouse and children, and thereby reduce their incentives for joining the shadow economy.

Another means of reducing the tax burden on lower wages would be the removal of the minimum social security base, which now stands at 35 % of the average wage. While its impact on people working full-time jobs is negligible since the minimum wage is far above this level, it increases labour costs for part-time workers with standard open-ended employment contracts.

In addition to removing the minimum base for social insurance, an important incentive to formalising informal employees working part-time jobs would be the introduction of less restrictive tax treatment of so-called 'mini jobs' and 'midi jobs', based on the positive experiences of Germany (Eurofound 2008) where healthcare and social security contributions for mini jobs (defined by the wages earned rather than by hours worked) are much lower than standard, while the rate of income tax can even equal zero. Midi jobs (where wages lie between those of mini jobs and standard employment) attract contributions that are greater than those for mini jobs but are still lower than standard. These rules ensure that workers in mini jobs avoid the trap of wage poverty and ease their transition into standard employment.

Seasonal workers in agriculture, tourism, and other seasonal activities may find the Montenegrin solution beneficial: employers there are required to pay a fixed amount per day for each seasonal employee.

Some countries have also introduced progressive contributions for social security or contribution rates that differ by sector, with labour-intensive, lower-paying sectors of activity (where the shadow economy is generally more widespread) paying contributions at lower-than-standard rates. Empirical, theoretical, and legislative arguments for and against the introduction of such differentiated rates in Serbia deserve careful consideration.

Minimum Wage Regulation

To avoid driving down the demand for formal work, the minimum wage should be reduced from the current level of 50 % to some 35 %–40 % of the average wage, as was the case in Serbia until several years ago and as recommended by the World Bank for middle-developed countries. Moreover, the introduction of a slightly lower minimum wage for youth under 25 years of age should be considered, to stimulate their open-ended employment. Similarly, the minimum wage could vary slightly by region so as to partly reflect regional differences in the cost of living (which is slightly higher in Belgrade than in the rest of Serbia).

Working Hours Regulation

The body of regulations governing working hours should be carefully analysed to see which of the current standards are more costly for employers or do not benefit workers, and an effort should be made to change them. The suggestions made below are based on comparative data on prevailing practices in OECD countries and on employers' most common complaints.

- Slightly reduce increased hourly rates for overtime and work on weekends and holidays.
- Allow more flexible re-allocation of working hours, both within the working week and for longer periods of time, subject to the consent of both employee and employer.
- Allow annual leave to be used as agreed between employee and employer.

Employment Protection Legislation

The most urgent requirement in this respect is the removal of the statutory provision obliging employers to pay employees severance in proportion to each employee's total years of service rather than only years of service spent with that employer. This would foster formal employment, primarily of elderly workers with work experience.

In addition, the maximum length of employment under individual fixed-term contracts should be extended from 1–2 or 3 years. This change would probably not have a major impact, as breaches of this rule are rife, with businesses extending such contracts beyond the statutory maximum by manipulating job titles. Nonetheless, this change must be made to give the most compliant businesses (frequently foreign investors, who are also the ones objecting the most to this provision) more flexibility in adjusting the volume and structure of their workforce. In addition, a better general principle is to comply with a good rule than not to comply with a bad one.

Retirement Rules

An increase in the formal employment of elderly workers, as well as a parallel drop in their undeclared work, would be achieved by raising the current retirement age threshold, introducing actuarial adjustment of pensions to reflect the life expectancy of people who retire earlier, and providing for actuarial rewards for those who continue to work and pay pension contributions after meeting conditions for full retirement, regardless of whether they receive pensions or not.

Welfare Benefits

In Serbian practice, welfare benefits are available almost exclusively to unemployed and inactive persons, which lead those who are able to work to combine welfare and informal employment. To incentivise employment in the formal sector, an in-work benefits programme should be introduced along the lines of the US Earned Income Tax Credit, which would make it possible for workers to combine formal employment and welfare benefits, with the latter gradually reduced as earnings increase.

Specific Measures Targeting Informal Employment

Evaluations show that various specific measures targeting informal employment are more beneficial than a blanket reduction in tax rates, which can have much broader implications and not sufficiently reflect a reduction in the shadow economy (Eurofound 2008).

An example of a targeted programme is support for formal self-employment. This measure is applied in Serbia by the National Employment Service (NES), and it involves a one-off non-repayable grant and some in-kind support, provided that the beneficiary regularly pays contributions and taxes for at least the following 2 years. On average, some 3,000–5,000 people per year become self-employed through this programme; NES staff estimate that most of them merely formalise their informal businesses. It is interesting to note that evaluations show that entrepreneurs who have been legalised have higher survival rates than those who start businesses without previous experience in the informal sector.

Some European countries apply a broader range of support measures to ease the shift from unemployment or informal employment towards formal self-employment. A special programme is available in the Netherlands that offers tax breaks for relatives and other persons who lend start-up money to those without jobs. Germany subsidises the unemployed who start their own business for 3 years; the subsidies decrease gradually over the course of the 3-year period (Eurofound 2008). In Serbia unemployed persons can receive the entire amount of unemployment benefits to which they are entitled in advance, on condition they use the money for self-employment.

Microlending is also a measure that facilitates the establishment of legal sole proprietorships, especially for those categories of people who cannot rely on their own funds or commercial credit. Formal borrowing is believed to increase the likelihood of a business becoming formal (Eurofound 2008).

Recommendations for Improving the Efficiency of the Labour Inspectorate in Tackling Undeclared Work

An analysis of the position, operation, and volume of activities undertaken by the Labour Inspectorate shows that this body has been achieving relatively good results in terms of addressing undeclared work, given the constraints on its operation imposed by regulations, limited human resources, and lack of other capacities. This finding is further borne out by the fact that 56 % of all respondents in the Survey on Conditions for Doing Business in Serbia awarded good marks (4 and 5 on a scale from one to five) to the Labour Inspectorate, while a mere 12 % gave it poor marks (1 and 2 on a scale from one to five). This result is slightly better than that achieved by the other two institutions in charge of tackling the shadow economy, the Tax Administration and Market Inspectorate.

As has already been demonstrated using a multitude of examples, one of the key problems in the operation of the Labour Inspectorate is the lack of co-ordination and integration with other inspection and oversight services. This problem could be overcome by integrating the various inspection services into an Inspectorate-General (of which the Labour Inspectorate would be a part) to achieve synergy and avoid duplication of activities, while at the same time establishing a consistent system that would be more efficient at preventing some of the most dangerous participants in the shadow economy (such as ‘phantom companies’) from operating with virtual impunity by using loopholes in existing legislation.

Changes to legislation should be considered that would allow labour inspectors to access and examine all premises where business is conducted, regardless of whether the entities in question are formally registered or not. In addition, it would be beneficial to allow labour inspectors to impose fines as part of a simplified procedure.

A long-standing complaint of the Labour Inspectorate is that they have too few people and too much work, and that the number of inspectors needs to be increased substantially if optimal results are to be achieved. Inspectors are well qualified, and nearly all of them have university degrees. The Inspectorate has limited Information and Communication Technology (ICT) capacity. There are electronic linkages with the Business Registries Agency and an internal analytics and planning database has been developed. However, the Inspectorate cannot establish direct links with business records, the Tax Administration, the National Employment Service, or social security organisations.

The key measures for removing administrative barriers are better co-operation between the Labour Inspectorate and the Tax Administration, social security organisations, the police, and courts. Moreover, co-operation with the National Employment Service is tenuous: the database of people receiving unemployment assistance is not available to the Inspectorate, which is an issue that needs to be resolved.

Recommendations for Improving the Efficiency of the Market Inspectorate in Tackling the Shadow Economy

The broadest recommendation in an institutional sense entails the drafting of a framework Inspections Law, harmonised with European Union regulations, to ensure better mutual co-ordination of inspection oversight and better delimitation of the powers of the various inspection services. This piece of legislation would also allow the closure of numerous loopholes in the powers of inspection bodies that have made it possible for the shadow economy to flourish and have hindered the implementation of activities designed to combat it. A commission to co-ordinate inspection oversight should be established as quickly as possible. The advantages of an integrated inspections approach are particularly obvious in the area of authority of the Market Inspectorate. A unified database of offenders and offences, accessible to all inspection services, the Tax Administration, the Customs Administration, and the police, would improve the efficiency of the fight against the shadow economy. The integration of powers would mean that inspectors that uncover an unregistered or unreported entity or person engaging in an activity under the remit of another inspection agency would be both authorised and required to demand that any deficiencies be remedied and to notify the Tax Administration of the infringement and the measures taken.

Specific recommendations for improving the efficiency of the Market Inspectorate have been made as part of the Regulatory Reform Project and USAID BEP. In addition to the above, these include the need to re-organise it along territorial lines and reduce the number of regional units, as well as to strengthen its functional organisation to ensure more complete oversight of the trade in specific goods throughout the country. Furthermore, inspectors should act solely pursuant to audit orders: this would avoid arbitrariness and guarantee adherence to the hierarchy and transparency of inspection oversight. A risk assessment system should be introduced (to focus on the likelihood of non-compliance or infraction), as should a risk management system for inspection oversight. Among the changes needed are more training for inspectors, new software development, and better public information about the work of the Inspectorate. Periodic outreach campaigns should be organised aimed at both offenders and the general public; we will go into this issue in greater detail at the end of this chapter.

9.2.4 Measures Relating to the Financial Sector

Curb Transactions in Cash and Incentivise Cashless Payments

Cash transactions involve money changing hands without the use of bank accounts, and are also termed 'cash-in-hand' payments. These transactions are not formally registered. In addition, in highly dollarised economies such payments are predominantly made and received in foreign currency.

Cashless and, particularly, electronic payments are among the means that can be used to reduce the volume of cash transactions, both formal and informal. Electronic payments therefore make it more difficult for parties to operate in the informal sector (Schneider 2011).

In the case of Serbia, an anti-crisis measure exempting certain entities from the requirement to use fiscal cash registers does not seem to have resulted in better reporting of cash transactions, nor in a decrease in the shadow economy. On the contrary, it has facilitated informal cash transactions.

In addition to reducing the volume of cash transactions, greater use of cashless payments would increase reporting, particularly by businesses and small entrepreneurs, and thereby make it impossible to conceal any portion of revenue generated in cash. Several measures can be implemented to boost the share of cashless (primarily electronic) payments in Serbia.

Incentives need to be preferred over repressive measures against the use of cash in financial transactions. Given the rapid pace of technological development, it is relatively easy to allow payments using electronic money so that sellers of goods and services are compelled to offer electronic payments in sectors presently dominated by cash payments (catering, taxi cabs, etc.). There are also many incentives that can be used, such as subsidising point-of-sale terminals for small and micro-businesses, limited tax incentives for electronic payments (as introduced by Argentina, Colombia, and South Korea), and prepaid cards for people without bank accounts to enable their inclusion in the formal sector. On the macroeconomic level, government subsidies and assistance could be paid out electronically, as could various types of contributions (as is the case in Russia). Further, all government payments could be limited to electronic channels only.

Cash payments can be constrained directly. For instance, an Italian law dubbed the *Decreto Bersani* (D. Lgs. 7/2007) imposes a €100 limit on cash payments for professional services on pain of a strict prison sentence.[3] Bulgaria is an interesting example when it comes to applying restrictive measures. In 2011, Bulgaria introduced a law restricting cash payments, which sets out conditions for limiting payments in cash in its territory, which should reduce the extent of the shadow economy (Bulgarian Ministry of Finance 2011). Besides the implementation of measures aimed at limiting cash payments, more effort should be put into educating users of payment cards about their uses and benefits.

Moreover, economic policymakers should reach a clear consensus on the application of a de-euroisation strategy. This would contribute to a substantial reduction in cash payments—particularly informal ones—throughout the system. The

[3] In addition to simplifying start-up procedures (Art. 9), the *Decreto Bersani*, adopted in 2007 (D. Lgs. 7/2007) introduced strict penalties for activities in the shadow economy. As such, it is a good example of measures designed to tackle informal activity. The penalty for a construction company employing undeclared workers is the closure of its construction site. A retail outlet caught not issuing fiscal receipts three times in 5 years can be closed down permanently. Finally, the *Decreto Bersani* prohibits cash payments of more than €100 for professional services rendered.

environment would then favourably affect macroeconomic stability, further driving down the shadow economy.

Finally, to ensure that the remaining cash transactions take place primarily within formal channels, field audits should be strengthened to ensure fiscal cash registers are used and receipts are issued for all transactions.

Formalise Remittances from Abroad Transferred Through Informal Channels

In the opinion of businesspeople, greater transfer of funds using formal channels (primarily the banking sector, money transfer agencies, and the post office) could be achieved by reducing transfer costs (commissions and fees). Greater formality would also increase transparency and facilitate the use of these funds to finance activities that contribute to the growth and development of the recipient country (Jongwanich 2007; Ratha and Mohapatra 2007; Ratha 2009; Ratha and Silwal 2012).[4] Serbia has high transfer costs compared with the global average, which has been estimated at about 9 % of funds remitted (World Bank 2012). What is more, in Serbia commission charges on incoming money transfers are higher for smaller amounts (in percentages), which disincentivises emigrants from sending money through formal channels.[5]

Greater competition of entities that transfer funds formally and lower transfer costs would increase migrant interest in sending remittances through formal channels and offer numerous benefits to recipients, who are mainly people with lower incomes. These benefits include easier access to financial institutions, cheaper finance available to a larger share of the population, lower investment risk due to easier diversification, and better education of recipients of remittances about alternative ways of using those funds.

Formal transfer channels should be easier to access, more reliable, faster, and cheaper than competing informal channels. The choice of more expensive formal and informal channels is often driven by the loss of anonymity inherent in bank transfers. Regulators of countries where funds are sent and received should enter into appropriate bilateral agreements to formalise and facilitate the transfer, channelling, and registration of funds received (see, for instance, the experience of Mexico in Hernández-Cos 2005). This process can take the form of a public-private partnership with the participation of financial institutions. Establishing closer co-operation between the banking sectors of countries where remittances

[4] The costs of transferring funds into Serbia using specialised money transfer agencies are, on average, 10–15 % (commission plus exchange rate difference), while the individual sums transferred average between €100 and €300 each.

[5] Several commercial banks in Serbia have, of their own accord, successfully cut remittance transfer costs severalfold to an average of 0.2–0.4 % of the sum remitted. This is an improvement, but still does not bring Serbia up to par with countries that apply fixed commission charges regardless of the amount remitted.

originate and receiving countries should reduce transaction costs and accelerate transfers using this formal channel.

To ensure adequate competition between institutions that participate in the transfer process, regulations governing the various players in the market need to be harmonised, giving due consideration to the protection of the services' clients. The role of the regulatory bodies would include oversight of transfers to reduce the risk of any form of abuse and mismanagement of funds and to increase client confidence in this transfer mechanism. A greater role for banks in the transfer of remittances should reduce transaction costs and increase the speed and reliability of the service. This could be achieved by developing a single clearing system to be shared by the participating countries.[6] Easier access by a greater share of the population to financial services provided by banks and other financial institutions should boost domestic savings and the use of remittances for investment.

Greater investment of remittance funds needs to be stimulated by a good investment climate in the migrants' country of origin and investment incentives (e.g., tax breaks). The Law on Foreign Exchange Operations (*Official Gazette of the Republic of Serbia*, No. 62/2006, Art. 29) and its amendments (*Official Gazette of the Republic of Serbia*, Nos. 31/2011 and 119/2012) make it possible to repatriate non-resident profits generated in the local economy after taxes are paid, unless otherwise specified.

Formalising the channels used for remittance inflows would also enhance the efficiency of the financial sector through economies of scale resulting from greater inflow of funds and more services provided (Gupta et al. 2009; Aggarwal et al. 2011). This would also allow for these institutions to become more involved in encouraging entrepreneurship and other investment by using the funds received to attract deposits and offer loans, advisory services, insurance, and custody operations. The largest banks would stand to benefit most from these transactions, as they could offer the greatest volume of services and reduce transaction costs the most. By providing affordable remittance transfer services, they could induce both migrants and their family members in the country of origin to purchase other profit-making services offered by the bank.

The stability of remittance inflows has led some developing countries (e.g., Turkey and countries in Latin America) to use them as collateral in new bank borrowing and on-lending cycles.

As the greatest share of remittances sent through formal channels are electronic transfers, appropriate infrastructure to access these funds needs to be put into place throughout the receiving country. The development of technical and IT infrastructure at the local level could be funded through public-private partnership, and the project approved by the development bank of the country in question or another regulatory body. A well-developed infrastructure to support money transfers from

[6] According to data made available by the Ministry of Religious Affairs and the Diaspora, the number of Serbian expatriates is estimated at about four million. Most remittances are sent from Western Europe, particularly Austria and Germany, as well as from Serbia's neighbours.

abroad would also facilitate access to other financial services (such as current accounts, savings accounts, and credit instruments) for a broader section of the population.

Further development of formal remittance transfer channels would, in time, lead to the development of innovative products to help migrants invest directly in their country of origin by, for instance, purchasing land or real estate.

Moreover, special programmes could be set up to combine remittances sent by groups of migrants with funds provided by the central government or local authorities to jointly finance infrastructure projects of local or public importance (such as schools, hospitals, roads, sports centres, churches, parks, irrigation, electricity supply, computers, medical supplies, etc.).

The sending and registration of remittances should be regulated gradually, so that these flows can be better studied and this segment of the market developed without excessive and hasty government intervention, which could retard or disincentivise additional remittance inflows.

These and other possible enhancements of the regulatory environment and the financial system would contribute to greater inflows of remittances into Serbia through formal channels and their more efficient channelling into investment, which can be expected to have a positive impact on the economic growth and development of the country.

9.2.5 Measures Related to the Business Environment

These measures that have an impact on the conditions for doing business will be examined from the point of view of whether they are aimed at business entities that already operate in the formal sector but carry out some or the majority of their activities in the shadow economy, or are directed at entities completely in the informal sector.

Measures Aimed at Business Entities Operating Partially in the Shadow Economy

Resolve the Issue and Consequences of 'Phoenix Companies'

'Phoenix companies', entities that transfer assets to a newly formed business while leaving debts vested in an old one, make a substantial contribution to the chain of illiquidity, primarily with regard to small and medium-sized businesses, which in these circumstances are forced to move part of their activities into the shadow economy. There are several options for resolving this issue. The first one involves the ex-post introduction of a special Registry of Bans, similar to the already extant Court Ban Registry, which would serve as a record of all bans imposed on managers and owners of businesses facing criminal or other proceedings (e.g., under

Art. 46 of the Misdemeanours Law, which provides for bans on the performance of a particular activity). Numerous countries have similar registration regimes in place (such as Estonia, Norway, the UK, Ireland, and Macedonia). Regardless of this, the Business Offences Law, Misdemeanours Law, and Criminal Code must begin to be consistently implemented, as they govern fraudulently causing insolvency and other business crimes that damage creditors and jeopardise the exercise of their rights. Another approach would ex-ante prohibit individuals from managing a business and establishing new entities when their existing business has been operating with a frozen bank account for in excess of a certain number of days, has not been filing financial reports, or has not been paying taxes. However, applying the second option might create the wrong incentives and penalise those who are not actually responsible so that introducing manager disqualification would prove counter-productive. In addition, regardless of which solution is adopted to ban operating in any capacity, both approaches will have shortcomings if regulations are not implemented consistently, as it will not be possible to prevent the establishment of new entities by other parties or foreign off-shore centres. Another option open to dishonest businesspeople is to establish several firms in advance as a precaution, and then use them one by one.

Impose Barriers to the Introduction of New Administrative Burdens by Requiring the Application of the SME Test and the Standard Cost Model[7]

The Small and Medium-Sized Enterprise (SME) Test is designed to assess the impact of new regulation on small and medium-sized businesses in order to avoid imposing disproportionately large burdens on them. Although Article 40(2) of the Rules of Procedure of the Serbian Government stipulates that a regulatory impact assessment should contain information on the costs that a new piece of legislation will impose on SMEs, this is not sufficiently comprehensive, and should be replaced by a provision requiring the inclusion of the SME Test as an integral part of the assessment. The SME Test should, above all, examine the proposed legislation from the point of view of its suitability for the SME sector to see whether SMEs should be partly or fully exempt from the new regulatory requirements, as well as estimate or quantify the annual costs faced by micro, small, and medium-sized enterprises. The Regulatory Reform Office has already developed the SME Test but it is yet to be implemented. The second approach involves the Standard Cost Model (SCM), which measures the overall administrative cost and the burden of new administrative requirements and has been developed by the Regulatory Reform Office in the form of a turnkey software application. The use of this tool is

[7] Since 2008 the European Union has been implementing the Small Business Act as a new framework for SME development policy. As the act is part of the *acquis communautaire*, its significance for EU candidate countries is also substantial. The SME Test is an integral part of the EU's regulatory impact assessment procedure.

yet to be mandated for amending administrative requirements or introducing new ones. The consistent and mandatory use of the SCM could prevent undue administrative burdens. Both methods have become integrated into the European Commission's regulatory impact assessments and are used in many EU member states.

Simplify Regulatory (Administrative) Requirements

The aim of the Comprehensive Regulation Reform effort and NALED's[8] (2012) *Grey Book V* is to identify, with the active participation of businesses themselves, administrative burdens and procedures that unduly constrain doing business and to find the simplest solutions for removing them. Practice has shown that the problems identified are resolved too slowly, which creates additional costs for business entities. Some issues, such as the removal of 'turnover and incoming payment ledgers' and the abolishing of complicated pregnancy and maternity leave procedures, have been in the pipeline for several years. Instead of acting on an ad hoc basis, the government needs to adopt a clear plan for removing unnecessary administrative requirements and report to the public on its realisation.

Regulate the Public Consultation Process

In contrast to European Union practice, stakeholder participation in the legislative process in Serbia is often unsatisfactory. In the EU a minimum of 8 weeks is set aside for public consultation. According to Transparency Serbia, statutory provisions governing public comment periods in Serbia are inadequate. Among other things, there is no pre-defined form of public debate and no sanctions if a public body fails to launch such a debate. Non-compliance with the law by public authorities is compounded by the frequently passive stance of business entities. There are multiple reasons for this behaviour. Businesses often lack the necessary time and resources or simply do not feel that they can change anything. Serbian laws stipulate that a public comment period is mandatory where a proposed piece of legislation significantly changes the statutory treatment of a particular area, or where the issues at hand are of particular interest to the public. Except for this requirement imposed on the legislator, public consultation is not governed in greater detail. In some cases there is no public comment period but it essentially takes place by other means (e.g., in roundtables, public gatherings, etc.). To improve the current situation the minimum requirement could be the posting of a proposed piece of legislation on the web site of a ministry or other regulator at least 8 weeks before that piece of legislation enters formal procedure. In addition, depending on the issues to be governed by the proposed regulations, as part of the

[8] National Alliance for Local Economic Development.

law drafting process consultation with local authorities and legitimate representatives of business and other professional associations must be improved.

Adopt Bylaws in a Timely Fashion

One of the fundamental causes of legal insecurity is lateness in the adoption of bylaws, which makes it impossible to implement laws. When bylaws are not adopted in due time, new laws cannot be implemented, while old legislation lapses.[9] Faced with this legal vacuum, business entities are often forced to make do without knowing whether they are operating in accordance with the law or if their activities fall within the scope of the shadow economy. The legal insecurity created by this situation has major consequences for the economy. There are several options that can be considered. One (admittedly extreme) option is not to allow a draft document (or bill) to begin the procedure of becoming law without all bylaws being ready. Another option is to make the existence of guidelines for drafting specific bylaws the minimum condition for beginning the procedure. A third option would be to make it impossible to implement a law without providing a detailed explanatory note stating how it will affect the private sector, including calculations of costs and a detailed consideration of the specific requirements to be governed by bylaws. Finally, realistic deadlines should be set for the adoption of bylaws.

Improved Protection from Unfair Competition

The Law on Trade prohibits unfair competition; that is, actions of a business aimed against another business that damage or may damage a competitor through untrue or insulting claims regarding that business, or through the sale of goods whose labels, packaging, or shape create justifiable confusion regarding the quality or other characteristics of such goods. However, there are substantial problems with the application of the law. The Ministry of Trade has introduced a Bill Amending and Supplementing the Law on Trade, currently undergoing parliamentary procedure, which includes a new article whereby businesses will be able to seek intangible damages for harm to their reputation arising from unfair competition. However, while this change will improve current legal framework, the implementation has to be substantially improved.

[9] According to an analysis carried out by NALED in 2012 (NALED 2012), only three bylaws were adopted before the deadline, 33 were adopted after the deadline, while in 163 cases the deadline expired before the bylaws were adopted.

Measures Directed at Business Entities Operating Wholly in the Informal Economy

Establish an E-Portal for Licences, Permits, Approvals, and Consents

Although reform of the registration process has made it much easier to incorporate a business entity, in some sectors of activity there remain a large number of administrative requirements that an entity must meet. When filing for permits and approvals, business entities often face administrative requirements that leave them unsure what to submit, which steps to take, or which body to contact. A solution already implemented in the region is an e-portal for licences, permits, approvals, and consents that would contain detailed information, directions, documents, and contacts to make it easier to start a business. Immediately after being incorporated, although formally registered, businesses often cannot legally engage in an activity while they wait for an approval or licence. To bridge this gap businesses begin doing part of their business in the informal sector, and continue doing so even when the licences are finally received. This e-portal could be made part of the e-Government web site and contain instructions for each individual sector. Another option would be to host it on the Business Registries Agency web site.

Remove Barriers to Entry in Particular Sectors

Over the past several years new requirements have appeared that business entities have to meet before they can begin operating in a particular sector of activity. While in some sectors these are justified, in others they are typical barriers to entry, set up to protect current participants in the market. Recent examples are the introduction of a solicitors' examination and the review of regulations governing the profession of tourist guide. If a portal for licences, permits, approvals, and consents is established, existing requirements could be analysed, some procedures could be simplified, and, finally, some requirements could be abolished. In addition, efficient implementation of the Competition Law plays a major role in removing barriers to entry and it must be substantially improved.

Establish an Authoritative Registry of Legislation Accessible to the Public Free of Charge

Among the constraints faced by new start-ups are the costs they must meet to obtain information that is, by its very nature, in the public domain. Small businesses usually rely on their bookkeepers or lawyers, but they should also be allowed to access a legislation database. Službeni Glasnik ('Official Gazette'), the public body tasked with publishing authoritative texts of legislation in the journal of the same name, has of its own initiative developed a database of legislation containing revised texts of current regulations and PDF files of the relevant issues of the Official Gazette where the regulations and their amendments are published. This database can be considered authoritative in the sense that all of its users are able to rely on the authenticity of the contents of the PDF files. Public access to this database would significantly reduce transaction costs at the level of the entire economy, and in particular would make it easier for new start-ups to operate and to reduce their expenses.

Construction Permits and 'Legalisation'

The construction permit procedure is inefficient and lengthy due to a very complicated system that involves filing for permits with a large number of entities. Unable to obtain permits, some business entities start construction illicitly, at great risk. Developers (or investors) hire workers from the informal sector and engage businesses and entrepreneurs that do not declare such work. Accelerating construction permit procedures, decentralising authority, establishing 'one-stop shops' at local authorities, changing the role of public entities in the permit procedure, harmonising procedures, drafting plans, etc. would all greatly contribute to shifting construction activities into the formal sector.[10]

Another serious issue is the 'legalisation' of buildings, i.e., the subsequent issuance of construction permits for unpermitted properties. According to available data, nearly 700,000 buildings constructed without permits have been reported to local authorities; sources indicate that there are 1.3 million unregistered buildings. This legalisation procedure must be simplified to incorporate clearly defined and restricted deadlines, while the fees for subsequent issuance of permits must be based on economic criteria.

9.2.6 *Outreach Campaigns*

Outreach campaigns should play a particularly important role in the implementation of the proposed measures, which should have an impact on reducing tax evasion and encourage entities to move from the informal to the formal sector. Outreach campaigns should clearly point out the risks and expenses associated with operating in the shadow economy and the benefits of formalisation, or aim to change their audiences' views of the morality of tax evasion.[11]

[10] Detailed proposals for resolving construction permit issues are presented in the Assessment of Constraints to Construction Permits in Serbia, prepared for the USAID Business Enabling Project (2012).

[11] The most important outreach campaigns in the region have been 'Take the Receipt' in Serbia in late 2004, and 'VAT is Your Money', which is still in progress in Montenegro.

These campaigns should be aimed at both participants in the transaction: where they focus on tax evasion their target should be both buyers and sellers and if the topic is employment they should target both employers and workers. The campaigns should be general but should focus on sectors where the shadow economy is most widespread (such as construction or transportation), or on particular social or demographic segments of the population (particularly on those groups, such as young people, who believe activities in the shadow economy are an acceptable form of behaviour).

The International Labour Organisation and the European Union recommend the use of information campaigns to combat the shadow economy. Education campaigns targeting taxpayers, the media, and the general public should be intensified to maximise impact.

References

Aggarwal R, Demirgüç-Kunt A, Martinez Peria MS (2011) Do workers' remittances promote financial development? J Dev Econ 96(2):255–264

Arsić M, Randjelović S (2012) Periodično oporezivanje imovine u Srbiji: Šta smo uradili i šta smo naučili. GIZ – studija u izradi

Arsić M, Altiparmakov N, Ranđelović S, Bućić A, Vasiljević D, Levitas T (2010) Tax policy in Serbia – looking forward. Foundation for the Advancement of Economics, Belgrade

Bulgarian Ministry of Finance (2011) The shadow economy: how to measure and model it. Brief methodological analyses. www.minfin.bg/document/9795:4

Eurofound (2008) Tackling undeclared work in the European Union. Eurofound, Dublin.

Gupta S, Pattilo CA, Wagh S (2009) Effect of remittances on poverty and financial development in sub-Saharan Africa. World Dev 37(1):104–115

Hernández-Cos R (2005) The U.S.–Mexico remittance corridor – lessons on shifting from informal to formal transfer systems. World Bank Working Paper No. 47. The World Bank, Washington, DC

Jongwanich J (2007) Workers' remittances, economic growth and poverty in developing Asia and Pacific countries. UNESCCAP Working Paper, WP/07/01

Krstić G et al (1998) Analysis of the grey economy in the FRY with estimates of its volume for 1997 and recommendations for its legalisation. Economics Institute Belgrade

NALED (2012) Siva knjiga 5 - Preporuke za uklanjanje administrativnih prepreka za poslovanje u Srbiji 2012/2013

Ratha D (2009) Remittances in development: a lifeline to poor countries. Finance and Dev 46(4)

Ratha D, Mohapatra S (2007) Increasing the macroeconomic impact of remittances on development. In: Development Prospects Group. The World Bank, Washington, DC

Ratha D, Silwal A (2012) The World Bank – migration and development brief, 18

Schneider F (2011) The shadow economy in Europe – using payment systems to combat the shadow economy. http://www.bblf.bg/uploads/files/file_378.pdf

Schneider F, Enste D (2000) Shadow economies: size, causes and consequences. J Econ Lit 38 (1):77–114

USAID Business Enabling Project (2012) Assessment of constraints to construction permits in Serbia
Williams CC (2005) Small business in the informal economy: making the transition to the formal economy – the evidence base. Small Business Service, London
Williams C, Horlings E, Renooy P (2008) Tackling undeclared work in the EU, European Foundation for the improvement of living and working conditions, 2008
World Bank (2012). Migration and development brief 19, November 2012

Chapter 10
Executive Summary

Gorana Krstić, Friedrich Schneider, Mihail Arandarenko, Milojko Arsić, Branko Radulović, Saša Ranđelović, and Irena Janković

10.1 Main Findings of the Study

10.1.1 Survey of the Informal Activities of Serbian Businesses and Entrepreneurs

Incentives to formalise the shadow economy should be based on knowledge of the causes and structure of informal activity. A specific problem in designing these incentives is the fact that information on the shadow economy is inherently unreliable and incomplete. A survey of the informal activities of Serbian businesses and entrepreneurs (Survey on Conditions for Doing Business in Serbia) was therefore carried out for the purpose of this study on a representative sample of 1,251 business entities (businesses and entrepreneurs). This made it possible for the first time to view the Serbian shadow economy from the point of view of businesses, to assess the various forms that the shadow economy takes, and to analyse them according to the relevant characteristics of business entities. The survey also allowed us to see the causes of and motives for informal activity, which is of particular importance in drafting recommendations for formalising the shadow economy.

G. Krstić (✉) • M. Arandarenko • M. Arsić • S. Ranđelović • I. Janković
Faculty of Economics, University of Belgrade, Belgrade, Serbia
e-mail: gkrstic@ekof.bg.ac.rs; arandarenko@ekof.bg.ac.rs; arsicm@ekof.bg.ac.rs; randjelovic@ekof.bg.ac.rs; irenaj@ekof.bg.ac.rs

F. Schneider
Department of Economics, University of Linz, Linz, Austria
e-mail: Friedrich.schneider@jku.at

B. Radulović
Faculty of Law, University of Belgrade, Belgrade, Serbia
e-mail: bradulovic@ius.bg.ac.rs

G. Krstić, F. Schneider (eds.), *Formalizing the Shadow Economy in Serbia*, Contributions to Economics, DOI 10.1007/978-3-319-13437-6_10

10.1.2 Causes of the Shadow Economy

We analysed the causes of the shadow economy using elementary theoretical analysis, comparative data, social partners' views on how institutions operate, and the results of the Survey on Conditions for Doing Business in Serbia. Among the fiscal causes of the shadow economy are the relatively high fiscal burden on labour; complicated and costly tax procedures; complicated and opaque tax system; poorly organised, under-staffed, and under-equipped Tax administration; poor quality of public services; and high tolerance for the shadow economy. The features of the labour market that are particularly significant in fostering and sustaining the shadow economy are high fiscal burden on labour for lower wage earners; a social security system that prevents entitlement to social welfare benefits and other transfers for people in formal employment; high minimum wage; and certain regulations governing employment protection legislation, working hours, unemployment benefits, and the pension system. There are many other institutional and economic factors that contribute to the large extent of the shadow economy. Owing to low productivity, many businesses can only operate at a profit if they evade paying taxes. The economic crisis and pervasive liquidity issues have forced even the more productive businesses to shift a portion of their operations into the informal sector, and inefficient enforcement and market exit mechanisms incentivise businesses operating in the informal sector to remain there. Among the other causes with a significant bearing on the extent of the shadow economy are high administrative burdens on doing business; low quality of the regulatory environment; and legal insecurity. In addition to these regulatory causes the decision to operate informally is affected by widespread corruption and low tax morality. The most important financial factors are the large share of cash transactions in the total volume of payments, informal financing, and the unregistered remittances of migrant workers.

10.1.3 Extent of the Shadow Economy in Serbia

The shadow economy in Serbia was estimated using three methods: (a) the MIMIC method, a modelling-based approach covering Serbia and ten other Central and Eastern European countries between 2001 and 2010; (b) the Household Tax Compliance (HTC) method based on 2010 data for Serbia, an indirect method based on macroeconomic data; and (c) the Survey on Conditions for Doing Business in Serbia. The methods used differ in their coverage of the shadow economy in terms of institutional sector, form of shadow economy, and methodology used. The MIMIC method has the broadest coverage since it covers all institutional sectors and all forms of the shadow economy. The HTC method estimates only those forms of the shadow economy that can be identified and estimated on the basis of household income and consumption data. The survey was used to estimate the most important forms of the shadow economy among business entities.

Table 10.1 Extent of the shadow economy according to the various methods of estimation

	Year	% of GDP
Shadow economy according to the MIMIC method	2010	30.1
Shadow economy—HTC method	2010	23.6
Shadow economy—Survey	2012	21.0

Source: Own calculations

The results of the assessment using the first method showed that all countries recorded a decline in the extent of the shadow economy over the observed period, with the exception of 2009 when there was a slight increase. In Serbia the shadow economy contracted from 33.2 % of official GDP in 2001 to 30.1 % in 2010 (Table 10.1). The results show that the shadow economy in Serbia (as % of GDP) declined over the period of economic growth and remained nearly unchanged after the beginning of the economic downturn. Serbia's levels were greater than the averages for the other selected 11 countries throughout the entire reporting period. Only Bulgaria had a larger shadow economy, as a percentage of GDP, than Serbia.

The HTC method estimated the extent of the shadow economy in Serbia at 24 % of GDP. The figure obtained using the HTC method is lower than that derived from using the MIMIC model, since data on household income and consumption cannot cover some forms of the shadow economy in the business sector (corporate income and property tax, charges, fees, etc.).

Data from the Survey on Conditions for Doing Business in Serbia made it possible to estimate the extent of the two key forms of informal activity in the sectors of businesses and entrepreneurs, trade in goods, and partly or wholly unreported employment. Using the findings of the survey we estimated that these two forms of informal activity amount to some 21 % of GDP. The extent of the shadow economy estimated using the results of the survey is the lowest, since businesses also take part in the shadow economy by evading the payment of other dues such as corporate income tax, property tax, fees, and charges, and there is also a portion of the shadow economy that takes place outside the business sector (home repairs, private tuition, trade in goods at flea markets, etc.). A comparison of these results with those obtained using the MIMIC method showed that businesses and entrepreneurs accounted for over two-thirds of all activity in the shadow economy, and that these were in the form of illicit transactions and the payment of wages without paying appropriate taxes and contributions.

10.1.4 Estimates of the Tax Evasion Gap

The tax gap is the difference between hypothetical (theoretical) tax revenue and taxes actually collected. Hypothetical tax revenues are the sums that would be collected over a particular period of time if all taxpayers paid their taxes in full compliance with tax legislation. The shadow economy is a broader concept than the

Table 10.2 Estimated tax gap and fiscal effects of formalisation

	Method/ coverage	Year	Amount
VAT gap (as % of GDP)	Macroeconomic data	2011	2.5
	Survey	2012	2.5
VAT gap (as % of hypothetical VAT)	Macroeconomic data	2011	21.3
	Survey	2012	21.6
Personal income tax and social contributions gap (as % of GDP)	Survey	2010	5.0
Personal income tax and social contributions gap (as % of hypothetical income tax and contributions)	Survey	2010	27.7
Fiscal effects of formalisation (short-term), as % of GDP	VAT	2013–2015	0.2–0.5
	Income tax and contributions	2013–2015	0.6
	Total	2013–2015	0.8–1.1
Fiscal effects of formalisation (long-term), as % of GDP	VAT	2013–2020	1.0
	Income tax and contributions	2013–2020	0.9
	Total	2013–2020	1.9

Source: Own calculations

tax gap, as it encompasses all taxable economic activities that take place informally. The tax gap, on the other hand, is the amount of tax that should be paid on those activities. The tax gap is mainly caused by tax evasion, which is why these two terms are often seen as identical. However, the tax gap can, to a lesser extent, reflect reported but unpaid taxes, as well as tax revenue lost due to taxpayer bankruptcy, write-offs of back taxes, etc. Having carried out a detailed analysis of tax rates, volumes of consumption, etc., we estimated the VAT gap at 2.5 % of GDP (Table 10.2). By combining the data from macroeconomic accounts with the findings of the survey, we estimated the tax gap for personal income tax and social security contributions at about 5 % of GDP. We then extrapolated these tax gap estimates to all taxes, and by using data from the Household Consumption Survey we arrived at the figure of 10 % as an approximation of the overall tax gap.

10.1.5 The Shadow Economy in the Business and Entrepreneur Sector

The Survey on Conditions for Doing Business in Serbia asked respondents to state their views on whether their own business was engaged in the shadow economy, and found that 28 % of all business entities in Serbia did so. These businesses and entrepreneurs employed workers informally and/or made payments in cash even though they were VAT payers. The term 'informal workers' is used to describe workers employed without a contract or those who do have contracts but only declare part of their wage officially, with the remainder paid in cash. The results of the survey show that entrepreneurs, new start-ups, construction businesses and businesses based in Central Serbia are more likely to engage in the shadow economy. Based on respondents' views on the participation of their own businesses in the shadow economy and their estimates of the extent to which other entities in the same industry take part in informal activities, we estimated the upper and lower limit of the extent of the shadow economy in this sector. The share of employees working without formal contracts ranged from 1.9 % (lower limit) to 23.9 % (upper limit) of the total number of employees. The share of employees with a portion of undeclared wages ranged between 3.8 and 24.7 %, while the share of cash transactions ranged between 11.3 and 21.6 % of the total volume of payments.

Econometric analysis based on the survey data identified specific factors that are statistically significant to a business's decision whether or not to engage in informal operations. The results obtained were in line with the findings of other studies, where entrepreneurs were seen to be more likely to take part in the shadow economy than other business entities. Business entities in the construction sector were almost twice as likely to operate informally than those in services, while entities in the trade sector were nearly twice less likely to do so. Finally, the attitude of the business entity towards the shadow economy was a major and statistically significant factor determining that entity's participation in the shadow economy.

The findings of the survey showed that competition from entities operating at least partly in the informal sector was extremely widespread. As many as 85.3 % of the business entities surveyed stated that unfair competition was present in their sector of economic activity. Construction and transportation again led the field, whilst the presence of competition was also determined to a large degree by the likelihood of detection. This shows that most problems appear in sectors where there are greater regulatory obstacles to formalisation and greater difficulty in detecting informally employed workers. Since such an environment is conducive to greater operating savings, the pressure of competition coming from the informal sector is thus also greater.

10.1.6 Effects of Formalising the Shadow Economy

Although the estimated extent of the shadow economy in Serbia is significant, comparative data show that the average is only about 5 percentage points greater in Serbia than in other Central and Eastern European countries. This leads to the conclusion that the tax gap in Serbia is greater by approximately the same amount as in these other countries. Therefore the optimal aim in reducing the extent of the shadow economy and the tax gap in Serbia would be to reduce them to the Central and Eastern European averages over the medium term, while the long-term goal would be to bring them down to the levels seen in developed Western European countries. The potential increase in public revenue that could be generated by reducing the Serbian shadow economy was estimated at between 0.8 and 1.1 % of GDP in the medium term (up to 3 years), or some 2 % of GDP in the long term (7–10 years).

These estimates are the upper limit of the potential additional public revenue that could be generated through the reduction of the shadow economy, since the institutional conditions for tackling the shadow economy and tax morality are far higher in Western European countries than in Serbia as a consequence of their long tradition of combating the shadow economy. These fiscal effects can only be achieved in Serbia if all the measures necessary to tackle the shadow economy are applied in a comprehensive, non-selective, and consistent manner. From the fiscal policy standpoint, a reduction in the shadow economy will not allow for any tax cuts or greater public expenditure. Taxing the shadow economy should contribute to a drop in the fiscal deficit and compensate for the decline in tax revenues due to the expected restructuring of the economy towards less-taxable activities such as exports and investment.

The findings of the MIMIC method applied to Serbia and the other 10 Central and Eastern European countries show that the effect of the shadow economy on registered GDP is statistically highly significant and has the expected negative sign: if GDP per capita falls by 1 percentage point, the shadow economy will increase by between 0.6 and 0.7 percentage points, depending on the model used. This means that any future decline in GDP will increase pressure on the shadow economy, since business entities will endeavour to compensate for fewer opportunities in the formal sector by shifting into the shadow economy. This finding underlines the importance of preserving macroeconomic stability and creating conditions for future growth in the future, which will be a major component in the successful strategy for formalising the shadow economy.

10.2 Recommendations for Formalising the Shadow Economy

10.2.1 Fiscal Policy Measures

Fiscal policy measures are aimed at reducing incentives for operating in the shadow economy and the benefits of doing so on the one hand, and increasing the associated costs and risks on the other. The most important fiscal policy measures for tackling the shadow economy are: reducing distortions introduced by the tax system; reducing tax compliance costs; reducing the return to tax evasion; and reducing tolerance for the shadow economy.

Distortions introduced by taxes in Serbia could be reduced by decreasing the fiscal burden on labour (since other general taxes are moderate), by reducing the number of tax rates applicable to income from different sources or trade in different types of goods, and by significantly reducing the number of tax exemptions (particularly when it comes to corporate income tax). Tax compliance costs could be lowered by reducing the number of tax procedures and simplifying them, and by introducing mandatory e-filing of tax returns and requiring electronic communication with tax authorities. Thus, the reduction in cost effectiveness of tax evasion could be achieved primarily by increasing the likelihood of the Tax Administration detecting tax evasion: to ensure this, the number of Tax Administration staff tasked with performing audits should be increased, and their training and case selection methodology improved. In addition, there should be more consistent implementation of statutory penalties for tax evasion, particularly by courts.

Moreover, there should be co-operation with other government bodies (such as the Municipal Police) to institute and enforce a ban on the sale of new products at farmers' and flea markets. Improving co-ordination between the Tax Administration and other government bodies, both in terms of exchange of information and of joint action in the field, is another important precondition for tackling the shadow economy and combatting tax evasion. The reach of property taxes should be widened in co-operation with the Property Cadastre and other government bodies, since a significant percentage of properties in Serbia are unregistered and as such not subject to property tax. Co-operation between the Tax Administration and other government bodies is of particular importance in successfully cross checking property and income, which would project a public message of the state's determination to tackle the shadow economy and the tax evasion associated with it. In order to combat the non-payment of taxes, the practice of periodically writing off nominal interest on back taxes should be finally abandoned. A portion of the principal debt is also written off along with nominal interest, which rewards undisciplined taxpayers and fosters moral hazard behaviour, as taxpayers will intentionally defer payment in expectation of a new round of interest write-offs.

Finally, in order to reduce the extent of the shadow economy, the education and public information system must be used to increase public awareness of the adverse effects of the shadow economy and so improve tax morality. An improvement in the quality of public goods and services provided by the state would also contribute to achieving this goal.

10.2.2 Measures Relating to Features of the Labour Market

In terms of the fiscal burden on labour, the tax wedge of labour (expressed as the ratio of total wage taxes and contributions to total labour costs) is high for low wages and relatively low for high wages, a consequence of the proportional wage taxation system with a relatively low tax-exempt allowance. At about the level of the minimum wage, the tax burden in Serbia is the fourth highest of all European countries. This is a natural incentive for the preservation and growth of informal employment, since informal businesses generally enter the formal economy at approximately that point. Thus, the most important recommendation in the field of labour taxation is the need to substantially reduce labour costs for lower-paying jobs. Any kind of reform of labour taxation (or, in a broader sense, of the taxation of income derived from work) should ideally entail an increase in the personal tax-exempt allowance to the level of the minimum wage. Most European countries employ this practice. In addition, introducing a tax exempt allowance for dependents would reduce the tax wedge for employees with unemployed spouses and children, and thereby reduce their incentives for joining the shadow economy.

The existence of the minimum social security contribution base makes open-ended, full-time labour contracts unpopular. Another means of reducing the tax wedge for lower wages would be to remove the minimum social security base, which now stands at 35 % of the average wage. While its impact on people working full-time jobs is negligible, since the minimum wage is far above this level, it increases labour costs for part-time workers with standard open-ended employment contracts. An important incentive for formalising informal employees working part-time jobs could be the introduction of less restrictive tax treatment of 'mini jobs' and 'midi jobs', based on the positive experiences of Germany where, for mini jobs, healthcare and social security contributions are much lower than standard, while the rate of income tax can even equal zero. Midi jobs attract contributions that are greater than those for mini jobs but still lower than standard, so that workers in mini jobs can avoid the trap of in-work poverty, and their transition into standard employment is eased.

Welfare benefits in Serbian practice are available almost exclusively to unemployed and inactive persons, which encourage those who are able to work to combine welfare and informal employment. To incentivise employment in the formal sector, an in-work benefits programme should be introduced along the lines of the US Earned Income Tax Credit, which would make it possible for workers to combine formal employment and welfare benefits, with the latter gradually reduced as earnings increase.

To avoid driving down demand for formal work, the minimum wage should be reduced from the current level of 50 % to some 35–40 % of the average wage, as used to be the case in Serbia until several years ago and as recommended by the World Bank for middle-developed countries. Moreover, the introduction of a slightly lower minimum wage for under-25 s should be considered in order to stimulate their open-ended employment. Similarly, the minimum wage could vary slightly by region so as to partly reflect regional variation in the cost of living.

The most urgent requirement in the area of employment protection legislation is the removal of the statutory provision obliging employers to pay employees severance in proportion to each employee's total years of service rather than only years of service spent with their current employer. This would foster formal employment, primarily of elderly workers with work experience. In addition, an extension of the maximum length of employment under individual fixed-term contracts from 1–2 or 3 years should be considered.

Retirement rules are characterised by relatively low standard and minimum retirement age thresholds. Moreover, there are no actuarial penalties for early retirement, which incentivises pensioners to continue working after retirement, particularly in the informal sector. The current retirement age threshold should thus be increased; in addition, actuarial adjustment of pensions should be introduced to reflect the life expectancy of people who retire earlier, while actuarial rewards should apply to those who continue to work and pay pension contributions after meeting conditions for full retirement, regardless of whether they receive pensions or not.

In order to support entrepreneurship, specific programmes targeted at reducing informal employment should be pursued more vigorously and with reference to experiences of other European countries. Self-employment is supported by the National Employment Service (NES); this assistance takes the form of a one-off non-repayable grant and some in-kind support, provided that the beneficiary regularly pays contributions and taxes for at least the following 2 years. On average, some 3,000–5,000 people per year become self-employed through this programme: NES staff estimate that most of them merely formalise their informal businesses. It is interesting to note that evaluations of such 'legalised' entrepreneurs show survival rates greater than for those who started their businesses without previous experience in the informal sector. Microlending is also a measure that facilitates the establishment of legal businesses, especially for categories of people who cannot rely on their own funds or commercial credit, but is as yet virtually non-existent in Serbia due to an inadequate statutory framework.

Inspection Oversight The Labour and Market Inspectorates are responsible for tackling informal employment and undeclared and illicit transactions, whilst the Tax Administration is responsible for preventing tax evasion. In addition to the lack of equipment and appropriately qualified staff, one of the key problems in the operation of these institutions is the absence of sufficient co-ordination and integration with other inspection and oversight services. Closer integration is therefore required between the various inspectorates, either through an Inspectorate-General, or, in less demanding form, by means of a co-ordinating body such as a Commission to Co-Ordinate Inspection Oversight. A framework Inspections Law should be adopted, harmonised with European Union regulations, to at least ensure better mutual co-ordination of inspection oversight and to better delimit the powers of the various inspection services, at the same time closing the loopholes in the powers of inspection bodies that have made it possible for the shadow economy to flourish and have hindered the implementation of activities designed to combat it. The advantages of an integrated inspections approach are particularly obvious in the area of the authority of the Market and Labour Inspectorates. A unified database of offenders and offences, accessible to all inspection services, the Tax Administration, the Customs Administration, and the police, would improve the efficiency of the fight against the shadow economy. The integration of powers would mean that inspections that uncover an unregistered or unreported entity or person engaging in an activity under the remit of another inspection would be both authorised and required to order any deficiencies to be remedied and to notify the Tax Administration of the infringement and the measures taken.

10.2.3 Measures Relating to the Financial Sector

Curb Transactions in Cash and Incentivise Cashless Payments Switching to cashless (and particularly electronic) payments would reduce the participation of parties to transactions in the shadow economy. In ensuring this, emphasis should be placed on incentives that will foster cashless transactions. The use of electronic money for payment operations can be fostered by allowing electronic payments in sectors dominated by cash (such as hospitality, taxi cabs, etc.). Other incentives could include subsidising point-of-sale terminals for small and micro-businesses, limited tax breaks for electronic payments, and prepaid cards for people without bank accounts to enable their inclusion in the formal sector. On the macroeconomic level, government subsidies and assistance could be paid out electronically, as could various types of contributions. Further, all government payments could be limited to electronic channels only. To ensure that all remaining cash transactions take place primarily within formal channels, field audits should be strengthened to ensure fiscal cash registers are used and receipts are issued for all transactions. A clear consensus among economic policymakers regarding the application of a de-euroisation strategy would contribute to a substantial reduction in cash payments—particularly informal payments—throughout the system.

Reduce the Share of Informal Sources of Finance in the Economy To further stimulate greater transfers of money through formal channels (and the inflow of significant funds from abroad in the form of remittances), transfer costs must be reduced, as was also pointed out by survey respondents. This would increase the transparency of these flows and make it easier to direct them into investment contributing to local growth and national development. Greater competition between formal transfer intermediaries and lower transfer service costs would increase migrant interest in sending remittances through formal channels, since these offer numerous benefits to recipients such as easier access to financial institutions, cheaper finance for the broader public, lower cost of investment due to more options for diversification, and better education of beneficiaries about alternate modes of employing funds. Regulatory authorities in sending and receiving countries should enter into bilateral agreements to formalise and facilitate transferring, channelling, and registering funds. This process could take the form of a public-private partnership, with the participation of financial institutions. Closer co-operation between banking sectors in sending and receiving countries should lower transaction costs of transfers and accelerate the sending of remittances through formal channels.

A greater role played by banks in the transfer of remittances should lower transaction costs and increase the speed and reliability of these services. This could also be achieved by developing a unified clearing system for all countries involved in this process. Investment using remitted funds could be stimulated by creating a better climate for investing, as well as by deploying a range of incentives for putting funds to productive use (e.g., tax breaks). A well-developed infrastructure to support channelling money transfers from abroad would also facilitate access to other financial intermediation services (such as current accounts, savings accounts, and credit instruments) for a broader section of the population, which would, in turn, foster the development of the country's financial sector. Further development of formal channels for transferring remittances could be harnessed to create innovative products that would make it possible for migrants to directly invest in their home countries by purchasing, for instance, land or real estate. Gradual regulation of sending and receiving remittances would be desirable, so that these flows could be better studied and this segment of the market developed without excessive and hasty government intervention, which could retard or disincentivise additional inflow of these funds.

10.2.4 Measures Related to the Business Environment

Measures related to the business environment are aimed either at business entities already operating formally or at those wholly in the shadow economy. The existing regulatory requirements for businesses operating formally need to be simplified and unnecessary new administrative burdens should be prevented administrative burdens. At between 3.8 and 4.2 % of GDP, Serbia's administrative costs are among the highest of all countries that have made similar measurements. Consistent application of methods such as the SME Test and the Standard Cost Model, as well as regular stakeholder consultation, could significantly reduce existing administrative costs, which would foster the shift of some activity from the informal to the formal sector. There are other areas of the regulatory process that could see major improvement; in particular, bylaws should be adopted in a timely fashion to reduce legal uncertainty.

Solving the issues of 'phoenix companies' and unfair competition are very important in tackling the shadow economy. The former would contribute to greater liquidity, primarily among SMEs, who are often unable to collect receivables from 'phoenix companies' and are thus forced to move part of their businesses into the shadow economy in order to survive. One possible solution would be to set up a special registry of all bans on operating imposed on managers and owners of businesses that face criminal or other proceedings. However, what is most needed to eliminate both 'phoenix companies' and unfair competition is greater consistency in applying the existing legal framework.

There are several steps that would facilitate the operation of business entities wholly in the informal sector and thus promote their integration into the formal economy. In addition to directly lowering costs by removing barriers to entry in particular sectors, an electronic registry of legislation accessible to the public free of charge should be established. Further, existing records should be improved, and a new e-portal for licences, permits, approvals, and consents should be established.

Integration into the formal sector is also affected by the issue of 'legalising' buildings and obtaining construction permits. Unclear and complicated 'legalisation', the subsequent issuance of construction permits for unpermitted properties–makes entry into the formal sector more difficult, which means that certain resources are made unavailable for legal transactions and cannot be used by the economy. In addition to legalisation, entry into the market is hindered by the very complex construction permit system, which involves filing for permits with a large number of entities. The resolution of these issues requires a number of measures to accelerate construction permit procedures, including establishing 'one-stop shops' at local authorities, changing the role of public entities in the permitting procedure, drafting plans in a timely manner, etc.

10.3 Policy Conclusions

The key prerequisites for a successful strategy for formalising the shadow economy are: (1) to complete the process of transition into a market economy, and (2) to stabilise the legal and institutional structures of society; these should be followed by (3) achieving and maintaining macroeconomic stability and (4) creating preconditions for economic growth. The impact of these factors on the shadow economy is just one among their many desirable effects. The econometric findings presented in Chap. 6 indicate that an increase in official GDP leads to a drop in the extent of the shadow economy. In other words, a decline in GDP will increase the shadow economy as business entities endeavour to compensate for fewer business opportunities in the formal sector by working in the shadow economy. In these circumstances the measures proposed above will not be fully effective.

References

Abdih Y, Chami R, Gapen M, Mati A (2009) Fiscal sustainability in remittance dependent economies. IMF Working Paper WP/09/190. International Monetary Fund, Washington, DC

Abdih Y, Barajas A, Chami R, Ebeke C (2012) Remittance channels and fiscal impact in the Middle East, North Africa, and Central Asia. IMF Working Paper WP/12/104. International Monetary Fund, Washington, DC

Adams RH, Page J (2005) Do international migration and remittances reduce poverty in development countries? World Dev 33(10):1645–1699

Aggarwal R, Demirgüç-Kunt A, Martinez Peria MS (2011) Do workers' remittances promote financial development? J Dev Econ 96(2):255–264

Ahumada H, Alvaredo F, Canavese A, Canavese P (2004) The demand for currency approach and the size of the shadow economy: a critical assessment. Discussion Paper. Delta Ecole Normale Superieure, Paris

Aigner D, Schneider F, Ghosh D (1988) Me and my shadow: estimating the size of the U.S. hidden economy from time series data. In: Barnett WA, Berndt ER, White H (eds) Dynamic econometric modelling. Cambridge University Press, Cambridge, pp 224–243

Alm J, Jackson B, McKee M (1992) Estimating the determinants of taxpayer compliance with experimental data. Natl Tax J 45(1):107–114

Andrews D, Caldera Sánchez A, Johansson Å (2011) Towards a better understanding of the informal economy. OECD Economics Department Working Papers, No. 873. OECD Publishing

Arandarenko M (2012) How to make informal work less normal in Serbia. In: Mutual learning programme peer review on tackling undeclared work: developing an effective system for inspection and prevention, 4–5 October 2012, Prague (Czech Republic)

Arandarenko M, Avlijaš S (2011) Behind the veil of statistics: Bringing to light structural weaknesses in Serbia. In: Schmidt V, Vaughan-Whitehead D (eds) The impact of the crisis on wages in South East Europe. ILO, Budapest

Arandarenko M, Stanić K (2006) Labor costs and labor taxes in Serbia. Background paper for World Bank report. Labor Market Assessment, Serbia

Arsić M, Randjelović S (2012) Periodično oporezivanje imovine u Srbiji: Šta smo uradili i šta smo naučili. GIZ – studija u izradi

Arsić M, Altiparmakov N, Ranđelović S, Bućić A, Vasiljević D, Levitas T (2010) Tax policy in Serbia – looking forward. Foundation for the Advancement of Economics, Belgrade

Arsić M, Ranđelović S, Pejić M (2012) Reform of the system of Quasi-Fiscal charges for the improvement of business conditions in Serbia. Quarterly Monitor, vol 29, April–June 2012

G. Krstić, F. Schneider (eds.), *Formalizing the Shadow Economy in Serbia*,
Contributions to Economics, DOI 10.1007/978-3-319-13437-6

Asea P (1996) The informal sector: baby or bath water? Carnegie-Rochester Conference Series on Public Policy 45: 163–171

Bajada C, Schneider F (eds) (2005) Size, causes and consequences of the underground economy: an international perspective. Ashgate, Aldershot

Bartlett B (2001) Tax reform and economic growth. Ripon Society

Belev B (2003) The informal economy in the EU accession countries: size, scope, trends and challenges to the process of EU enlargement. Center for Study of Democracy, Sofia

Bhattacharyya DK (1999) On the economic rationale of estimating the hidden economy. Econ J 109(456):348–359

Bisić M (2011) Akcizna politika u Srbiji: značaj i ključna pitanja. Radni papir

Borseli F (2011) Organised VAT fraud: features, magnitude, policy perspectives. Banka D'Italia

Breusch T (2005a) The Canadian Underground Economy: An Examination of Giles and Tedds. Can Tax J 53(2):367–391

Breusch T (2005b) Estimating the underground economy using MIMIC models. Working Paper. National University of Australia, Canberra

Buehn A, Schneider F (2009) Corruption and the shadow economy: a structural equation model approach. Discussion Paper, 2009/1. Department of Economics, University of Linz, Linz

Buehn A, Karmann A, Schneider F (2009) Shadow economy and do-it-yourself activities: the German case. J Inst Theor Econ 165:701–722

Bulgarian Ministry of Finance (2011) The shadow economy: how to measure and model it. Brief methodological analyses. www.minfin.bg/document/9795:4

Centar za liberalno demokratske studije – CLDS (2012) Rast privatne domaće štednje u cilju ubrzanja privrednog rasta Srbije. Beograd

Chami R, Barajas A, Cosimano T, Fullenkamp C, Gapen M, Montiel P (2008) Macroeconomic consequences of remittances. IMF Occasional Paper No 259. International Monetary Fund, Washington, DC

Chami R, Barajas A, Gapen M, Fullenkamp C, Montiel P (2009) Do workers' remittances promote economic growth? IMF Working Paper WP/09/153. International Monetary Fund, Washington, DC

Christie E, Holzner M (2004) Household tax compliance and shadow economy in central and southeastern Europe. The WIIW Balkan Observatory Working Papers No. 038

Contini B (1981) The second economy of Italy. Taxing Spending 3:17–24

Contini B (1992) The irregular economy in Italy: a survey of contributions, guide book to statistics on the hidden economy. United Nations, New York

Cox H (2005) Intra-EU differences in regulation-caused administrative burden for companies. CPB Netherlands Bureau for Economic Policy Analysis, Memo 136, December

De Soto H (1989) The other path. Harper and Row, New York

De Soto H (2000) The mystery of capital: why capitalism triumphs in the west and fails everywhere else. Basic Books, New York

Dell'Anno R (2003) Estimating the shadow economy in Italy: a structural equation approach. Working Paper 2003-7. Department of Economics, University of Aarhus, Aarhus, Denmark

Dell'Anno R (2007) The shadow economy in Portugal: an analysis with the MIMIC approach. J Appl Econ 10(2):253–277

Dell'Anno R, Schneider F (2004) The shadow economy of Italy and other OECD countries: what do we know? Discussion Paper. Department of Economics, University of Linz, Linz, Austria

Dell'Anno R, Schneider F (2005) Estimating the underground economy by using MIMIC models: a response to T. Breusch's critique. Discussion Paper. Department of Economics, University of Linz, Linz

Dell'Anno R, Schneider F (2009) A complex approach to estimate shadow economy: the structural equation modelling. In: Faggnini M, Looks T (eds) Coping with the complexity of economics. Springer, Berlin, pp 110–130

Djankov S, Lieberman I, Mukherjee J, Nenova T (2002) Going informal: benefits and costs. The World Bank, Draft

Eilat Y, Zinnes C (2000) The evolution of the shadow economy in transition countries: consequences for economic growth and donor assistance. CAER II Discussion Paper, No. 83

Enste DH (2010) Regulation and shadow economy: empirical evidence for 25 OECD-countries. Constit Polit Econ 21:231–248

European Commission (2007) Undeclared work in the European Union, Special Eurobarometer

Feld LP, Schneider F (2010) Survey on the shadow economy and undeclared earnings in OECD countries. German Econ Rev 11(2):109–149

Fiscal Council (2012a) Predlog mera fiskalne konsolidacije 2012–2016

Fiscal Council (2012b) Ocena predloga Zakona o budžetu za 2013. godinu

Frey BS, Weck-Hannemann H (1984) The hidden economy as an unobserved variable. Eur Econ Rev 26(1):33–53

Friedman E, Johnson S, Kaufmann D, Zoido-Lobatón P (2000) Dodging the grabbing hand: the determinants of unofficial activity in 69 countries. J Public Econ 76:459–493

Geruber A, Parsche R (2003) Evasion of value-added taxes in Europe: Ifo approach to estimating the evasion of value-added taxes on the basis of National Account Data (NAD), Research report. CES Ifo, Munich

Gerxhani K (2007) Did you pay your taxes? How (not) to conduct tax evasion in transition countries. Soc Indic Res 80(3):555–581

Giles DEA (1997a) Causality between the measured and underground economies in New Zealand. Appl Econ Lett 4(1):63–67

Giles DEA (1997b) Testing the asymmetry in the measured and underground business cycles in New Zealand. Econ Rec 71(2):225–232

Giles DEA (1999a) Measuring the hidden economy: implications for econometric modeling. Econ J 109(3):370–380

Giles DEA (1999b) Modeling the hidden economy in the tax gap in New Zealand. Empir Econ 24 (4):621–640

Giles DEA, Tedds LM (2002) Taxes and the Canadian underground economy. Canadian Tax Paper, vol 106, Canadian Tax Foundation, Toronto

Giles DEA, Tedds LM, Werkneh E (2002) The Canadian underground and measured economics. Appl Econ 34(4):2347–2352

Giuliano P, Ruiz-Arranz M (2009) Remittances, financial development and growth. J Dev Econ 90 (1):144–152

GIZ (2010) Addressing tax evasion and tax avoidance in developing countries. Study prepared by GIZ and the German Federal Ministry of Economic Cooperation and Development

Gonzalez AS, Lamanna F (2007) Who fears competition from informal firms? Evidence from Latin America. Policy Research Working Paper Series 4316. The World Bank

Gupta S, Pattilo CA, Wagh S (2009) Effect of remittances on poverty and financial development in sub-Saharan Africa. World Dev 37(1):104–115

Hanlon M, Mills L, Slemrod J (2007) An empirical examination of corporate tax noncompliance. In: Auerbach A, Hines JR, Slemrod J (eds) Taxing corporate income in the 21st century. Cambridge University Press, Cambridge, pp 140–162

Hanousek J, Palda F (2004) Quality of government services and the civic duty to pay taxes in the Czech and Slovak Republics and other transition countries. Kyklos 57(2):237–252

Helberger C, Knepel H (1988) How big is the shadow economy? A re-analysis of the unobserved-variable approach of B.S. Frey and H. Weck-Hannemann. Eur Econ Rev 32:965–976

Hernández-Cos R (2005) The U.S.–Mexico remittance corridor – lessons on shifting from informal to formal transfer systems. World Bank Working Paper No. 47. The World Bank, Washington, DC

HM Revenue & Customs (2011) Methodological annex for measuring tax gaps

Hosmer D, Lemeshow S (2000) Applied logistic regression, 2nd edn. Wiley, New York

Hudson J, Williams C, Orviska M, Nadin S (2012) Evaluating the impact of the informal economy on businesses in South East Europe: Some lessons from the 2009 World Bank Enterprise Survey. South East Eur J Econ Bus 7(1):99–110

IMF (2010) Balance of payments manual, 6th edn. International Monetary Fund, Washington, DC
IMF (2011) Republic of Serbia: request for stand-by arrangement. IMF Country Report 11/311. International Monetary Fund, Washington, DC
Institute for Fiscal Studies (2010) A retrospective evaluation of EU VAT system. Final report
International Labour Office (2011) Statistical update on employment in the informal economy. ILO Department of Statistics
Irving J, Mohapatra S, Ratha D (2010) Migrant remittance flows: findings from a global survey of central banks. Working Paper 94. The World Bank, Washington, DC
Janković I, Gligorić M (2012) Remittances as a stable source of foreign currency inflow in Serbia. In: Jovanović-Gavrilović B, Rakonjac Antić T, Stojanović Ž (eds) Thematic collection of papers "Economic Policy and Development". Faculty of Economics, Belgrade, pp 215–236
Johnson S, Kaufmann D, Shleifer A (1997) The unofficial economy in transition, Brookings papers on economic activity. World Bank, Washington DC
Johnson S, Kaufmann D, Zoido-Lobaton P (1998a) Regulatory discretion and the unofficial economy. Am Econ Rev 88(2):387–392
Johnson S, Kaufmann D, Zoido-Lobatón P (1998b) Corruption, public finances and the unofficial economy. Research Paper. The World Bank, Washington, DC
Jongwanich J (2007) Workers' remittances, economic growth and poverty in developing Asia and Pacific countries. UNESCCAP Working Paper, WP/07/01
Kanniainen V, Paakkonen J, Schneider F (2004) Fiscal and ethical determinants of shadow economy: theory and evidence. Discussion Paper No. 30. Helsinki Center for Economic Research
Kaufmann D, Kaliberda A (1996) Integrating the unofficial economy into the dynamics of post socialist economies: a framework of analyses and evidence. In: Kaminski B (ed) Economic transition in Russia and the new states of Eurasia. M.E. Sharpe, London, pp 81–120
Kazemier B, van Eck R (1992) Survey investigations of the hidden economy. J Econ Philos 13
Keen M, Smith S (2007) VAT fraud and evasion: what do we know, and what can be done? Working Paper 07/31 IMF
Koettl J (2012) Does formal work pay in Serbia? The role of labor taxes and social benefit design in providing disincentives for formal work. In: Laderchi CR, Savastano S (eds) Poverty and exclusion in the Western Balkans. New directions in measurement and policy, vol 8. Springer
Kovtun D, Cirkel AM, Murgasova Z, Smith D, Tambunlertchai S (2014) Boosting job growth in the Western Balkans. IMF WP/14/16
Krstić G (2001) Reintegracija sive ekonomije i razvoj privatnog sektora u Srbiji. Ekonomski institut i Liga eksperata, Beograd
Krstić G (2012) Labour force flows and informal economy in Serbia. In: International conference from global crisis to economic growth. Which way to take? The Faculty of Economics, University of Belgrade, September 2012
Krstić G, Sanfey P (2011) Earnings inequality and the informal economy: evidence from Serbia. Econ Transit 19(1)
Krstić G et al (1998) Analysis of the grey economy in the FRY with estimates of its volume for 1997 and recommendations for its legalisation. Economics Institute Belgrade
Kyle S et al (2001) The shadow economy in Bulgaria. Harvard University, Agency for Economic Analysis and Forecasting and Institute for Market Economics
Labour Inspectorate (2011) Annual Report
Lackó M (1996) Hidden economy in East-European countries in international comparison. Working Paper. International Institute for Applied Systems Analysis (IIASA), Laxenburg (Austria)
Loayza NV (1996) The economics of the informal sector: a simple model and some empirical evidence from Latin America, vol 45. Carnegie–Rochester Conference Series on Public Policy, Washington, DC, pp 129–162

Loayza N, Oviedo AM, Serven L (2006) The impact of regulation on growth and informality, cross-country evidence. In: Guha-Khasnobis B, Kanbur R, Ostrom E (eds) Linking the formal and informal economy, concepts and policies. Oxford University Press, Oxford
Loayza V, Serven L, Sugawara N (2010) Informality in Latin America and the Caribbean. World Bank Policy Research Working Paper Series 4888
Lokshin M, Jovanović B (2003) Wage differentials and state-private sector employment choice in Yugoslavia. Econ Transit 11
Long JS, Freese J (2006) Regression models for categorical dependent variables using Stata, 2nd edn. Stata Press, College Station
Luedtke J (Hrsg.) Otto-von-Freising-Tagungen der Katholischen Universität Eichstätt. Leske + Budrich, Opladen
NALED (2012a) Businesses can run, but they cannot hide – the system of non-tax and para-fiscal charges in Serbia: inventory, analysis of effects and recommendations for reform
NALED (2012b) Siva knjiga 5 - Preporuke za uklanjanje administrativnih prepreka za poslovanje u Srbiji 2012/2013
NBS (2011) Godišnji izveštaj o stabilnosti finansijskog sistema. http://www.nbs.rs/export/sites/default/internet/latinica/90/90_4/finansijska_stabilnost_2011.pdf
NBS (2012) Report on the Dinarisation of the Serbian financial system. www.nbs.rs
OECD (2008) Serbia – a labour market in transition. OECD, Paris
Oviedo et al (2009) Economic informality: causes, costs and policies – a literature survey. World Bank Working Paper No. 167, Washington, DC
Pedersen S (2003) The shadow economy in Germany, Great Britain and Scandinavia: a measurement based on questionnaire service, study no. 10. The Rockwell Foundation Research Unit, Copenhagen
Perry G, Maloney W, Arias O, Fajnzylber P, Mason A, Saavedra-Chanduvi J (2007) Informality: exit and exclusion. World Bank, Washington
Pozo S (ed) (1996) Exploring the underground economy: studies of illegal and unreported activity. W.E. Upjohn, Institute for Employment Research, Michigan
Putninš TJ, Sauka A (2011) The size and determinants of shadow economies in the Baltic States. Baltic J Econ 11(2)
Radisavljević G (2010) Lična potrošnja u Republici Srbiji 2000–2009. Statistical Office of the Republic of Serbia
Radulović B (2011a) Merenje administrativnih troškova primenom modela standardnog troška – Kritički osvrt i moguća poboljšanja. u S. Tabaroši, ur. "Razvoj pravnog sistema Srbije i harmonizacija sa pravom EU". Pravni Fakultet, Beograd
Radulović B (2011b) Standard cost model – baseline measurement. Serbia, Mimeo
Ramey G, Ramey VA (1995) Cross-country evidence on the link between volatility and growth. Am Econ Rev 85(5):1138–1151
Ranđelović S (2011) Smanjenje sive ekonomije kao instrument fiskalne konsolidacije. Kvartalni monitor. FREN, Beograd, pp 25–26
Ranđelović, S, Đorđević A (2012) Unapređenje performansi malih i srednjih preduzeća u Srbiji kroz reformu sistema oporezivanja. Istraživački rad pripremljen za potrebe Istraživačkog foruma Evropskog pokreta u Srbiji
Rao BB, Hassan GM (2011) A panel data analysis of the growth effects of remittances. Econ Model 28(1–2):701–709
Rao BB, Hassan GM (2012) Are the direct and indirect growth effects of remittances significant? World Econ 35(3):351–372
Ratha D (2009) Remittances in development: a lifeline to poor countries. Finance Dev 46(4)
Ratha D, Mohapatra S (2007) Increasing the macroeconomic impact of remittances on development. In: Development Prospects Group. The World Bank, Washington, DC
Ratha D, Silwal A (2012) The World Bank – migration and development brief, 18
Reckon (2009) Study to quantify and analyse the VAT gap in the EU-25 member states, London

Renooy P, Ivarsson S, van der Wusten-Gritsai O, Meijer R (2004) Undeclared work in an enlarged union: an analysis of undeclared work – an in-depth study of specific items. European Commission, Brussels
Rice E (1992) The corporate tax gap: evidence on tax compliance by small corporations. In: Slemrod J (ed) Why people pay taxes: tax compliance and enforcement. University of Michigan Press, Ann Arbor, pp 24–39
Russell B (2010) Revenue administration: managing the shadow economy. Technical Notes and Manuals, IMF
Sauka A (2008) Productive, unproductive and destructive entrepreneurship: a theoretical and empirical exploration. Peter Lang GmbH, Frankfurt am Main
Schneider F (1994) Measuring the size and development of the shadow economy: can the causes be found and the obstacles be overcome? In: Brandstaetter H, Güth W (eds) Essays on economic psychology. Springer, Berlin, pp 193–212
Schneider F (1997) The shadow economies of Western Europe. J Inst Econ Aff 17(3):42–48
Schneider F (1999) Der Sozialstaat zwischen Markt und Hedeonismus? In: Lamnek S, Luedtke J (Hrsg.) Otto-von-Freising-Tagungen der Katholischen Universität Eichstätt. Leske Budrich, Opladen
Schneider F (2003) The shadow economy. In: Rowley CK, Schneider F (eds) Encyclopedia of public choice. Kluwer Academic Publishers, Dordrecht
Schneider F (2004) Shadow economies around the World: what do we really know? IAW-Diskussionspapiere 16
Schneider F (2005) Shadow economies around the World: what do we really know? Eur J Polit Econ 21(3):598–642
Schneider F (2010) The influence of public institutions on the shadow economy: an empirical investigation for OECD countries. Eur J Law Econ 6(3):441–468
Schneider F (eds) (2011a) Handbook on the shadow economy. Edward Elgar, Cheltenham
Schneider F (2011b) The shadow economy in Europe – using payment systems to combat the shadow economy. http://www.bblf.bg/uploads/files/file_378.pdf
Schneider F, Enste D (2000) Shadow economies: size, causes and consequences. J Econ Lit 38 (1):77–114
Schneider F, Enste D (2002) The shadow economy: theoretical approaches, empirical studies and political implications. Cambridge University Press, Cambridge
Schneider F, Buehn A, Montenegro CE (2010) New estimates for the shadow economies all over the world. Int Econ J 24(4):443–461
Slemrod J (2007) Cheating ourselves: the economics of tax evasion. J Econ Perspect 21(1):25–48
Socio-Economic Council of the Republic of Serbia (2010) Efikasno suzbijanje sive ekonomije, Beograd
Statistical Office of the Republic of Serbia (2012) Statistical Yearbook 2012
Tanzi V (1999) Uses and abuses of estimates of the underground economy. Econ J 109(456):338–340
Tedds LM (2010) Keeping it off the books: an empirical investigation of firms that engage in tax evasion. Appl Econ 42(19):2459–2473
The Foreign Currency Operations Law (Official Gazette of the Republic of Serbia, Nos. 62/2006 and 31/2011)
Thomas JJ (1992) Informal economic activity, LSE, handbooks in economics. Harvester Wheatsheaf, London
Transparency Serbia (2012) Public comment periods in the Republic of Serbia – analysis of the statutory framework and practice
United Nations (2008) Non-observed economy in national accounts – survey country practices. United Nations Economics Commission for Europe, New York and Geneva
Urban J, Brümmerhoff D (2005) Möglichkeiten und Grenzen der Schätzung der Schattenwirtschaft: Eine kritische Auseinandersetzung mit den Schätzergebnissen der Bargeldmethode nach Schneider, Diskussionspapier, Universität Rostock

USAID (2005) Removing barriers to formalization: the case for reform and emerging best practice
USAID (2012a) Financing the growth of small and medium-sized enterprises: critical issues and recommendations for Serbia
USAID Business Enabling Project (2012b) Assessment of constraints to construction permits in Serbia
Varma KN, Doob AN (1998) Deterring economic crimes: the case of tax evasion. Can J Crim 165
Williams CC (2005) Small business in the informal economy: making the transition to the formal economy – the evidence base. Small Business Service, London
Williams CC (2006) The hidden enterprise culture: entrepreneurship in the underground economy. Edward Elgar, Cheltenham
Williams C, Horlings E, Renooy P (2008) Tackling undeclared work in the EU, European Foundation for the improvement of living and working conditions, 2008
Woon Nam C, Parsche i R, Schaden B (2001) Measurement of value added tax evasion in selected countries on the basis of national account data. Working Papers No. 431. CESifo, Munich
World Bank (2006) Serbia: labor market assessment. Report no. 36576-YU, Washington, DC
World Bank (2009) Serbia – doing more with less: addressing the fiscal crisis by increasing public sector productivity. Report no. 48620-YU, Washington, DC
World Bank (2011) Republic of Serbia – country economic memorandum: the road to prosperity: productivity and exports, vol 2. Report no. 65845-YF, Washington, DC
World Bank (2012a) Doing business 2012. World Bank, Washington, DC
World Bank (2012b) Migration and development brief 19, November 2012
Zoido-Lobaton P, Johnson S, Kaufmann D Corruption, public finances, and the unofficial economy. Available at: http://siteresources.worldbank.org/INTWBIGOVANTCOR/Resources/wps2169.pdf; http://www.nbs.rs/export/sites/default/internet/latinica/15/konferencije_guvernera/prilozi/20100512_BM_prezentacija.pdf; http://data.un.org/Data.aspx?q=households&d=SNA&f=group_code%3a406; http://www.nbs.rs/internet/cirilica/15/mediji/cl/DS-C-20120725.html; http://www.fren.org [access 22/10/2012]; http://www.nbs.rs [access 20/11/2012]; http://web.worldbank.org [access 25/11/2012]; http://webrzs.stat.gov.rs/WebSite/userFiles/file/Nacionalni/Adhoc.pdf [access 16/11/2012]; http://www.stat.gov.rs/nacionalni_racuni

About the Author

Gorana Krstić is an Associate Professor at the Faculty of Economics, University of Belgrade. She obtained her Ph.D. in Economics at the School of Social Sciences, Sussex University in 2002. Her main research interests are the labour markets, informal economy, poverty and social policy. She has published (and edited) 16 monographs in these fields and has had more than 40 articles published in both national and international journals. She has been consulting short and long term for leading international agencies, including the World Bank, UNDP, ILO, EC and USAID.

G. Krstić, F. Schneider (eds.), *Formalizing the Shadow Economy in Serbia*,
Contributions to Economics, DOI 10.1007/978-3-319-13437-6

MIX
Papier aus verantwortungsvollen Quellen
Paper from responsible sources
FSC® C105338

If you have any concerns about our products,
you can contact us on
ProductSafety@springernature.com

In case Publisher is established outside the EU,
the EU authorized representative is:
Springer Nature Customer Service Center GmbH
Europaplatz 3, 69115 Heidelberg, Germany

Printed by Libri Plureos GmbH
in Hamburg, Germany